Achieving Sustainable Business Excellence

Flevy Lasrado • Vijay Pereira

Achieving Sustainable Business Excellence

The Role of Human Capital

palgrave
macmillan

Flevy Lasrado
University of Wollongong in Dubai
Dubai, United Arab Emirates

Vijay Pereira
University of Wollongong in Dubai
Dubai, United Arab Emirates

ISBN 978-3-030-10354-5 ISBN 978-3-319-73314-2 (eBook)
https://doi.org/10.1007/978-3-319-73314-2

Printed on acid-free paper

This Palgrave Macmillan imprint is published by the registered company Springer International Publishing AG part of Springer Nature
The registered company address is: Gewerbestrasse 11, 6330 Cham, Switzerland

Foreword

The Micro-foundation of a Company's Strategy or Performance is its Human Capital

In today's dynamic technological and global economy,

$$\text{Tobin's Q Ratio} = \frac{\text{Market Value of a Firm}}{\text{Book Value of Its Replacement Assets}}$$

is a large number. What explains why the numerator is typically a large multiple of the denominator? The difference is the intangible assets, knowledge and human capital of its employees that give a firm its competitive capabilities, and a market value well above the book value of its tangible replacement assets. In short, the competence of firms and the modern knowledge economy are substantially explained by its intangible assets, the thoughts of its personnel, and organization.

What exactly is meant when persons say that we are in a "knowledge economy"? Where does the knowledge reside? Raw data, however "big" or copious, is not knowledge until it is coded and analyzed, and deductions are drawn from it (Provost and Fawsett 2013). Knowledge, in turn, has no commercial value until it is registered as intellectual property with a government, or applied to a business problem. Knowledge can be classified into three categories (Contractor and Ra 2002): (i) coded and registered (e.g., patents or copyrights), (ii) codified but not registered (i.e., knowledge which is written but deliberately not shared, such as proprietary algorithms and confidential technology, corporate organization or routines, and trade secrets), and (iii) knowledge which is neither codified nor registered (e.g., tacit knowledge that exists within the minds of company employees, engineers, or craftspersons, and is difficult to explain or codify in its entirety). As we move from category (i) to (iii) the tacitness of the knowledge increases—that is to say, it is embedded in the minds of employees, corporate routines, and organization. The resource-based view of the firm, that competitive advantage stems from rare, inimitable, and non-substitutable resources internalized within the firm, is in effect saying that it is the thinking of managers, employees, and leadership of the firm that ultimately matters (Wernerfelt 1984).

Business excellence and performance then depend on the quality of the thoughts of a company's personnel, or the quality of its human capital. Human capital can be measured with physical metrics, such as health, longevity, disease, infant mortality, etc. Happily, with improvements in health worldwide over the past century, the measurement of human capital no longer emphasizes physical attributes (although many nations near the bottom of the 193 members of the UN badly lag those at the top). Instead, the measurement of human capital these days focuses more on education, skill sets of the population, managers and employees, and the efficiency of a nation's or company's processes.

This volume therefore focuses on some of the most important aspects of business management, with its emphasis on quality standards, HRM practices, organizational processes, and knowledge management, as well as consideration for other stakeholders such as customers and suppliers, these being the keys to competitive success.

In today's dynamic global business environment, two additional aspects are critical: (a) the fostering of an organizational learning capability and (b) alliance partnerships. Knowledge today is developing so rapidly, and is so fragmented over various companies and countries, that even the biggest firms cannot internally develop and combine the multiple technologies that go into today's complex products. Even a giant pharmaceutical firm may have competencies only in some of the many therapeutic areas (e.g., oncology, gastroenterology, hematology, immunology, nephrology, and neurology). Moreover, modern drugs need to draw from different scientific disciplines (e.g., genomics, physiology, biochemistry, and nanotechnology). No single firm, however large, encompasses all these fields. Hence the need for learning from alliance partners, or joint development with them.

The end-market applications of technologies are also fragmenting. A computer chip machinery manufacturer has sensing capabilities at the molecular level that can be very useful in improving the efficiency of solar panels. But it has no prior marketing expertise in solar panels. In such a case, an alliance between the computer chip machinery firm and a solar panel company can enable synergistic complementarities. Similarly, a European firm that lacks cultural or marketing understanding in Asian or African markets may need to partner with a local firm which provides local knowledge of distribution methods, culture, and government contacts.

The two foregoing themes—learning and cooperativeness in alliances—are ultimately human traits, and a considerable literature exists to show that companies that cultivate behavioral traits fostering organizational learning and cooperative relationship-building outperform rivals (Contractor and Reuer 2014; Nilesen 2001).

I laud the authors, Flevy Lasrado and Vijay Pereira, whose book takes a micro-foundational perspective—linking strategic success or performance, with its underlying root cause, namely the human factor, or the quality of human capital in a company.

Rutgers Business School
Newark/New Brunswick, NJ, USA

Farok J. Contractor

References

Contractor, F. J., & Ra, W. (2002). How knowledge attributes influence alliance governance choices: A theory development note. *Journal of International Management*, *8*(1), 11–27.

Contractor, F. J., & Reuer, J. J. (2014). Structuring and governing alliances: New directions for research. *Global Strategy Journal*, *4*(4), 241–256.

Nielsen, B. B. (2001). *Trust and learning in international strategic alliances* (No. 8–2001). https://ideas.repec.org/p/hhb/cbsint/2001-008.html

Provost, F., & Fawcett, T. (2013). Data science and its relationship to big data and data-driven decision making. *Big Data, 1*(1), 51–59.

Wernerfelt, B. (1984). A resource-based view of the firm. *Strategic Management Journal, 5*(2), 171–180.

The original version of this book was revised. A title has been included to the foreword of this book.

Contents

List of Figures

List of Tables

1

Introduction to Business Excellence

Aristotle stated that it is not enough to know about excellence, we must try to have and use it. In the twenty-first century, it is impossible to rely exclusively on financial parameters to measure, monitor, and sustain an organisation's success. Up to 75% of a company's value can no longer be measured by standard accounting techniques (Zdrilić and Dulčić 2016). A standard accounting technique, for example, will describe how a firm prepares and presents its business income, expenses, assets, and liabilities. Further, due to competition at a global level in all spheres of business activity, organisations that want to survive and lead in an industry today must continuously improve their processes, services, and products to achieve a competitive advantage, or, in other words, its business excellence (BE). Thus, in these increasingly competitive business environments, BE allows organisations to assess their competitive strengths, understand and manage their performance, develop and implement strategic plans, and, above all, find opportunities to learn (Ahmed 2015).

Through the empirical analysis in this book we contribute to our current state of knowledge by asking the following questions: What is BE? How can organisations achieve sustained BE? How does human capital relate and contribute to BE?

F. Lasrado, V. Pereira, *Achieving Sustainable Business Excellence*,
https://doi.org/10.1007/978-3-319-73314-2_1

In this introductory chapter, we define these questions and more. We define BE and analyse its underlying principles, present an overview of global BE models (BEMs) and identify the common themes within them, and provide best practice examples of the ways in which high-performing organisations have implemented various excellence principles.

Introduction to Business Excellence

Simply put, *excellence* means taking steps to ensure that the techniques and strategies that work today will be implemented in an even better and wiser way tomorrow. In an organisational context, excellence manifests itself through leaders and the management, who are dedicated to the continuous improvement of their organisation's key processes, working conditions, morale, and general organisational culture. While a 'good' organisation uses sustainability, innovation, diversity, and risk management to provide product and process quality, a truly excellent organisation goes above and beyond by satisfying its customers, employees, and any other stakeholders while at the same time presenting a clear vision for achieving the same or greater outcomes in the future. Mann et al. (2011) described excellent organisations as those that strive to be not only ahead in their profits, but also outstanding in everything they do by implementing 'improvement programs, initiatives and quality tools' (p. 10) to develop and strengthen management practices and organisational processes, thereby improving their overall performance and creating value for their stakeholders. More precisely, the idea behind BE is that quality should not be focused only on the products and services produced by the organisation; it should be the fundamental value of the organisation's management strategy (Evans 2008).

BE is therefore a philosophy of management or management approach that emphasises the importance of transformation in business processes and of striving for continuous improvement within an organisation to yield superior performance. On the other hand, total quality management (TQM) (also known as total productive maintenance) 'defines a management approach to long-term success through customer satisfaction. In a TQM effort, all members of an organisation [i.e. its human capital] participate in improving processes, products, services, and the culture in which they work' (ASQ 2017). While the TQM movement that began in the late 1980s has admittedly run its course, TQM organisations that implemented BE early on in their life cycles have long reported consistently high performance and market success, providing valuable examples for companies that wish to achieve similar excellence (Matias and Coelho 2011; Zairi and Alsughayir 2011). Thus, BE principles developed in and modelled by TQM organisations provide a 'jumping-off' point for organisations that wish to identify opportunities and capitalise on their learning.

Given its broad applicability, BE has a variety of definitions and connotations. Simply put, it refers to doing things better than one's competitors and constantly improving staff, systems, processes, and organisations in a competitive environment (Arasli 2012). Its primary focus is determining how to achieve excellence in everything that an organisation does. In an early study of BE, Kanji (1998, p. 633) described it as a technique for scaling the 'well-being' of employers, customers, shareholders, or stakeholders while simultaneously providing a means to comprehensively evaluate business performance. More recently, Aras and Crowther (2010) defined BE according to four fundamental concepts: profitability, sustainability, good governance, and corporate reputation. Along similar lines, the European Foundation for Quality Management (EFQM n.d.-a) stated that BE is reflected in outstanding practices based on eight fundamental concepts: leading with vision, harnessing creativity, agile management, encouraging their staff, adding customer value, developing their organisational capability, being sustainable (in society as well as the organisation), and sustaining their results.

It has also been argued that BE produces different outcomes according to how long it is/has been implemented and at what stage of development an organisation is when it begins using it. In the short term, BE can help a company reach a return on investment (Mann and Grigg 2006) and in the long term it can both generate and strengthen an organisation's competencies. However, it is important to note that there is no 'universal rule' or one single path to successful BE implementation in business (Harrington 2004; Oakland and Tanner 2008).

Fortunately, organisations that aspire to achieve higher levels of excellence can choose one or more existing BEMs to ensure that they continue to improve and hold a competitive advantage. BEMs are frameworks that, when applied within an organisation, can help to focus thought and action in a systematic and structured way. These models are holistic in that they focus on all areas and dimensions of an organisation and, in particular, factors that drive performance. They provide a framework to assist in the adoption of BE principles and serve as a reliable means to measure how effectively this adoption has been executed.

Foundations of Human Capital

The principal questions we aim to probe in this book relate to defining what BE means for firms across the globe, and how these firms achieve sustained BE. But more importantly, we contribute by investigating how human capital relates and contributes to BE, through best practice examples in which high-performing organisations have implemented various excellence principles. In other words, we investigate the role of human capital in achieving business excellence. Put simply, human capital is the extent of the commercial worth of an employee's or team's skills, knowledge, experience, attitude, value, and motivation to an organisation (micro level), industry (meso level), or nation (macro level). In Chap. 2, we discuss in detail how various theoretical foundations of human capital, alongside other relevant management theories, collectively help a firm in its pursuit of achieving greater BE.

Global Business Excellence Frameworks

During the TQM movement of the late 1980s and early 1990s, the strategic significance of quality in business became universally recognised. Drawing on early innovations in Japan, which launched the Deming Prize to identify quality practices in 1951, organisations began to implement award programmes to increase quality and excellence in business. The frameworks and criteria for ensuring quality developed during this time laid the groundwork for contemporary BE principles. As Adebanjo (2001, p. 39) astutely remarked, 'BE took off where TQM failed'.

Today, organisations follow updated BEMs in every aspect of their day-to-day operations to achieve quality, value, and sustainability both for themselves and for their stakeholders. The two most commonly used BEMS are the Baldrige Criteria for Performance Excellence (BCPE), developed in the United States, and the EFQM Excellence Model, developed in Europe. These BEMs provide highly structured managerial approaches. They also ensure that organisational review remains holistic; that is, they consider all levels of the organisation and all factors that can influence performance. They enable any organisation to clarify factors that inhibit or accelerate organisational advancement and provide tools to implement targeted strategies. Moreover, these models, which acknowledge the distinct nature of the enterprise in which they are used, have proven relevant to all types and sizes of organisation: multinational, small to medium-sized enterprise (SME), not-for-profit, public sector, and so on.

Administered by the National Institute of Standards and Technology (NIST), the BCPE is non-prescriptive and provides comprehensive criteria for BE, requiring organisations to diagnose overall performance management systems, identify opportunities for improvement, and assess their improvement efforts (NIST 2017a). Its scope is also wide and takes in the whole organisation using 11 core values which are assessed across the model's categories. Systemic processes make up six of the seven categories used (operations focus; leadership; workforce focus; strategic planning; measurement, analysis, and knowledge; and customer focus) which contribute to the seventh category, performance results. Each area of organisational performance is measured and scored according to a 1000-point system (Asif and Gouthier 2014).

The EFQM (n.d.-b) administers the EFQM Excellence Model. This model consists of three categories: underlying principles, nine criteria for excellence, and a management tool, RADAR (Results, Approach, Deployment, Assess, and Refine); this tool is used to power continuous improvement. Like the BCPE, the EFQM's model is non-prescriptive; it acknowledges and exploits the fact that an outcome is not necessarily limited to the use of one particular method but can be achieved via multiple approaches. The model consists of five 'enablers' used to achieve results. The enablers—leadership; people; strategy; partnership and resources; and processes, products, and services—represent the processes, structures, and means required to achieve results. The model is based on the premise that organisations must have processes and structures in place to drive excellent results. The global BE frameworks thus encourage high performance and provide tools to develop effective performance practices and create value.

The EFQM model is widely used in Europe and the Middle East. Similarly, according to NIST (2016), over four million copies of the *Baldrige Criteria for Performance Excellence* were distributed in the United States from 2010 to 2014 alone, and this does not include copies downloaded from the Web or those available as books or at state and local award programmes.

Across the globe, many countries took cues from these models and adopted national quality and excellence awards. In the early 2010s, the number of national quality awards was estimated to be approximately 100 (Mann et al. 2011). Only a few years later, however, a study conducted by the Center for Organizational Excellence showed that there were only 61 excellence awards in place (Ahmed 2015). While there has been an overall decline in the number of award frameworks, global frameworks for quality and excellence are being updated regularly. The Malcolm Baldrige National Quality Award (MBNQA) criteria were updated every five years from 1988 to 2003, and, since 2009, the criteria have been formally revised every two years, with the latest revisions made in 2017. The latest revisions to the EFQM model were made in 2013. As these frequent changes suggest, the general concept of BE has not been static over the years, but is instead dynamic and constantly evolving. We now discuss how organisations achieve sustained BE by identifying core themes of excellence.

Achieving Sustained Business Excellence: Core Themes

World-class organisations often owe their achievements and excellence to specific innovative practices that fit their specific business environment, be they unique strategies, unique business models, or unique operational processes. These practices are developed as organisations engage in self-reflection on their journey to excellence—reflection that asks how the organisation performs as an organisation, what it is best at, what it needs to improve upon, what the role of BE is, and how human capital contributes to BE, and so on. BEMs provide a framework, as well as tools and techniques, to guide organisations in these processes of evaluation (Zapata-Cantu et al. 2016). More specifically, they facilitate the full integration of improvement activities into an organisation (e.g. Porter and Tanner 2004; Zdrilić and Dulčić 2016).

Accordingly, it has long been recognised that sustained, high-performance results in business can be derived from the systematic adoption of the core principles of BE. Porter and Tanner (2004) have defined core excellence values as leadership, customer focus, strategic alignment, organisational learning, people focus, partnership development, fact-based processes management, results focus, and personal responsibility. We will look at each core principle in depth, followed by an example of that principle in practice.

Leadership

According to Porter and Tanner (2004, p. 6), '[t]he specific leadership behaviours of setting a clear direction and values for the organization, creating customer focus, and empowering the organization and its people in the pursuit of excellence are key to all excellence approaches'.

This theme basically emphasises that leaders are responsible for aligning an organisation's resources towards achieving benefits for all its stakeholders. In this sense, they will direct their organisations through well-thought-out strategies and utilisation of human capital as well as other resources in gaining customer satisfaction that result in superior organisational performance.

Leadership in Practice

According to the NIST website (2017b), MBNQA winner Don Chalmers Ford (DCF) is a business that places importance on leadership that follows a customised leadership framework. This systematic framework was improved five times over a period of 20 years to arrive at the successful model that it is today. Organisational sustainability and employee satisfaction are achieved by identifying stakeholder expectations and using them to direct final results. Communication and interaction are key elements of this framework. DCF utilises employee and customer interaction platforms, which begin with an expectation that is then developed into a goal. Areas of improvement are identified along the way, as well as avenues for intelligent risk-taking or new products, processes, and services. DCF also supports their corporate governance in being ethical and socially responsible leaders by aligning projects and sales with community partnerships. Employee engagement, vision deployment, and commitment to core competencies are enforced by every member of the official organisational structure and team efforts are always recognised. DCF also makes a notable annual corporate contribution by mentoring other companies and sharing knowledge of their quality-based experiences. Thus, the vision, mission, and values of the company are reflected in every stage of the leadership system model.

Customer Focus

According to Porter and Tanner (2004, p. 6),

> [t]he customer is the final judge of product quality and service delivery. Customer loyalty and retention are best achieved by understanding the current and future needs of current and prospective customers. The voice

of the customer is critical in designing the product or service 'offer', and in designing the processes that impact on the customer.

So, it is the kind of thinking that ensures 'the customer is in the driver's seat'. Hence, when customer requirements are understood and fulfilled by setting up appropriate end-to-end processes, product or service satisfaction is likely to be high. Organisations therefore have to strive to achieve this.

Customer Focus in Practice

According to NIST (2017b), customers are the focal point of the Charleston Area Medical Center (CAMC), which is thriving in the health-care industry. By broadly classifying four different patient groups and customer or market segments via a wide range of qualitative and quantitative data-listening methods, it has developed a customer communication and response system, along with a service excellence team to supervise it. Customer feedback and customer support is used to track performance measures and manage customer expectations. Social media and Web technology are also used to listen to customer compliments and grievances. A customer touchpoint committee then uses a standardised method to evaluate the comments and thus further understand customer requirements. A monthly meeting is also held in which the service excellence team discusses the metrics of trends and top issues related to patient experience enhancement. Mapping and benchmarking these trends and issues helps service leaders improve customer response as well as determine other market segments, which are differentiated according to service groups analysed through forecasting and aggregation. Finally, existing programmes and their relevance are reviewed for quality assurance. Key driving points for customer satisfaction/dissatisfaction and engagement are assessed to eliminate dissatisfying processes.

Strategic Alignment

Porter and Tanner (2004, p. 6) point out that '[a]ll the excellence models stress the importance of strategic development, alignment and planning. In this respect, an excellence approach can be differentiated from many TQM-type programmes, where a lack of strategic integration frequently results in bolt-on quality programmes'.

Organisations have to give clear importance to strategic planning. This is the fundamental ingredient to improving quality. It is only when you have a plan, and integrate your resources with the plan, that good results can be achieved.

Strategic Alignment in Practice

MidwayUSA, a rare two-time winner of the MBNQA (in 2009 and 2015), carries out strategic planning for its overall company and individual departments by consistently reviewing the organisation's strategic planning process and its ability to meet organisational goals. The strategic plan requirements range from sales growth to customer retention to meeting quality standards.

Data gathered and presented through balanced scorecards and projected trends is analysed using category matrix analysis, and any blind spots in the planning are addressed by conducting company- and department-based SWOT (strengths, weaknesses, opportunities, threats) analyses. These data are also employed to develop action plans which are used to develop an overall key growth plan as well as to address goals *en route* to completing strategic objectives. Suppliers, partners, and competitors are carefully considered when building the key growth plan, along with both internal and external costs and barriers (NIST 2017b).

Organisational Learning, Innovation, and Improvement

> Stimulating individual and organizational learning, innovation and improvement through the effective sharing of knowledge and information is a critical element in an excellence approach. (Porter and Tanner 2004, p. 6)

Human capital is indeed vital to organisational success. Creativity and innovation are the core elements nurtured though an organised process.

Organisational Learning, Innovation, and Improvement in Practice

The Charter School of San Diego (CSSD), winner of the MBNQA in 2015, offers quality academic programming for all students and has been particularly successful in implementing redirective programmes to address the needs of students at higher risk of dropping out. As a business, CSSD concentrates its efforts on sustainability and fair practices.

CSSD uses research to develop and hone its sustainability plan and organisational structure. Electronic data are collected and integrated into a knowledge management system; this information then informs employees' team and individual scorecards. Social media is monitored daily by the communications department, which enables CSSD to provide immediate responses and feedback to customers and stakeholders. Further, organisational data are made immediately available to the appropriate stakeholders through fully integrated information technology systems. CSSD also utilises outside research (such as a survey of charter schools' successful ventures) to inform its practices. CSSD thus obtains organisational data and information through a wide range of approaches, and manages these data to ensure accuracy and validity, integrity and reliability, and currency. Overall, here too, the role and importance of human capital is visible (NIST 2017b).

People Focus

According to Porter and Tanner (2004, p. 6),

> [a]n organization's success is highly dependent upon the knowledge, skills, creativity and motivation of its people. This 'people potential' is best harnessed through shared values supported by a culture of trust and empowerment. Valuing people is a critical element in an excellence approach.

Thus, people are a great resource which cannot easily be imitated by a competitor. Organisations should therefore constantly develop strategies to make their workforce, that is, human capital, a key competitive advantage.

People Focus in Practice

Mid-America Transplant Services (MTS), a 2015 MBQNA winner, utilises systematic strategic discussions to cultivate a mission-driven workforce and address business, market, and regulatory challenges and opportunities. The reinforcement of customer and business needs is a priority for MTS and is managed by its leadership system. MTS's mission statement is also a key factor in staff engagement, satisfaction, and retention.

Through its workforce planning process, MTS manages the needs of its workforce and the overall organisation, assesses its workforce capability and capacity, ensures continuity, and prevents workforce reductions. During hiring, necessary skills are identified in job descriptions and innovative recruiting methods are utilised to ensure that the workforce, that is, its human capital represents the diverse cultures of the community; these methods include recruiting via local community colleges and universities as well as social networking outlets such as Facebook, Twitter, LinkedIn, and CareerBuilder.

Once hired, employee competencies are monitored through a performance evaluation process. MTS assesses staff by soliciting feedback through monthly as well as ongoing strategic discussions at work system meetings, leadership team meetings, and executive leadership team meetings. MTS also gathers feedback from staff focus groups that are representative of all workforce segments, effectively allowing the organisation to validate engagement drivers for all of its employees.

MTS further systematically assesses workplace environmental factors to ensure and improve workforce health by utilising a comprehensive wellness programme. Additional organisational policies that support the well-being of the workforce include a generous paid leave plan, an emergency medical bank plan, paid holidays, tuition assistance, and an organisation-wide incentive plan. MTS thus organises and manages its workforce at individual, key process, and work system levels, as seen in its work system alignment. The culture of MTS reinforces intelligent risk-taking to achieve innovation, allowing the organisation to ensure that all goals and targets are closely monitored and that accountability is achieved, all of this through its focus on human capital (NIST 2017b).

Partnership Development

Porter and Tanner (2004, p. 6) write that '[o]rganizations need to develop longer-term strategic mutually beneficial partnerships with a range of external partners, including customers, suppliers and education organizations. Successful longer-term partnerships focus on delivering sustained value for the partners'.

Partners are central to any business today. Organisations can succeed when they deploy mutual long-term relationships with their partners.

Partnership Development in Practice

MidwayUSA, the 2009 and 2015 winner of the MBNQA, recognises that suppliers and key partners are critical to maintaining customer satisfaction and organic company growth. By implementing a variety of strategies, MidwayUSA promotes collaboration with and among suppliers and partners to improve performance, results, and overall satisfaction.

MidwayUSA selects suppliers using a supplier relationship management and setup process, which assesses estimated performance according to specific criteria directly related to stakeholder requirements as well as merchandising strategies, sales quotas, profit margins, inventory turnover requirements, and customer needs and values. The organisation also manages its supply chain according to a recurring process cycle that begins with supplier programme management and supplier relationship management. In addition to suppliers making site visits, and sales representative communication processes, Midway gathers feedback from key suppliers and partners, known as the Top 10 or Next 10, via annual surveys regarding their requirements and satisfaction as well as annual planning meetings.

MidwayUSA also utilises a monthly supplier performance evaluation process to assess and maintain effective supplier and partner relationships. The results of these evaluations are published in supplier performance reports, which include data on inventory analysis and aging, in transits, in stock rate, and overall performance. These data are then integrated with Midway's dashboards, merchandising scorecard, company scorecard, and monthly category sales reviews by product line. Suppliers are notified when they fail to meet performance criteria. All these excellence practices are supported by its human capital (NIST 2017b).

Fact-Based Processes Management

According to Porter and Tanner (2004, p. 7),

> [p]rocesses are the 'engines' that deliver every organization's value proposition. The focus of all excellence approaches is on designing processes to meet customer requirements, systematically managing processes on the basis of facts and improving processes on the basis of customer feedback and feedback from the process itself. Process capability is based on the ability of the organization's processes to meet customer requirements.

So processes are hard-factor mechanics for improving quality. These are to be designed and managed by effective and efficient human capital.

Fact-Based Processes Management in Practice

At MidwayUSA, services are developed using process design to align key performance indicators with business needs and direction. Process effectiveness audits, as well as LEAN and Six Sigma projects, are used to improve process effectiveness and efficiency while reducing performance variability. MidwayUSA conducts an annual review to analyse processes and facilitate integration and improvement. It also implements the International Organization for Standardization (ISO) audit process to assess ISO compliance and determine if processes are meeting requirements. Improvements and corrective actions are identified, implemented, and refined through reviews, audits, and improvement projects. Effectiveness and efficiency measures are reviewed on a monthly and in-process basis at both the company and department level, and dashboards are used to monitor the daily performance of operations. MidwayUSA has also established productivity measures for individual employees where appropriate, and these individual performance measures are integrated with the overall performance management process. Additionally, MidwayUSA's process design system uses LEAN principles to prevent defects, service errors, and rework. Processes are developed with an eye to minimising the cost of inspections and audits, as well as variances or non-compliance, by including automated system checks, in-process reports, and alerts. This also reduces the costs of inspections, tests, and audits. These efforts, taken in total, have led to improvements in key measure performance. For example, the implementation of the Nitro Express shipping system in 2010 resulted in efficiency and productivity improvements from 2011 to 2014 and increased system throughput from 780 to 1765 invoices per hour, a 126% improvement (NIST 2017b).

Results Focus

Porter and Tanner (2004, p. 7) write that '[e]xcellence is concerned with creating value for all the key stakeholders, including customers, employees, suppliers and partners, the public and the community at large. Balancing the needs of all these key stakeholders is a critical part of developing successful strategies'.

Results signal the performance of the organisation. These are the outcomes achieved as a result of integration of human capital into business excellence themes.

Results Focus in Practice

St. David's HealthCare, an MBNQA winner in 2014, is reported by the NIST (2017b) website to have

> exhibited exceptional performance in net revenue growth through expanded operations and operational discipline between 2007 and 2013, with an increase of more than 70 percent. Additionally, the return on assets has increased from approximately 17 percent in 2007 to 33 percent in 2013, far exceeding the 4.7 percent average benchmark for Moody's AA-rated organizations. [Its] financial strength allows it to reinvest in its facilities each year without incurring any long-term debt.

Further, Hill Country Memorial (HCM), a 2014 award recipient,

> demonstrated significant improvements in its financial performance from 2010 to 2013. During that period, HCM's net income increased from $10 million to nearly $20 million, cash flow to total debt ratios improved from 50 to 60, and cash and investments to debt ratios improved from less than 1.5 to higher than 3. (NIST 2017b)

Social Responsibility

According to Porter and Tanner (2004, p. 7), '[r]responsibility to the public, ethical behaviour and good citizenship are important in an excellence approach, and are critical to the longer-term interest of the organization'.

Thus, achieving results in a social arena is an important element of business excellence and, more importantly, human capital has a key role to play in obtaining such results, in particular by influencing the decision-making that has an impact on society as a whole.

Social Responsibility in Practice

At the BMW Plant in Regensburg, Germany, winner of the EFQM Excellence Prize in 2013, '[t]argets for 'carbon free energy supply' and activities behind that (skills, technical developments) have reduced carbon emissions by about 25% from 2006 to 2012' (EFQM 2013a). Similarly, Wakefield and District Housing, another 2013 EFQM Excellence Prize winner, reduced carbon emissions by over 18% from 2008 to 2011 (EFQM 2013b).

Conclusion

This introductory chapter has explored the influence of BE through the role of human capital and its values in business organisations. BE frameworks are a way forward for organisations that seek to carry out effective evaluations and build improvement plans for ongoing sustainable excellence. This aspect has already been demonstrated by organisations across the world using the previously discussed BEMs as the basis for continuous performance improvement.

Additionally, global frameworks, such as the MBNQM and EFQM, have been used as the basis for many national quality awards developed worldwide. Although the number of quality award models has seen a decline in recent years, the number of global frameworks has remained consistent and the criteria for these frameworks have undergone substantial revision, ensuring that they remain relevant and can be adapted to specific industries.

Common themes in BEMs, with some case examples, were also discussed. The core themes of excellence are: leadership, customer focus, strategic alignment, organisational learning, people focus, partnership development, fact-based processes management, and results focus. Each of these values needs to be integrated to achieve performance or business excellence within an organisation where the role of human capital is seen to be paramount. In Chap. 2, we will explore relevant theories that link to business excellence.

Overall, the key points emerging from this chapter are that BE frameworks are a way forward for organisations that seek to carry out effective evaluations. The core themes of BE stated here are linked to the TQM approach. There needs to be a mechanism to assess organisations' overall values besides financial standards. The BE frameworks help organisations to build improvement plans for ongoing sustainable excellence. Although a special excellence model may not suit the needs of an organisation, global excellence frameworks can be a starting point to carry out a self-assessment based on non-tangible aspects. The core themes of excellent leadership, customer focus, strategic alignment, organisational learning, people focus, partnership development, fact-based processes management, and results focus have to be integrated to achieve performance or BE within an organisation. Organisations can develop unique business models that reflect relevant measures and values based on which an improvement roadmap can be drawn for sustaining business results.

References

Adebanjo, D. (2001). TQM and business excellence: Is there really a conflict? *Measuring Business Excellence, 5*(3), 37–40.

Ahmed. (2015). New research shows 61 countries with national business excellence awards. Retrieved April 20, 2017, from http://blog.bpir.com/latest-news/new-research-shows-67-countries-with-national-business-excellence-awards/

Aras, G., & Crowther, D. (2010). Sustaining business excellence. *Total Quality Management, 21*(5), 565–576.

Arasli, H. (2012). Towards business excellence in the hospitality industry: A case for 3-, 4-, and 5-star hotels in Iran. *Total Quality Management & Business Excellence, 23*(5–6), 573–590. https://doi.org/10.1080/14783363.2012.669539

Asif, M., & Gouthier, M. H. J. (2014). What service excellence can learn from business excellence models. *Total Quality Management & Business Excellence, 25*(5–6), 511–531.

ASQ. (2017). *What is total quality management (TQM)?* Retrieved from http://asq.org/learn-about-quality/total-quality-management/overview/overview.html

EFQM. (2013a). *Process and results.* Retrieved from http://www.efqm.org/success-stories/process-and-results

EFQM. (2013b). http://www.efqm.org/members-area/knowledge-base/wakefield-and-district-housing-uk-efqm-prize-winner-2013

EFQM. (n.d.-a). *Fundamental concepts.* Retrieved from http://www.efqm.org/efqm-model/fundamental-concepts

EFQM. (n.d.-b). *The EFQM excellence model.* Retrieved from http://www.efqm.org/the-efqm-excellence-model

Evans, J. R. (2008). *Quality & performance excellence: Management, organization and strategy* (5th ed.). Mason: Thomson South Western.

Harrington, H. J. (2004). The fallacy of universal best practices. *Total Quality Management & Business Excellence, 15*(5–6), 849–858.

Kanji, K. G. (1998). Measurement of business excellence. *Total Quality Management, 9*(7), 633–643. https://doi.org/10.1080/0954412988325

Mann, R. S., & Grigg, N. P. (2006). *A study of national strategies for organizational excellence.* Paper presented at the 5th multinational alliance for the advancement of organizational excellence conference-oxymorons, empty boxes, or important contributions to management thought and practice, Sydney, Australia.

Mann, B., Mohammad, M., & Agustin, M. T. A. (2011). *Understanding business excellence-An awareness guidebook an awareness guide book for SMEs.* Asian Productivity Organization. Retrieved from http://www.apo-tokyo.org/coe/files/Understanding-Business-Excellence.pdf

Matias, J. C. O., & Coelho, D. A. (2011). Integrated total quality management: Beyond zero defects theory and towards innovation. *Total Quality Management & Business Excellence, 22*(8), 891–910.

NIST. (2016). *Four U.S. organizations receive nation's highest honor for performance excellence*. Retrieved from https://www.nist.gov/news-events/news/2016/11/four-us-organizations-receive-nations-highest-honor-performance-excellence

NIST. (2017a). *Baldrige*. Retrieved from https://www.nist.gov/baldrige/how-baldrige-works

NIST. (2017b). *Baldrige award recipient information*. Retrieved from http://patapsco.nist.gov/Award_Recipients/index.cfm

Oakland, J. S., & Tanner, S. J. (2008). The relationship between business excellence and performance–an empirical study using Kanji's leadership excellence model. *Total Quality Management, 19*(7–8), 733–749.

Porter, L., & Tanner, S. (Eds.). (2004). *Assessing business excellence*. London/New York: Routledge.

Zairi, M., & Alsughayir, A. A. (2011). The adoption of excellence models through cultural and social adaptations: An empirical study of critical success factors and a proposed model. *Total Quality Management & Business Excellence, 22*(6), 641–654.

Zapata-Cantu, L., Cantu Delgado, J. H., & Gonzalez, F. R. (2016). Resource and dynamic capabilities in business excellence models to enhance competitiveness. *The TQM Journal, 28*(6), 847–868.

Zdrilić, I., & Dulčić, Ž. (2016). Business excellence as a success factor for the performance of large Croatian enterprises. *Management: Journal of Contemporary Management Issues, 21*(1), 145–162.

2

Theoretical Frameworks

Introduction

The goals or objectives of human resource management (HRM) are multifold. From a business perspective, the foremost are economic objectives, which lead organisations to follow cost-effectiveness, organisational flexibility, and sustained competitive HR advantage. Thus, a fundamental economic goal in HRM is for managers to try to stabilise an effective production system at a cost that is competitive in their industry. There are differences in what this means across different industries. Thus, capital-intensive (high-tech and knowledge-intensive) contexts and labour-intensive (manufacturing and low-skill) services will need different strategies. Similarly, when it comes to organisational flexibility, some element of flexibility is important in an organisation's HRM if it is to cope with change. The five aspects of flexibility are numerical flexibility, financial flexibility, functional flexibility, short-term responsiveness, and long-term agility. Achieving business excellence requires recognising which flexibility is needed for the organisation, which in turn will help address particular areas. Lastly, when it comes to sustained competitive (HR) advantage, there is a need for a higher-order economic goal which involves achieving sustained, superior profitability despite the efforts of

F. Lasrado, V. Pereira, *Achieving Sustainable Business Excellence*,
https://doi.org/10.1007/978-3-319-73314-2_2

competitors. This is achieved through human capital advantage (HCA) and social capital advantage (SCA) and more specifically through labour-cost advantage (LCA) and labour-differentiation advantage (LDA).

Other objectives of HRM are sociopolitical, and these include areas such as social legitimacy and managerial autonomy or power. Social legitimacy is the fundamental sociopolitical goal in HRM. It covers compliance with legal requirements and adaptation to important social norms: regulative, normative, and cultural-cognitive. In practice, the legitimacy goals of employers vary from non-compliance to compliance, through to 'employer of choice' objectives. These have all been known to lead to superior business excellence in firms. Similarly, when it comes to managerial autonomy and power, management also has an underlying motive to enhance its power. Much of this is a natural and necessary impulse but it carries the potential to undermine employee motivation and may set managers at odds with the interests of other stakeholders.

Human Capital

When it comes to the role of human capital in business excellence, we argue here that human capital can impact on two determined levels: individual and organisational. On an organisational level, we extend the arguments made by Boxall (1998), that human resource advantage (HRA), the positive differentiation through human resources, is portrayed in two ways: first, by HCA, through superior forms of human capital (i.e. recruiting and retaining people with high-value tacit knowledge and skills); and second, by organisational process advantage (OPA), through superior social capital, systems, and processes (i.e. managing people in ways that create higher levels of trust, cooperation, and commitment). The argument here is that the outcomes to attaining greater business excellence will be achieved when these two sources reinforce each other, that is, HRA = f (HCA.OPA).

On the individual level, managing people, that is, HRM, is an inevitable process in organisations. HRM is about managing work and people, including both individual and collective dimensions, which is also an aspect of all management jobs. HRM can thus be usefully understood as a set of activities aimed at building individual and organisational performance (P). Further, at the individual level, HRM consists of managerial attempts to influence individual ability (A), motivation (M), and the opportunity to perform (O). At the group or collective level, HRM plays an important role in building workforce organisation and capabilities and the general climate of employee attitudes. Thus, the following formula becomes pertinent when it comes to achieving greater business excellence through superior performance:

$$P = f\left(A.M.O\right), \text{where } P = \text{Performance}; A = \text{Ability};$$
$$M = \text{Motivation}; O = \text{Opportunity}$$

Resource- and Knowledge-Based View

Another important theory we link to business excellence is the resource-based view (RBV) of the firm. For many years, the internal side of the SWOT model (strengths, weaknesses), including operations management and critical HR issues, was devalued by models of strategy that focused only on external aspects (opportunities, threats) (e.g. Porter 1990). The RBV has helped to rebalance that situation, as it looks at the internal characteristics of a firm and is a major branch of the theory of strategic management. One of the first proponents of the RBV, Edith Penrose (1959), argued as follows:

- The firm is an administrative structure and a bundle of productive resources.
- The knowledge and experience of the management team and their subjective interpretation (or 'images') of the firm's environment make a major difference to how firms evolve.
- Firms are 'heterogeneous' rather than 'homogeneous': they retain important differences even when competing closely.

This perspective was picked up by Wernerfelt (1984) and then by a series of other strategy writers from the late 1980s (e.g. Barney 1991). They argued that resources could be both tangible and intangible semi-permanent assets of a firm. For example, these could include in-house knowledge of technology, brands, skilled employees (and quality of employee know-how), trade contacts, machinery and equipment, capital, efficient processes, and reputation with customers—to name a few. In the RBV, the desirable resources or 'strategic assets' possess specific characteristics. Such resources are argued to be

- Valuable: helpful in grasping opportunities or countering threats in competitive markets, to deliver superior results
- Appropriable: capable of benefiting the firm's shareholders (if internal bargaining by managers and employees soaks up the superior productivity of a firm's resources, shareholders will not benefit through greater profits)
- Inimitable: very hard to imitate or copy, either directly or indirectly (i.e. by substitution)

The literature further argues that 'resources' will not deliver superior value if they are easily imitated. Barriers to imitation include the following:

- Unique timing and learning: path dependence; getting to the action ahead of others and learning more quickly from experience
- Social complexity: the network of relationships that grows as people work together inside and across organisations (social architecture/social capital)
- Causal ambiguity: the uncertainty, inside and outside a high-performing organisation, as to what exactly makes it successful

Hamel and Prahalad (1994) developed the idea of 'core competencies' (earlier referred to as 'distinctive' competencies) for the application of RBV in a firm to, for example, business excellence. A core competence

- Includes a bundle of skills and technologies that enables a company to provide particular benefits to its customers.
- Is not product-specific.
- Represents the sum of learning across individual skill sets and individual organisational units.
- Must be competitively unique.
- Is not just an asset in the accounting sense of the word.
- Represents a broad opportunity arena or gateway to the future.

Hamel and Prahalad (1994) state that to apply RBV two important aspects have to be understood by firms: first, an emphasis on developing a knowledge-based rather than a product-based understanding of a firm; and second, whatever the terminology, human and social capital is clearly an essential aspect of a company's special competencies. Leonard (1998), too, came up with four dimensions of what she called 'core capabilities'. She identified these as employee knowledge and skill; physical technical systems; managerial systems; and values and norms. Her model illustrates the HR implications more clearly: for example, each strength can become a weakness, continuous renewal is required to avoid 'core rigidities', and recognising the strategic importance of capabilities to a firm.

One example of the application of RBV through the core competency argument is Apple, which can be said to be 'making user-friendly user interfaces and design'. Similarly, the core competency of Walmart can be said to be 'groceries at a low cost' and that of Dell 'custom-made PCs direct from the manufacturer at a low cost'. Note that these overarching competencies and service strategies, in effect, lead organisations to identify several such core competencies that contribute and are valuable and inimitable. These could be in HR, marketing, operations, finance, IT, supply chain, processes, R&D, and so on, or could involve a combination of these functions. The key question then is how do these core competencies/capabilities lead to greater business excellence? The RBV thus encourages a focus on the know-how of firms, both technical and managerial. Such know-how focuses on the creation and exploitation of knowledge and organisational learning. In this context, some speak of the knowledge-based view (KBV) of the firm, although firms vary in knowledge intensity, with some operating effectively with fairly stable know-how while others work in knowledge-intensive conditions. For all firms, however, the environment can change. Therefore, the need to build the capacity for learning, or the firm's dynamic capability (Teece et al. 1997), is a critical issue, and people are naturally central to this process. It is also argued that sources of superior value will not come from individual HR policies but rather from astutely crafted and consistently enacted HR systems. Thus, HR systems are an especially valuable part of social capital when they enable the firm to recruit and retain highly talented people and to optimise their interactions. These individuals become the elite group of core employees, who lead in achieving business excellence for a firm.

Corporate Social Responsibility

Corporate social responsibility (CSR) is part of every business strategy and has grown with increasing recognition within business and academic circuits in recent years (Anderson and Bieniaszewska 2005; Doku and Appiah-Kubi 2014; Egri et al. 2004; Kuada and Hinson 2012; Lynes and Andrachuk 2008; Tullberg 2005). CSR as a strategy has also received the attention of the popular press through magazines and journals as it captures some aspects of information in the areas of conferences, seminars, campaigns, advocacy, and technical advice (Carroll and Shabana 2010). CSR strategies are needed to correct or minimise the impact of business operations within society, and they also enhance cordial relations between the two in order to attain an environment conducive to operations. Arguably, investing in one's business society is not parallel to the shareholder objective of wealth creation. Thus, can advancing business excellence through the role of an organisation's human capital be the bridge that creates CSR that is inclusive to all stakeholders?

Empirical evidence has established that enterprises that work towards meeting stakeholders' expectations, for example through business excellence, have a high propensity to increase profit, which helps to achieve the shareholder objective (Economist Intelligence Unit 2008; Kim and Statman 2011; KPMG International 2011; Darnall et al. 2008; Marom 2006). For instance, a highly motivated workforce (human capital) may employ innovative skills to manage costs efficiently to the benefit of shareholders. Again, as reiterated by the United Nations, where CSR is carefully managed, certain operational costs are avoided as there is the tendency to record fewer lawsuits, public protests, and other interruptions by local communities, and to a large extent, the global business community. The United Kingdom Department of Trade and Industry reinforces this and posits that the era when CSR was perceived to be in conflict with shareholders' interests is past; the new order is that while continuing to work for the interests of its investors, firms must embrace the well-being of society as a whole. Apart from working to attain the objectives of those who provide financial resources for investments, corporate bodies are to meet the expectations of other key stakeholders. For a multinational mining enterprise (MNE), key stakeholders apart from the shareholders may include local and national governments, employees, local communities, contractors, environmental advocacy groups, and financial market operators. Each of these stakeholders has particular expectations that need to be satisfied by the company. For example, employees are generally interested in job security and conditions of service; the government and environmental activists may want firms to adhere to laws relating to the environment, labour, and taxation. Similarly, the local community may expect minimal environmental footprint from industry, job creation activities, and, perhaps, the provision of certain social amenities. Schoenberger-Orgad and McKie (2005) contend that it is imperative for those in charge of governance to constantly address and review the subject of CSR at the decision table. Governments in both advanced and developing countries continue to formulate policies around CSR to show their commitment to protecting the environment and society (Wiggins et al. 2004; Sugiyama and Takeuchi 2008; Zhang and Wen 2008; Yuan et al. 2009; Solangi et al. 2011). Various stakeholder groups including international bodies, civil societies, non-governmental organisations, and local communities are promoting the need for corporate bodies to act responsibly (Aguilera et al. 2007). Despite the multitude of literature on CSR, scholars and interested parties alike have not settled on a common definition for the concept (Crane et al. 2008; Matten and Moon 2008). Perhaps the difficulty in agreeing on a common definition lies in the fact that CSR is dynamic, and cannot be confined to a fixed list of activities. As the Economist Intelligence Unit (EIU) (2008) puts it, CSR approaches are seen differently among industries, job functions, and even geographical locations. In a recent survey that examined the impact of sustainability on enterprises, KPMG International (2011) defined CSR as being about adopting business strategies that meet the current expectations of an organisation and its stakeholders while sustaining both human and natural resources, which will be needed in the foreseeable future. This definition is in conformity with an earlier study by the EIU (2008, p. 4) that posits that CSR is 'those policies and processes which enhance the financial, environmental, societal, human, and other resources on which the company involved depends for its long-term health'. In other words, greater business excellence can be achieved through CSR activities that are inclusive and driven by human capital.

For the past decade, academic literature on CSR has been dominated by the importance and benefits of the concept for shareholders (Servaes and Tamayo 2013; Holtbrügge and Dögl 2012; Kuada and Hinson 2012; Carroll and Shabana 2010; Du et al. 2010; Vaaland and Heide 2008). Unfortunately, there has been little research on effective CSR implementation strategy that will deliver optimum gains to the shareholder (Rangan et al. 2012). In a study of CSR partnerships among mining companies in South Africa, Hamman (2004) found that certain enterprises implemented their CSR programmes independently of the indigenous people. He emphasises that some companies narrowly view their CSR responsibilities as doing 'the right thing' by donating towards charitable causes. Thus, companies do not consider any other way of 'doing' CSR other than donating. They wouldn't consider taking active environmental measures to clean up their industry themselves, or being in dialogue with the indigenous people to find out what they want. Proper engagement of local communities or their appointed representatives by MNEs will ensure the former's views are taken on board during the planning of developmental projects (Shift 2013). The lack of stakeholder engagement could affect the impact of the project and also increases the risk of conflict between the two parties (Shift 2013).

Signalling Theory

Signalling theory is useful for describing behaviour when two parties have access to different types of information (Connelly et al. 2011). That is, the sender may select or signal some information whilst the other party, the receiver, may choose how to interpret the signal. Accordingly, signalling theory holds a prominent position in a variety of management literatures, including strategic management, entrepreneurship, and HR. Signalling theory is thus fundamentally concerned with reducing information asymmetry between two parties (Spence 2002).

Whilst developing the signalling theory, its architect utilised the labour market to model the signalling function on education of a workforce. Its effectiveness explains the pervasive nature of the theory which has been used in a health-marketing context in India (Spence 1973, 2002). Furthermore, in Spence's classic example (1973), the characteristic of quality refers to the underlying, unobservable ability of the signaller to fulfil the needs or demands of an outsider observing the signal or the ability of the individual to complete the signalled action. Hence, in the context of this book, we argue that the signals about its business excellence strategies and priorities that the organisation sends out to its internal (human capital) and external (end users) customers will ascertain its success.

Conclusions

We now bring together the discussed theoretical strands to formulate a thematic model for our book (Fig. 2.1).

We argue that firms can achieve greater levels of business excellence through the intervention of human capital at two levels: the individual and the organisational. On an individual level, performance equals the sum of an individual's ability, motivation, and opportunity, that is, P = f (A.M.O), where P = performance, A = ability, M = motivation, and O = opportunity; and on an organisational level, HRA = f (HCA.OPA), where HRA = human resource advantage, HCA = human capital advantage, and OPA = organisational process advantage. The RBV of a firm helps to

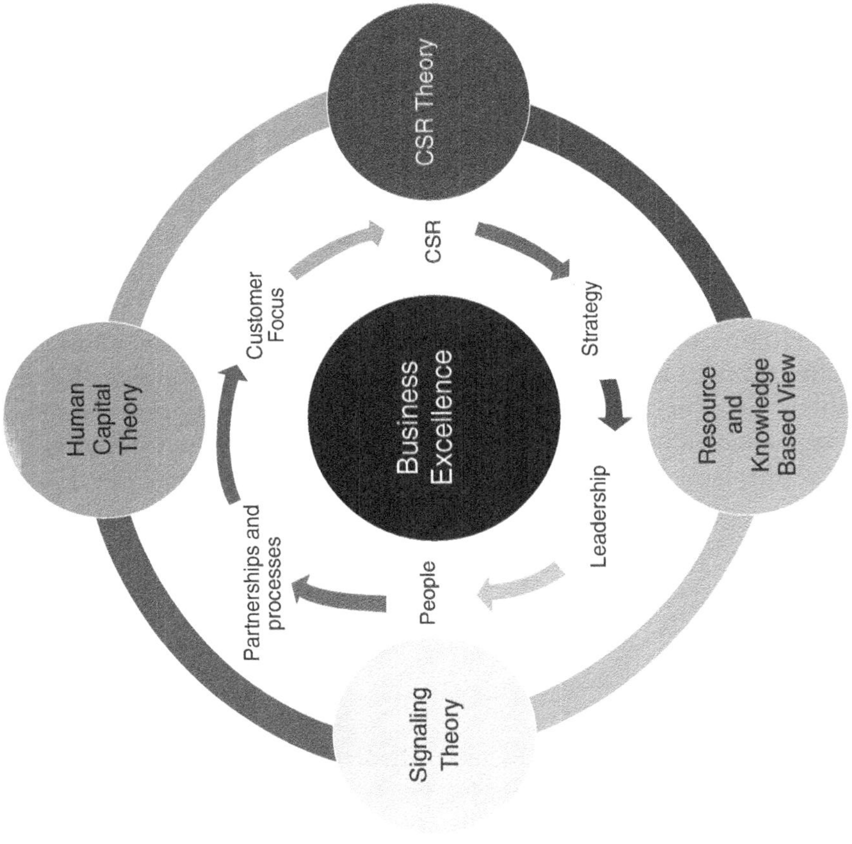

Fig. 2.1 Theoretical strands of excellence

rebalance both the internal characteristics of the firm (strengths and weaknesses) and the external environment (opportunities and threats) and, in the context of human capital, it helps identify a firm's core competencies in a way that is valuable, rare, inimitable, and organised so that it can achieve greater business excellence. The role of human capital in business excellence can also be viewed through a CSR lens in that each stakeholder has particular expectations that need to be satisfied by the firm. Thus, shareholders, employees, suppliers, partners, the government, environmental activists, the local community, and so on would all benefit if the firm pursues and achieves greater business excellence through human capital. Lastly, signalling theory as a lens is important in the context of our book for the following reason: with regard to the role of human capital in business excellence, as a signaller or sender of its business excellence strategy, the firm may select or signal some information whilst the other party, the receiver, who could be any of the stakeholders discussed earlier, may choose how to interpret the signal. The role of human capital here becomes pivotal in this tangible and intangible communication process, as humans need to identify and communicate the correct 'signals' in the context of business excellence to the various stakeholders.

References

Aguilera, R. V., Rupp, D. E., Williams, C. A., & Ganapathi, J. (2007). Putting the S back in corporate social responsibility: A multilevel theory of social change in organizations. *Academy of Management Review, 32*(3), 836–863.

Anderson, C. L., & Bieniaszewska, R. L. (2005). The role of corporate social responsibility in an oil company's expansion into new territories. *Corporate Social Responsibility and Environmental Management, 12*(1), 1–9.

Barney, J. (1991). Firm resources and sustained competitive advantage. *Journal of Management, 17*(1), 99–120.

Boxall, P. (1998). Achieving competitive advantage through human resource strategy: Towards a theory of industry dynamics. *Human Resource Management Review, 8*(3), 265–288.

Carroll, A. B., & Shabana, K. M. (2010). The business case for corporate social responsibility: A review of concepts, research and practice. *International Journal of Management Reviews, 12*(1), 85–105.

Connelly, B. L., Certo, S. T., Ireland, R. D., & Reutzel, C. R. (2011). Signaling theory: A review and assessment. *Journal of Management, 37*(1), 39–67.

Crane, A., McWilliams, A., Matten, D., Moon, J., & Siegel, D. (2008). *The Oxford handbook of CSR*. Oxford: Oxford University Press.

Darnall, N., Henriques, I., & Sadorsky, P. (2008). Do environmental management systems improve business performance in an international setting? *Journal of International Management, 14*(4), 364–376.

Doku, A. K., & Appiah-Kubi, B. (2014). Internalizing the negative externalities of mining in ghana: Should corporate social responsibility be voluntary? *Developing Country Studies, 4*(15), 76–83.

Du, S., Bhattacharya, C. B., & Sen, S. (2010). Maximizing business returns to corporate social responsibility (CSR): The role of CSR communication. *International Journal of Management Reviews, 12*(1), 8–19.

Economist Intelligence Unit. (2008). *Doing good: Business and the sustainability challenge*. London: The Economist Publication.

Egri, C. P., Ralston, D. A., Milton, L., Naoumova, I., Palmer, I., Ramburuth, P., Wangenheim, F., Fu, P., Kuo, M. H., Ansari, M., Carranza, M. T. G., Riddle, L., Girson, I., Elenkov, D., Dabic, M., Butt, A., Srinivasan, N., Potocan, V. V., Furrer, O., Hallinger, P., Dalgic, T., Thanh, H. V., Richards, M., & Rossi, A. M. (2004). *Managerial perspectives on corporate environmental and social responsibilities in 22 countries*. Paper presented at the academy of management conference proceedings, New Orleans.

Hamel, G., & Prahalad, C. K. (1994). *Competing for the future*. Boston: Harvard Business School Press.

Hamman, R. (2004). Corporate social responsibility, partnerships, and institutional change: The case of mining companies in South Africa. *Natural Resources Forum, 28*(4), 278–290.

Holtbrügge, D., & Dögl, C. (2012). How international is corporate environmental responsibility? A literature review. *Journal of International Management, 18*(2), 180–195.

Kim, Y., & Statman, M. (2011). Do corporations invest enough in environmental responsibility? *Journal of Business Ethics, 105*(1), 115–129.

KPMG International. (2011). *Corporate sustainability: A progress report*. Switzerland: KPMG International.

Kuada, J., & Hinson, R. E. (2012). Corporate social responsibility (CSR) practices of foreign and local companies in Ghana. *Thunderbird International Business Review, 54*(4), 521–536.

Leonard, D. (1998). The role of tacit knowledge in group innovation. *California Management Review, 40*(3), 112–132.

Lynes, J. K., & Andrachuk, M. (2008). Motivations for corporate social and environmental responsibility: A case study of Scandinavian airlines. *Journal of International Management, 14*(4), 377–390.

Marom, I. Y. (2006). Toward a unified theory of the CSP–CFP link. *Journal of Business Ethics, 67*(2), 191–200.

Matten, D., & Moon, J. (2008). Implicit and explicit CSR: Conceptual framework for a comparative understanding of corporate social responsibility. *Academy of Management Review, 33*(2), 404–424.

Penrose, E. T. (1959). *The theory of the growth of the firm*. Oxford: Oxford University Press.

Porter, M. E. (1990). *The competitive advantage of nations*. New York: Free Press.

Rangan, K., Chase, L. A., & Karim, S. (2012). *Why every company needs a CSR strategy and how to build it* (Harvard Business School working paper 12–088). Retrieved from http://www.hbs.edu/faculty/Publication%20Files/12-088.pdf

Schoenberger-Orgad, M., & McKie, D. (2005). Sustaining edges: CSR, post-modern play, and SMEs. *Public Relations Review, 31*(4), 578–583.

Servaes, H., & Tamayo, A. (2013). The impact of corporate social responsibility on firm value: The role of customer awareness. *Management Science, 59*(5), 1045–1061.

Shift. (2013). *Stakeholder engagement and the extractive industry under the OECD guidelines for multinational enterprises*. Discussion paper. Retrieved from http://shiftproject.org/sites/default/files/Discussion%20Paper_Stakeholder%20Engagement%20and%20the%20Extractive%20Industry.pdf

Solangi, K. H., Islam, M. R., Saidur, R., Rahim, N. A., & Fayaz, H. (2011). A review on global solar energy policy. *Renewable and Sustainable Energy Reviews, 15*(4), 2149–2163.

Spence, M. (1973). Job market signaling. *Quarterly Journal of Economics, 87*(3), 355–374.

Spence, M. (2002). Signaling in retrospect and the informational structure of markets. *American Economic Review, 92*(3), 434–459.

Sugiyama, N., & Takeuchi, T. (2008). Local policies for climate change in Japan. *The Journal of Environment Development, 17*(4), 424–441.

Teece, D. J., Pisano, G., & Shuen, A. (1997). Dynamic capabilities and strategic management. *Strategic Management Journal, 18*(7), 509–533. https://doi.org/10.1002/(SICI)1097-0266(199708)18:73.0.CO;2-Z

Tullberg, J. (2005). Reflections upon the responsive approach to corporate social responsibility. *Business Ethics: A European Review, 14*(3), 261–276.

Vaaland, T. I., & Heide, M. (2008). Corporate social responsibility: Investigating theory and research in the marketing context. *European Journal of Marketing, 42*(9), 927–953.

Wernerfelt, B. (1984). A resource-based view of the firm. *Strategic Management Journal, 5*(2), 171–180.

Wiggins, S., Marfo, K., & Anchirinah, V. (2004). Protecting the forest or the people? Environmental policies and livelihoods in the forest margins of southern Ghana. *World Development, 32*(11), 1939–1955.

Yuan, Z., Bi, J., & Moriguich, Y. (2009). The circular economy: A new development strategy in China. *Journal of Industrial Ecology, 10*(1–2), 4–8.

Zhang, K., & Wen, Z. (2008). Review and challenges of policies of environmental protection and sustainable development in China. *Journal of Environmental Management, 88*(4), 1249–1261.

3

Impacts of Business Excellence Models: Empirical Evidence from the UAE

Introduction

The first two chapters discussed business excellence (BE) and its links to human capital and the relevant theories. In this chapter, we will investigate how excellence frameworks help businesses grow efficiently and effectively in many ways. Such frameworks integrate technology, infrastructure, and personnel successfully to achieve the organisation's overall goals. According to *In Search of Excellence* by Thomas Peters and Robert Waterman, a survey showed that over the course of 20 years, organisations that had adopted an organisational excellence framework performed above average on both the Dow Jones Industrial Average and Standard & Poor's 500 Index.

Chapter 1 demonstrated that BE can provide an organisation with a foundation for long-term organisational success. Business excellence frameworks (BEFs) synthesise best business practices and management concepts from a variety of disciplines and organisational contexts to provide tools that support an organisation in achieving its overall goals. These tools allow organisations to integrate technology, infrastructure, and human capital to coordinate skills and resources, drive tangible

F. Lasrado, V. Pereira, *Achieving Sustainable Business Excellence*,
https://doi.org/10.1007/978-3-319-73314-2_3

growth, and reduce non-value-adding procedures (Boulter et al. 2005). Another study (Link and Scott 2011) was conducted amongst 273 organisations to study the impact of the Baldrige programme on organisational performance. This showed that companies that had adopted the organisational framework practices attained a benefit-to-cost ratio of 3:1. They also achieved a 107:1 benefit-to-cost ratio when considering the financial gains linked to higher customer satisfaction and a ratio of 820:1 in financial gains linked to higher sales value in excess of resource costs.

Further positive effects associated with Baldridge winners include the following:

- Organisations that have won the Baldrige Award twice demonstrate (a) a median growth in jobs at a rate nearly 20 times greater than the average business over the same time frame, (b) a 92.6% increase in median revenue growth, and (c) a 67% median growth in their number of sites.
- Hospitals that adopt and use the Baldrige criteria were linked to successful operations, management practices, and overall performance in a study by Truven Health Analytics.
- According to survey results reported in Futurescan 2013, 65% of surveyed hospitals are likely to 'use the Baldrige Criteria for Performance Excellence as a systematic framework for performance improvement or as an internal assessment tool' by 2018. The same survey states that 41% of hospitals are likely to apply for the Baldrige Award or a state-level Baldrige-based award by 2018. (NIST 2017)

This chapter will present both theoretical and empirical research on the effects of business excellence awards (BEAs) to illustrate the relevance of BE principles in contemporary business contexts.

Research on Businesses Excellence Awards

On a broader spectrum, the excellence framework can help an organisation in many ways:

- By providing an integrated and coordinated way of achieving tangible results—the organisational excellence framework provides efficient and effective business practices for all business management areas, as well as tools to measure the business's success or failure rate (Pattison 2011), where the role of human capital is paramount.
- By identifying the interdependencies and interrelationships between management areas—in the organisational excellence model, every department is related and depends on other departments to guarantee complete implementation of a successful excellence programme (Schaefer 2011).
- By reducing non-value-added activity—activities which reduce the pace of the organisation's performance (such as repetition, errors, duplication of tasks, activities which lead to dissatisfied customers and employees, and activities that do not help employees achieve the organisational goals) are not just highlighted by the application of the excellence framework but also reduced (Boulter et al. 2005), and this is where the contribution of human capital can count.
- By contributing to becoming an employer of choice—a successful implementation of the organisational excellence model also brings an awareness of employee well-being and greater improvements in organisational performance. This eventually results in efficient and effective human capital (Stoehr 2010), again through human capital.
- By providing a performance-benchmarking programme—an employee performing a task is usually best aware of the mechanics of the task and knows where there is potentially room for improving those mechanics. An organisational excellence framework gives employees the freedom to improve the performance of their tasks. It also allows employees to analyse the productivity of the task both internally and externally and to benchmark it in order to attain human capital efficiency (Mann et al. 2011).
- By providing a platform for long-term organisational success—once the organisational excellence framework has been implemented the organisation tends to grow over time due to the excellence culture that has been developed within it. The leaders in such organisations continually ensure that their human capital follows the principles of the

excellence framework and is motivated to achieve more (Peters and Waterman 1982).

- By increasing the value of the business—according to the financial sector, implementing an organisational excellence framework results in a higher value for the business (Peters and Waterman 1982).

Overall, the benefits of the excellence framework and the motives of companies in applying for the Baldrige and other similar awards have been demonstrated by rigorous research in recent years. The early years of the total quality management (TQM) era focused on the Baldrige Award, but in recent years further extensive research on the European Foundation for Quality Management (EFQM) BEF has been conducted. In this chapter, we compile the empirical research to show the benefits that an organisation can gain from adopting a BE philosophy. Our aim is to present those studies conducted within the last decade to understand the impact and relevance of the BEFs in today's competitive world.

Our main observation taken from the research is that BE delivers a competitive advantage. Many researchers have shown a link between quality activities and organisational performance. Although in the past, most of the research was focused on the American Baldrige framework, other parts of the world (especially Asia) have received attention. We will explore some of these studies and present the motives and benefits associated with BEFs and the role of human capital theories.

Studies Conducted in Recent Years

The empirical research examining the results of BE implementation from 2005 to 2016 is highlighted below. Porter and Tanner (2004) shortlisted a range of studies conducted from 1983 to 2002. The following are some of the more relevant ones reviewed for their paper:

- A study on the benefits of the JUSE (Union of Japanese Scientists and Engineers) (1983)
- A review of Baldrige winners (Wisner and Eakins 1994)

- The first major study on the uses of EFQM Model across Europe
- A 1999 survey of 4000 firms to determine the benefits of business excellence (Samson and Terziovski 1999)
- Examples from various organisations conducting self-assessment using the EFQM Excellence Model
- A review of the effectiveness of business excellence within the automotive industry (Curkovic et al. 2000)
- A study on the impact of quality awards taken from a 2001 survey of hospitals in the USA to examine how business excellence implementation affected organisational performance (Douglas and Judge 2001)
- An investigation into the impact of stakeholder management and social initiative participation on shareholder returns (Hillman and Keim 2001)

In recent years, the empirical research has included the following studies:

- European Foundation for Quality Management Business Excellence Model: An integrative review and research agenda (Young et al. 2010)
- Including Sustainability in Business Excellence Models (Asif et al. 2011)
- A Comparison and Usage Overview of Business Excellence Models (Sampaio et al. 2012)
- A Perspective on Small and Medium-Sized Enterprises in the United Arab Emirates where Management Utilised the European Foundation for Quality Management Concepts of Excellence (Rowland-Jones 2013)
- 'What Service Excellence Can Learn From Business Excellence Models' (Asif and Gouthier 2014)
- Project to Improve Knowledge Management and Key Business Results through the EFQM Excellence Model (Calvo-Mora et al. 2015)
- Modern Analytics and the Future of Quality and Performance Excellence (Evans 2015)

- Criteria for Excellence in Business (Ghicajanu et al. 2015)
- Developing an Agile Business Excellence Model for Organisational Sustainability (Dubey 2016)
- What Characterises Leading Companies Within Business Excellence Models? An Analysis of 'EFQM Recognised for Excellence' Recipients in Spain (Escrig and de Menezes 2015)
- Deploying Business Excellence – Success Factors for High Performance (Tickle et al. 2016)

The United Arab Emirates: A Case Study

In this section, we will discuss the case of the United Arab Emirates (UAE). The UAE was chosen as the case study because while research on excellence impacts is now carried out extensively in the Western world, the UAE has a 22-year history of excellence that has not yet been fully studied and reported. A recent study conducted by Lasrado (2017) examined the factors that motivated organisations in the UAE to participate in BEAs. The participants for this research comprised attendees of the Best Practices and Benchmarking Forum, an annual event hosted by the UAE Department of Economic Development. A questionnaire was distributed to all attendees and a total of 107 responses were received. The profiles of the participants included senior managers, quality managers, and BE managers. The main objective of the questionnaire was to identify the sources of motivation for participation in the Dubai Quality Award (DQA) as well as the perceived benefits of BEAs.

The main impetus for participation in the BEA was corporate image. This has the highest mean of 4.5, and 91% of respondents strongly agreed that it was very important. Other highly valued motives were market advantage (78%), benefits experienced by others (77%), relations with communities (73%), and relations with authorities (70%). Less valued but still important motives included cost reductions (63%), customer pressure (66%), and benefits received by others (62%). These factors suggest that BE adaptation occurs mainly to enforce the company's commitment to excellence and to serving as role models, while indirectly improving market share.

All respondents stated that they had benefited from applying BE principles, and none indicated that the BEA was completely without benefit. However, the respondents differed on the nature of the benefits achieved. For example, the most important perceived benefits were an improved corporate image and improvement of internal procedures. Of the participants, 91% said that their corporate image and internal procedures had improved. Interestingly, while improved internal procedure was valued relatively low as a motive, it was the highest rated benefit. Other significant reported benefits were improved customer satisfaction (cited by 88% of respondents), improved employee morale (85%), improved relations with communities (82%), improved relations with authorities (79%), and improved market share (75%). The benefits least noted by respondents were improved productivity (73%) and increased profit margin (71%).

Motives and Benefits Associated with Other Sources

Much literature has been published on the factors that motivate companies to adopt a BEF within their organisations. Generally, the BEFs are implemented to develop positive attitudes towards quality, to encourage companies to introduce TQM, and to allow organisations to assess themselves in comparison to TQM models so that they can identify their strengths and areas of improvements (Wilkes and Dale 1998; Talwar 2011; Ghobadian and Woo 1996). The frameworks acknowledge the successes of business organisations and recognise the achievements of those organisations (Brown 2013). Hughes and Halsall (2002) explain that the excellence model draws best practice and management thinking from a variety of sources and offers them as a template against which organisations can be assessed and ranked for the purposes of achieving and awarding prizes.

Boys et al. (2005) suggested that motivations for companies to adopt BE fall into one of two categories: endogenous and exogenous. Endogenous motives include attuning to employees' satisfaction, standardising the internal operations process, and increasing process stability and capability. Exogenous drivers are meant to be recognised by the customers, for example by establishing a good relationship between the company suppliers and stakeholders and complying with social, environmental, and safety issues.

Araújo and Sampaio (2014) studied the motivations of Portuguese companies and found that they were predominantly internal, which is common amongst European organisations. These companies sought to assess their progress in TQM and excellence, but not just to win a prize.

Metaxas and Koulouriotis (2014) argued that awards are an excellent opportunity for assessment. They offer recognition, especially to firms who use quality in their marketing programmes, and allow examination of the organisation from a global perspective to help it achieve a world-class level. Similarly, Mann et al. (2011) reported several reasons for adopting BE that are related to (1) improved company competitiveness needed to achieve world-class status, (2) continuous improvement, (3) quality improvement, and (4) performance measurement. Talwar (2011) showed that companies in China, India, and Thailand all strive to achieve high performance and to become world-class by using the national quality award (NQA) criteria as a means for improvement.

In addition, organisations may tend to adapt BEFs as a way to enhance relationships with consumer groups and communities as well as to improve customer recognition and fulfil external stakeholder expectations (Tutuncu and Kucukusta 2007). The aim may be to win a prestigious award (Metaxas and Koulouriotis 2014) or to enhance marketing by demonstrating to customers the excellence of their products (Alsaleh 2007).

Winning quality awards can also be viewed as a credible and low-cost mechanism to signal to the market and to customers that a firm has implemented an effective quality programme. Araújo and Sampaio (2014) consider awards to be more than an end in themselves. They posit that such rewards are important tools used to improve the management systems of public and private organisations and to enable the implementation and continuous improvement of shareholder requirements and expectations. Many researchers agree that organisations gain a competitive advantage by implementing BEFs as doing so directly helps to implement and increase their quality efforts (Talwar 2011; Zárraga-Rodríguez and Alvarez 2013; Link and Scott 2012).

In recent years, other motives have been revealed. A study by Ashraf (2016) in Pakistan reported the following:

- Increased global competition
- Globalisation
- The need for cost reduction
- Multiplication of profits and retention of customers
- Increasingly complex business environment

Akyuz's (2015) study on EFQM models also identified other possible motives:

- Business pressures, such as competition
- Megatrends shaping modern supply chains
- Increasingly complex and highly interdependent Web-enabled supply networks

A study by Zdrilić and Dulčić (2016) on Croatian organisations reported the following motives:

- The possibility of global economic crises
- An intense competition between tourist destinations and the expected (re)structuring of the world's income and demographics
- The need to improve the use of market information throughout the hotel organisations
- The inefficient use of technology with a resulting failure to provide adequate information for decision-making
- An increase in hotel-sector participation in social responsibility

A study by Akdağ (2011) conducted in Kazakhstan reported the following motives for adopting excellence criteria:

- Avoiding financial crises
- The need to ensure the quality of programmes for newcomers
- Supporting and strengthening employee professional development
- Increased demands from society and employees

In New Zealand, Corbett and Angell (2011) reported the following motives:

- The challenge of remaining competitive in a fast-changing environment
- The need to guide efforts towards becoming top-tier performers
- Providing guidelines for comparison and auto-evaluation
- Raising the profile of the organisation and generating pride amongst employees
- Acquiring valuable data for prospective customers looking for reliable companies
- Obtaining significant operational and financial benefits
- Achieving and improving customer satisfaction, financial and market results, human resource results, and organisational effectiveness results
- The need for assisting in delivering long-term stretch goals and building competencies

Kanji (2008) reported motives focused mainly around the following:

- The complexity of present-day business
- Low-cost opportunities
- Quickly expanding global markets
- The boosting of operating efficiencies
- The delivery of better and more personalised customer service

Overall, our analysis of the literature demonstrates that the primary motivations for pursuing BE include achieving internal quality improvements, enriching competitiveness, gaining recognition and publicity from authorities and communities, and acquiring marketing advantages that result in improved market share and better overall organisational performance. There is no clear consensus amongst researchers as to which are the main drivers, and it seems that many sources and motivations may lead to implementation and become associated with the perceived benefits.

Benefits of the Quality Awards

The results and benefits associated with BEAs have been analysed extensively in the academic literature. Most contributions are empirical in nature. For example, Hendricks and Singhal, York and Miree (2004), and Boulter et al. (2005) all reported on the positive financial effects experienced by NQA winners. Specifically, Hendricks and Singhal (1997) explored the performance of firms over ten years and found that quality award-winning firms present better operational performance, a greater increase in sales, and better cost control. Similarly, Eriksson's study (2004), based on interviews of 29 organisations that had participated in the Swedish Quality Award process, reported that most of the organisations considered process orientation, customer orientation, and improvement work to have all been enhanced by their participation in the quality award process. Lin et al. (2013) reported the effect of NQAs on the market value of the award-winning companies and concluded that well-implemented BE programmes could provide a long-term return on the market value of the firms. The Spanish firms study also confirmed that implementation of quality awards leads to improvement in performance under any circumstances (Corredor and Goñi 2010). Overall, these studies also portrayed the positive role of human capital in achieving their goals.

Indeed, when overall quality is improved, the company improves both its market share and its benefits (Lin et al. 2013). For example, Mann et al. (2011) reported that organisations that had adopted BE programmes improved their processes and business results performance from approximately industry average to approximately above average. Organisations often report adopting such programmes as a result of positive and sustained involvement of its human capital to maintain a competitive position in the industry and hopefully to capture a greater market share (Link and Scott 2012; Fonseca 2015; Jacob et al. 2012).

A BE model can be a powerful tool in both improving organisational performance and enhancing business efficiency by bringing together the people, processes, strategies, and technologies needed to produce outstanding results (Lee et al. 2003). Accordingly, organisations benefited from improved operations, management control, and quality awareness amongst its human capital (Rawabdeh 2008).

Many scholars believe that BEAs provide a roadmap for excellence and present companies with an opportunity for self-assessment, identifying areas for improvement, benchmarking, and taking actions needed for improvement (Talwar 2011). Many organisations have adopted BE models because they recognise that they promote the adoption of best practices and tools that allow achieving a strategy of quality, benchmarking of best practices, self-assessment, and continuous improvement (Sampaio et al. 2012; Martin et al. 2011).

To summarise the overall results from the literature studies, the types of performance noted in the theories include quality performance, operating performance, market and financial performance, employee performance, customer satisfaction, innovation performance, project performance, and aggregate firm performance.

Practical Evidence that Excellence Models Are Beneficial

Evidence from US Firms

In the United States, the Baldrige Award has been used widely as an excellence benchmark, and its various winners have demonstrated many achievements resulting from implementation of such an excellence framework. We highlight the achievements of a few prominent award winners in this section as reported on the website of the National Standards Institute (NIST) (Table 3.1).

Table 3.1 List of award winners

Advocate Good Samaritan Hospital (2010)
Overall extremely good clinical results, including a 0.13 reduction to 0.42 (1 = standard) in risk-adjusted mortality between 2007 and 2010. This measure exceeded the six-county top-decile level.
In 2009, achieved 100% compliance with the Centre for Medicare and Medicaid Service recommendation that all pneumonia patients should receive blood cultures before being given antibiotics.
AtlantiCare (2009)
From 2002 to 2009, system revenues increased from $280 million to $651 million, an 11% compound annual growth rate. Over the same time, AtlantiCare's medical centre volume grew at a rate twice that of the state.
Primary service market share increased to a six-year high of 62% in the second quarter of 2008. The regional service area also saw a growth of 57% from 2000 to 2009.
Cargill Corn Milling North America (2008)
Improved financial results due to $7.5 million annual cost savings from implementing innovative ideas for two years.
Customer complaints reduced by 23% annually over three years.
A 19% annual improvement rate in overall worker satisfaction over four years.
A 42% improvement in operational asset health over a five-year period to 85% (world-class level).
City of Coral Springs (2017)
Customer satisfaction: 75% of customer relationships exceeded ten years.
Improved financial results: cost avoidance of $3.22 billion over five years.
Satisfied workforce: 53% decrease in employee turnover over nine years.
Excellent service: 100% of complaints closed within seven business days.
Eastman Chemical Company (1993)
Over 70% of customers ranked Eastman as their number one supplier.
Shipping reliability was near 100% for the four years prior to the award.
Between 1982 and 1993, Eastman received 97 awards from its customers.
Federal Express Corporation (1990)
Annual revenues topped $1 billion within ten years of the company's founding.
Federal Express revenues totalled $7 billion in fiscal year 1990.
The company has received 195 awards in the 13 years prior to the award.
Henry Ford Health System (2011)
From 2004 to 2011, inpatient market share increased by an average of 3% per year.
From 2007 to 2010, net operating income exceeded $25 million per year despite significant increases in uncompensated care.

(*continued*)

Table 3.1 (continued)

Hill Country Memorial (2004)
Significant improvements in financial performance from 2010 to 2013.
Almost double net income to nearly $20 million in the same period, improved cash flow to total debt ratios from 50 to 60, and cash and investments to debt ratios from less than 1.5 to higher than 3.
Lockheed Martin Missiles and Fire Control (2012)
Maintained a major global market position in each of its key lines of business in a shrinking market for the four years preceding its award.
Return on investment grew at a 23% compound annual rate, faster than the industry-best competitor (13.7%).
Memorial Hermann Health System (2016)
Recorded 90% retention for employee partners, 100% for physician partners, and 90% for volunteer partners, all comparable to or exceeding national benchmarks.
Also 90th percentile for patients saying they were 'likely to recommend' day surgery, emergency care, gynaecology, orthopaedics, and women's health.
Nestlé Purina PetCare Co (2010)
Ranked #1 in market share for pet care products in North America and has twice the market share of its closest competitor.
Market share increased by over 3% from 2001 to 2010 in a mature industry.
Pewaukee School District (2013)
PSD achieved a 97.4% graduation rate in 2012–2013; between 2008 and 2012, it also had a higher graduation rate than other county, state, and nearby high-performing districts.
Outperformed national average (74%) in parent and student satisfaction surveys; PSD parent satisfaction with communication ranged between 91.5% and 94.8% in 2012–2013.
Over 12% increase in percentage of PSD students attending a two- or four-year college course, reaching 91.9% in 2011–2012.
Poudre Valley Health System (2008)
Achieved a 24% reduction over three years in risk-adjusted mortality rate.
Achieved 24% increase in net operating margin over two years.
Over a five-year period recorded 725% improvement in medical-group patient satisfaction with urgent care and 100% improvement in overall medical-group patient satisfaction.
Recorded 260% increase in training hours per full-time equivalent (FTE) over three years.

(*continued*)

Table 3.1 (continued)

Premier Inc. (2006)
In a four-year period saw almost 20% average annual increase in consolidated pre-tax operating income.
Reported 95% customer loyalty and 97% customer retention in the year of the award.
Employee turnover reduced to 16%, 11% better than the industry average.
Recorded 22% average drop in industrial customer operating costs over two years.
PRO-TEC Coating Company (2007)
Annual revenue growth of 12% to 16% between 2003 and the year of award.
Over five years, improved employee satisfaction rates by 28% and increased training hours by 12% over two years.
Improved accuracy with a 54% decrease in warehouse errors/orders billed over five years.
Achieved 97% on-time delivery.
Increased ROA and productivity: manufacturing productivity up by 150%, 33% increase in weekly average output, and 39% return on assets.
Ritz-Carlton Hotel Company (1999)
Revenue increased by 40% over five years to $1.5 billion.
Return on investment up 4.5% from 1995 to 1998.
Reported 100% customer loyalty.
Recorded zero customer difficulties.

Evidence from European and Middle Eastern Companies

Amongst European organisations, the EFQM award is generally more widely known than the Baldrige Award. Organisations that have won the EFQM award demonstrate numerous benefits, some of which are presented here to illustrate how BE has benefited these organisations (Table 3.2).

The Motives of the Winning Organisations that Applied for the EFQM and Malcolm Baldrige Awards

Several companies and organisations across the world which have previously won Baldridge Awards were studied, and their reasons for adopting BEFs reviewed. A list of those companies and their motives for adopting BEFs is presented in Table 3.3.

Table 3.2 Evidence from European and Middle Eastern companies

Alpenresort Schwarz, Austria (2013)
Operating profit and cash flow performance has improved yearly over the past decade in line with targets and comparing favourably with local and national competitors.
BMW Plant Regensburg, Germany (2012)
Employee surveys reported 99% overall satisfaction and 'trust in leadership'.
Increasing numbers of targets being met and positive customer reactions reported.
Ongoing improvement in the most important financial business results.
Carbon emissions reduced by about 25% from 2006 to 2012.
Nilufer Municipality, Turkey (2012 Finalist)
Benchmarks and assessment/review of Nilufer Municipality's approaches had significant positive effects on budget realisation through effectiveness and efficiency improvements.
Income shows a positive trend, increasing by 78% from 2008 to 2012.
St Mary's College, Northern Ireland, UK (2013)
Since 2005, over 70% of pupils from St Mary's College have gone on to further/higher education, exceeding the Northern Ireland average.
Increase in people satisfaction, from 75% in 2002 to over 90% in 2010.
Sustained good perception trends over eight years for all society result areas with most achieving perception levels of 90%. Service providers (local libraries, swimming pools, sport complex, buses, etc.) show a satisfaction level of over 99%.
Wakefield and District Housing, England, UK (2013)
Overall customer satisfaction with WDH between 2009–10 and 2012–13 ranged between 86% and 90%.
People overall satisfaction percentages are continually increasing.
Stakeholder positive perceptions of WDH at local, regional, and national level increased from 77% in 2010 to 84% in 2012.
Carbon emissions reduced by over 18% from 2008–09 to 2011–12.

Similarly, from a European perspective, the motives identified by the EFQM award winners are presented in Table 3.4.

Conclusion

BE is a phenomenon that, while it does not *guarantee* definite success, does enable an organisation to grow. Successful implementation of a BEF results in higher goodwill and a more positive image for the organisation that benefits all the stakeholders present, both inside and outside.

Table 3.3 Motives for business excellence

No.	Motives for adopting BEFs for Baldrige Award winners
1	**MidwayUSA Glossary (Small Business 2015)**
	Large swings in demand for the products offered
	Impacted by political uncertainty
	Market volatility and the emergence of other competitors
	Competitive product pricing
	Reduced margins driven by price pressure from competitors
	Loss of identity in crowded market
	Changing customer expectations about delivery times
	Inconsistent supplier pricing policies (minimum advertised price)
	Inventory management of products that are both hard to produce and hard to get
	Computer viruses, malware, phishing, and hacking
	Credit card data breach and credit card fraud
2	**Charleston Area Medical Centre (Health Care 2015)**
	Located in a rural, economically challenged state
	Limited workforce pool and difficulty recruiting from out of state (recruiting and retaining competent staff)
	Governmental pressure to continuously increase quality and decrease cost
	Medical staff alignment and integration
	Redesigning patient work processes to reduce waste, increase direct time at the patient's bedside, and improve the overall quality of care
3	**Hill Country Memorial (Health Care 2014)**
	Acquiring direct competitor performance data is a challenge
	Ability to recruit and retain talented physicians
	Transition to population health management
	Meeting increasing patient expectations
	Revenue pressures and reorientation of economic models
	Out-migration
	New competitors entering the market
4	**St. David's HealthCare (SDH 2014)**
	The need to strategically position the hospital for the rapidly changing health-care environment
	To support its mission of providing exceptional care and to drive improvement
	Patient expectations for service and quality
	Changing reimbursement environment
	New and maturing competition
	To identify opportunities for innovation
	To standardise the process for evaluating innovation pilots and to define the process to communicate best practices across the system
	To drive greater employee and customer engagement
	The need for a performance analysis and review platform

(*continued*)

Table 3.3 (continued)

No.	Motives for adopting BEFs for Baldrige Award winners
5	**PricewaterhouseCoopers (Public Sector 2014)** A sharp decrease in spending on federal contractors and a tremendous increase in work directed to small businesses Opportunities for collaboration with teaming partners and for innovation The federal consulting industry experienced major challenges over the previous few years due to significant federal budget cuts, continuing resolutions, a government shutdown, and sequestration The challenges to obtain reliable comparative data from competitors Federal regulations The need to distinguish the company from competitors in the crowded market

Although the organisation may incur additional costs to build new infrastructure and frameworks, these are recouped through higher productivity from employees, happier customers, more efficient operations for the organisation, and ultimately more profits. Overall, the most common benefits that organisations obtain are better organisational performance and improved customer and employee results.

In the context of the UAE, organisations find similar motives and benefits by adopting the requirements of an NQA. Amongst the many benefits that they perceive, improving internal procedures and building their corporate image are the two most highly valued. Overall, the sources of motivations in fact are also consistent with the rest of the world.

BEFs also have a social impact and account for both tangible and non-tangible benefits. Ultimately, different organisations may have multiple motives in pursuing the excellence framework, and these overarching motives guide organisations towards adopting a systematic improvement programme, which will yield sustained results.

This chapter has shown several examples of winning organisations and their key performance indicators based on either the EFQM or the Baldrige Award. If BEFs are implemented properly, organisations can reap the benefits of excellence; the frameworks also provide a holistic

Table 3.4 Motives for EFQM award

No.	Motives for EFQM award
1	**Wakefield and District Housing, England, UK**
	Increasing employee engagement
	Developing a strategy that goes beyond core business activity to 'create confident communities'
	Increasing customer satisfaction
	Responding to new legislation that calls for reduced carbon emissions
	Increasing revenue
2	**Glasco Housing Association, Scotland, UK**
	Identifying priorities for improvement
	Ensuring a sustainable and growing business
	Increasing employee satisfaction
	Supporting and improving leadership style
	Creating a system to improve complaint handling
	Satisfying society and improving the local neighbourhood
	Increasing work efficiency through improved performance levels to reduce the total work cost
3	**Nilufer Municipality, Turkey**
	Building a structured review of the overall performance to measure achievements and strengths
	Identifying improvement opportunities
	Achieving political goals through the electoral process
	Decreasing the response time for key services
	Increasing employee satisfaction and engagement
	Developing and improving HR policies and strategies
4	**GC Europe, Belgium**
	Increasing product safety and consumer safety (and especially, oral health)
	Using and following the latest scientific knowledge
	Pursuing greater market share despite increased competition
	Increasing customer satisfaction
	Improving customer retention
	Addressing legislation regarding the environment (i.e. carbon footprint)
	Maintaining economic stability and business reliability

solution for continuous improvement even in highly competitive environments.

Finally, overall it has been reported that the BEFs have many benefits, both financial and non-financial, for organisations. They have successfully created an economic impact in many countries. There needs to be a mechanism to assess the overall organisational value besides financial standards. Hence, organisations opting to adopt the excellence framework highlight many internal and external motives and the framework has very often been associated with the improvement of quality and services. Moreover, BEFs also have a social impact and account towards both tangible and non-tangible benefits. Indeed, BE is a phenomenon which, while it does not guarantee definite success, does enable an organisation to grow towards achieving higher maturity on the road to BE. The argument thus made is that organisations should prioritise their motives and work towards reaping the potential benefits available by utilising the excellence frameworks.

References

Akdağ, H. C. (2011). Business excellence in Kazakh higher education institutions. *EMAJ: Emerging Markets Journal, 1*(1), 33–40.

Akyuz, G. A. (2015). Quality excellence in complex supply networks: EFQM excellence model reconsidered. *Total Quality Management & Business Excellence, 26*(11–12), 1282–1297.

Alsaleh, N. A. (2007). Application of quality tools by the Saudi food industry. *The TQM Magazine, 19*(2), 150–161.

Araújo, M., & Sampaio, P. (2014). The path to excellence of the Portuguese organisations recognised by the EFQM model. *Total Quality Management & Business Excellence, 25*(5–6), 427–438.

Ashraf, A. A. (2016). Total quality management, knowledge management and corporate culture: How do they synchronized [sic] for performance excellence. *Pakistan Journal of Commerce and Social Sciences, 10*(1), 200–211.

Asif, M., & Gouthier, M. H. (2014). What service excellence can learn from business excellence models. *Total Quality Management & Business Excellence, 25*(5–6), 511–531.

Asif, M., Searcy, C., Garvare, R., & Ahmad, N. (2011). Including sustainability in business excellence models. *Total Quality Management & Business Excellence, 22*(7), 773–786.

Boulter, F., Bendell, T., Abas, H., Dahlgaard, J., & Singhal, V. (2005). *Report on EFQM and BQF funded study into the impact of the effective importance of organizational excellence strategies on key performance results*. Leicester: The Centre of Quality Excellence, University of Leicester.

Boys, K., Wilcock, A., Karapetrovic, S., & Aung, M. (2005). Evolution towards excellence: Use of business excellence programs by Canadian organizations. *Measuring Business Excellence, 9*(4), 4–15.

Brown, A. (2013). Managing challenges in sustaining business excellence. *International Journal of Quality & Reliability Management, 30*(4), 461–475.

Calvo-Mora, A., Navarro-García, A., & Periañez-Cristobal, R. (2015). Project to improve knowledge management and key business results through the EFQM excellence model. *International Journal of Project Management, 33*(8), 1638–1651.

Corbett, L. M., & Angell, L. C. (2011). Business excellence in New Zealand: Continuous improvement, learning, and change. *Total Quality Management & Business Excellence, 22*(7), 755–772.

Corredor, P., & Goñi, S. (2010). Quality awards and performance: Is there a relationship? *The TQM Journal, 22*(5), 529–538.

Curkovic, S., Vickery, S., & Dröge, C. (2000). Quality-related action programs: Their impact on quality performance and firm performance. *Decision Sciences, 31*(4), 885–902.

Douglas, T. J., & Judge, W. Q. (2001). Total quality management implementation and competitive advantage: The role of structural control and exploration. *Academy of Management Journal, 44*(1), 158–169.

Dubey, M. (2016). Developing an agile business excellence model for organizational sustainability. *Global Business and Organizational Excellence, 35*(2), 60–71.

Eriksson, H. (2004). Organisational value of participating in a quality award process: A Swedish study. *The TQM Magazine, 16*(2), 78–92.

Escrig, A. B., & de Menezes, L. M. (2015). What characterizes leading companies within business excellence models? An analysis of "EFQM recognized for excellence" recipients in Spain. *International Journal of Production Economics, 169*, 362–375.

Evans, J. R. (2015). Modern analytics and the future of quality and performance excellence. *The Quality Management Journal, 22*(4), 6–17.

Fonseca, L. M. (2015). Relationship between ISO 9001 certification maturity and EFQM business excellence model results. *Quality Innovation Prosperity, 19*(1), 85–102.

Ghicajanu, M., Irimie, S., Marica, L., & Munteanu, R. (2015). Criteria for excellence in business. *Procedia Economics and Finance, 23*, 445–452.

Ghobadian, A., & Woo, H. S. (1996). Characteristics, benefits and shortcomings of four major quality awards. *International Journal of Quality & Reliability Management, 13*(2), 10–44.

Hendricks, K. B., & Singhal, V. R. (1997). Does implementing an effective TQM program actually improve operating performance? Empirical evidence from firms that have won quality awards. *Management Science, 43*(9), 1258–1274.

Hillman, A. J., & Keim, G. D. (2001). Shareholder value, stakeholder management, and social issues: What's the bottom line? *Strategic Management Journal, 22*, 125–139.

Hughes, A., & Halsall, D. N. (2002). Comparison of the 14 deadly diseases and the business excellence model. *Total Quality Management, 13*(2), 255–226.

Jacob, R. A., Madu, C. N., & Tang, C. (2012). Financial performance of Baldrige award winners: A review and synthesis. *International Journal of Quality & Reliability Management, 29*(2), 233–240.

Kanji, G. K. (2008). Leadership is prime: How do you measure leadership excellence? *Total Quality Management, 19*(4), 417–427.

Lasrado, F. (2017). Perceived benefits of national quality awards: A study of UAE's award winning organizations. *Measuring Business Excellence, 21*(1), 50–64.

Lee, S. M., Rho, B. H., & Lee, S. G. (2003). Impact of Malcolm Baldrige National Quality Award criteria on organizational quality performance. *International Journal of Production Research, 41*(9), 2003–2020.

Lin, C. S., Chen, L. F., Su, C. T., & Kon, T. C. (2013). Stock price impact on the Taiwan national quality award. *Total Quality Management & Business Excellence, 24*(1/2), 158–170.

Link, A. N., & Scott, J. T. (2011). *Economic evaluation of the Baldrige Performance Excellence Program* (NIST planning report 11–2). Retrieved from https://www.nist.gov/baldrige/economic-evaluation-baldrige-performance-excellence-program-december-2011

Link, A. N., & Scott, J. T. (2012). On the social value of quality: An economic evaluation of the Baldrige performance excellence program. *Science and Public Policy, 39*(5), 680–689.

Mann, R., Adebanjo, D., & Tickle, M. (2011). Deployment of business excellence in Asia: An exploratory study. *International Journal of Quality & Reliability Management, 28*(6), 604–627.

Martin, C., Bulkan, A., & Klempt, P. (2011). Security excellence from a total quality management approach. *Total Quality Management, 22*(3), 345–371.

Metaxas, I. N., & Koulouriotis, D. E. (2014). A theoretical study of the relation between TQM, assessment and sustainable business excellence. *Total Quality Management & Business Excellence, 25*(5/6), 494–510.

NIST. (2017). *The Baldrige Criteria 101*. Retrieved from http://www.nist.gov/baldrige/publications/upload/The-Baldrige-Criteria-101.docx

Pattison, Z. (2011). *Implementing the Australian business excellence framework: Eight local government case studies*. Australian Centre of Excellence for Local Government, UTS: CLG Centre for Local Government, SAI Global, Sydney, NSW. Retrieved from http://apo.org.au/node/26028

Peters, T. J., & Waterman, R. H., Jr. (1982). *In search of excellence: Lessons from America's best-run companies*. New York: Harper & Row.

Porter, L., & Tanner, S. (Eds.). (2004). *Assessing business excellence*. London/New York: Routledge.

Rawabdeh, I. A. (2008). Jordan quality award (King Abdullah II award for excellence (KAIIAE)) characteristics, assessment and benchmarking. *Benchmarking: An International Journal, 15*(1), 4–243.

Rowland-Jones, R. (2013). A perspective on United Arab Emirates small and medium-sized enterprises management utilising the European Foundation for Quality Management concepts of excellence. *Total Quality Management & Business Excellence, 24*(1–2), 210–224.

Sampaio, P., Saraiva, P., & Monteiro, A. (2012). A comparison and usage overview of business excellence models. *The TQM Journal, 24*(2), 181–200.

Samson, D., & Terziovski, M. (1999). The relationship between total quality management practices and operational performance. *Journal of Operations Management, 17*(4), 393–409.

Schaefer, C. (2011). *Baldrige 20/20: An executive's guide to the criteria for performance excellence*. USA: ASQ Quality Press.

Stoehr, A. (2010). *Stock market roller coaster*. Retrieved from http://excellence.ca/en/knowledge-centre/articles/stock-market-roller-coaster

Talwar, B. (2011). Business excellence models and the path ahead.... *The TQM Journal, 23*(1), 21–35.

Tickle, M., Mann, R., & Adebanjo, D. (2016). Deploying business excellence–success factors for high performance. *International Journal of Quality & Reliability Management, 33*(2), 197–230.

Tutuncu, O., & Kucukusta, D. (2007). Relationship between organizational commitment and EFQM business excellence model: A study on Turkish quality award winners. *Total Quality Management, 18*(10), 1083–1096.

Wilkes, N., & Dale, B. G. (1998). Attitudes to self-assessment and quality awards: A study in small and medium-sized companies. *Total Quality Management, 9*(8), 731–739.

Wisner, J. D., & Eakins, S. G. (1994). A performance assessment of the US Baldrige Quality Award winners. *International Journal of Quality & Reliability Management, 11*(2), 8–25.

York, K. M., & Miree, C. E. (2004). Causation or covariation: An empirical re-examination of the link between TQM and financial performance. *Journal of Operations Management, 22*(3), 291–311.

Young Kim, D., Kumar, V., & Murphy, S. A. (2010). European foundation for quality management business excellence model: An integrative review and research agenda. *International Journal of Quality & Reliability Management, 27*(6), 684–701.

Zárraga-Rodríguez, M., & Alvarez, M. J. (2013). Exploring the links between information capability and the EFQM business excellence model: The case of Basque country quality award winners. *Total Quality Management & Business Excellence, 24*(5–6), 539–560.

Zdrilić, I., & Dulčić, Ž. (2016). Business excellence as a success factor for the performance of large Croatian enterprises. *Management: Journal of Contemporary Management Issues, 21*(1), 145–162.

4

Global Excellence Frameworks and Human Capital

Introduction

According to the business excellence (BE)- and return on investment (ROI)-based Process Maturity–Global Insights 'global survey 2014' conducted by KPMG, over 60% of organisations invest in people-related practices to maintain employee motivation, learning, and career growth, while minimising attrition. In recent years, it has been recognised that the ways in which human resources (HR) are treated and developed affect their performance, and that, consequently, the general organisational performance is also affected. Given these considerations, many organisations have shown interest in global excellence frameworks such as the Baldrige or European Foundation for Quality Management (EFQM) models for quality. A study conducted by the New Zealand Centre for Organisational Excellence Research reported that there are currently about 61 excellence frameworks around the world (Ahmed 2015). These are the results of various national efforts of many countries to increase organisational competitiveness. However, in broader terms, many excellence frameworks are based on popular awards, such as the Deming Prize (DP), Baldrige Award, and EFQM Award. The latter two have provided foundations for many national-level excellence awards. These awards and

F. Lasrado, V. Pereira, *Achieving Sustainable Business Excellence*,
https://doi.org/10.1007/978-3-319-73314-2_4

their criteria are described in detail in this chapter. In addition, we illustrate how the excellence frameworks are linked to human capital and discuss the 'people' and 'workforce' criteria of the EFQM and Baldrige award models. Organisations seeking improvement in their HR management (HRM) also rely on known best practices, hoping they will benefit and improve their HRM policies and practices.

The Baldrige Excellence Framework and Award

The Malcolm Baldrige National Quality Award (MBNQA) is the most prestigious quality award in the United States. It was established in 1987 with the key aim of improving competition and quality management practices amongst US companies by providing a strong system for understanding performance management that was guided by certain core concepts and values. The Malcolm Baldrige Criteria for Performance Excellence are jointly overseen and administered by the National Institute of Standards and Technology (NIST), a governmental organisation, and the American Society for Quality (ASQ), a non-profit organisation in charge of the review process and documentation. The award is categorised into three eligibility tiers for manufacturing companies, the service sector, and small businesses, and up to two awards may be allocated in each category. The winners of this award are encouraged to publicise and promote their triumphs and best practices with other organisations, and they are predominantly required to educate and inform other companies about their excellence strategies.

The purpose of the Baldrige Excellence Framework is to help an organisation to innovate and improve its operations. The framework aims to empower organisations to reach their goals, improve results, and become more competitive. The Baldrige framework takes a systems perspective in the sense that it is designed to manage all the components of an organisation as a unified whole, ensuring that plans, processes, measures, and actions are consistent. The framework suits a variety of businesses/non-profit organisations, including those in the manufacturing, services, small business, non-profit, government, education, and health-care sectors. The Baldrige Excellence Framework includes the Criteria for Performance Excellence, core values and concepts, and guidelines for evaluating processes and results. The revised 2017–2018 criteria focus on the following aspects:

- Managing all components of the organisation as a unified whole
- Managing cybersecurity risks to data, information, and systems
- Understanding the role of risk management from a systems perspective on organisational performance management

The MBNQA is the highest level of national recognition for performance excellence that a US-based organisation can receive. The Baldrige Award was established by Congress in 1987 and since the first group was recognised in 1988, 113 awards have been presented to 106 organisations, including seven repeat recipients. Up to 18 awards are given annually across six eligibility categories (a maximum of three in each), namely manufacturing, service, small business, education, healthcare, and non-profit. The following are some of the effects of receiving the award:

- Median growth in revenue for two-time Baldrige Award winners of 92%
- Median job growth for two-time Baldrige Award winners of 63% (compared with 3.5% for a matched set of industries and time periods)

Over the years, organisations have used the Baldridge criteria to assess organisational performance, thereby helping them identify their strengths, weaknesses, and opportunities for improvement. There are various examples of how the criteria have been used: as the basis for internal performance programmes; to determine the quality of suppliers; to manage culture shifts and engage the workforce during mergers and acquisitions; brand management, guiding organisational learning and the improvement of performance outcomes; and ensuring the efficiency and effectiveness of resources (NIST 2015, p. 2).

The criteria definitely make a difference in overall organisations' business performance, as evidenced by several winners, as explained in Chap. 3. Examples include results bucking the economic trend; cost savings through improved processes (including changes suggested by employees); increased revenues and positive customer feedback/satisfaction; growth and results exceeding that of close competitors; and better than normal rates of industry staff retention (for further detailed examples, see NIST 2015).

Further, there have been numerous studies to assess the effects of the criteria on the overall economy, and all results have been positive. For instance, Fisher et al. (2001) assessed the effects of the award for MBNQA winners compared to Standard and Poor's 500 (S&P500) companies. They showed that MBNQA recipients received an 841% ROI compared to the 222% ROI for the S&P500. Interestingly, it has been reported that Baldrige Award applicants cite the feedback report as the most significant benefit of applying for the award. Hendricks and Singhal (1997) show similar results; companies that adopt a total quality management (TQM) approach had a 48% higher operating income compared to the control sample. Interestingly, this growth started to occur even before the companies won the award, and often remained for as long as six years after the award was received. Another effect of the MBNQA is an increase in investor valuation (Jacob et al. 2004). The literature shows that compared with non–award winners, companies that have received the MBNQA attain higher investor valuation, resulting in a higher economic effect.

The Baldrige Award Criteria

The Baldrige Award Criteria provide a systems perspective, ensuring alignment and integration across an organisation. They are divided into process and results categories, representing all the components of a performance management system. The criteria include core values and concepts that represent the embedded beliefs and behaviours found in high-performing organisations, as shown in the seven criteria listed in Fig. 4.1. The categories represent seven critical aspects of managing and performing as an organisation, core principles, and the organisation profile. The organisational profile is a snapshot of the organisation,

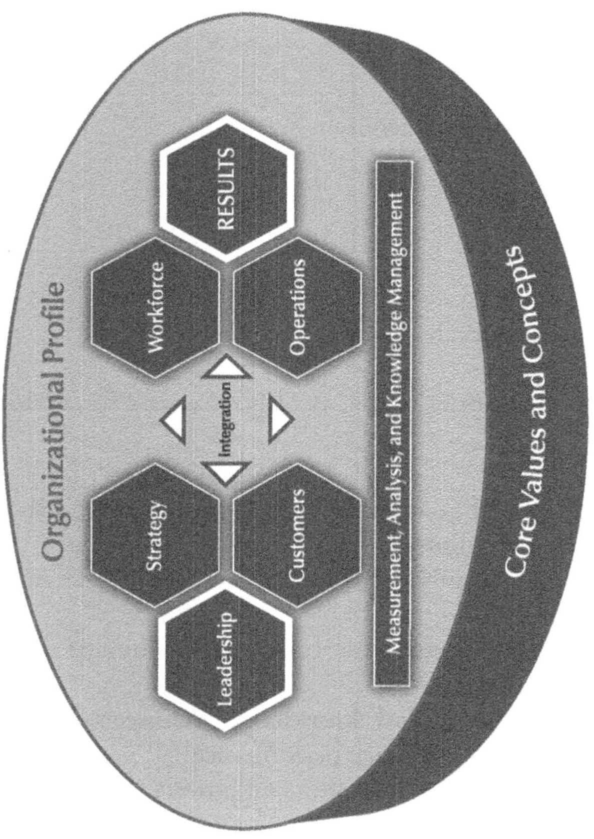

From Baldrige Performance Excellence Program. 2017. *2017–2018 Baldrige Excellence Framework: A Systems Approach to Improving Your Organization's Performance.* Gaithersburg, MD: U.S. Department of Commerce, National Institute of Standards and Technology. https://www.nist.gov/baldrige.

Fig. 4.1 Baldrige model (Cited permission not needed as confirmed by Lucy earlier)

illustrating the key influences on how it operates and the competitive environment. The following are core values and concepts that represent beliefs and behaviours found in high-performing organisations:

- A systems perspective
- Visionary leadership
- Customer-focused excellence
- Valuing people
- Organisational learning and agility
- A focus on success
- Managing for innovation
- Management by fact
- Social responsibility
- Ethics and transparency
- Delivering value and results

There are seven categories of the Baldrige Criteria for Performance Excellence:

1. **Leadership**: How management leads an organisation and the organisation leads the community
2. **Strategy:** How an organisation establishes and plans to implement strategic directions
3. **Customers:** How an organisation builds and maintains strong relationships with customers
4. **Measurement, analysis, and knowledge management:** How an organisation uses data to manage performance
5. **Workforce:** How an organisation empowers and involves its workforce
6. **Operations:** How an organisation designs, manages, and improves key processes
7. **Results:** How an organisation performs in terms of customer satisfaction, finances, HR, supplier and partner performance, operations, governance, and social responsibility, and how these characteristics compare with those of competitors

The first category, Leadership, asks how senior leaders' personal actions and the governance system guides and sustains the organisation. This item asks about the key aspects of the senior leaders' responsibilities, with the aim of creating an organisation that is successful now and in the future. Indeed, to direct a successful organisation, a strong, clear leader is needed. The objectives and goals are set by the leaders, who can effectively attract and motivate employees and ensure that the goals are achieved.

The Strategy category relates to the development and implementation of strategic objectives and action plans. This includes the recognition that, depending on circumstances and initial results, plans may have to be changed to achieve the desired outcome. Plans should include measures to address long-term organisational success, a competitive environment, core competencies, and work systems.

The Customers category emphasises the importance of listening to and engaging with customers. Knowing customers' needs and expectations—and acting on this valuable information—assists an organisation in its quest to achieve excellence and have that excellence reflected in its business results through increased customer loyalty and attracting new customers.

The fourth category—Measurement, Analysis, and Knowledge Management—is, essentially, the nerve centre where the organisation matches its operations with its strategic objectives. It requires data that are both available and of high quality in order to be able to effectively move the organisation forward. The data are used to drive internal changes and also to assess how the organisation measures up against competitors, and thus also include a strategic element.

The Workforce category looks to overhaul workforce practices in order to enhance workers' buy-in of quality initiatives and produce an environment that actively supports better worker performance. It, too, has a strategic element—the overall planning of workforce management to reinforce the organisation's overall strategic planning.

The sixth category, Operations, focuses on an organisation's work, product design and delivery, innovation, and operational effectiveness. These elements help to achieve organisational success now and in the future.

The final category, Results, provides a systems focus that encompasses all results necessary to sustain an enterprise. These include key process and product, customer focus, workforce, leadership and governance system, and overall financial and market performance results.

The latest edition of the Baldridge framework focuses on two important key areas in alignment with the new ISO standard 9001:2015. These are cybersecurity and enterprise risk management.

The EFQM Excellence Model and EQA/EEA Award

The idea of the EFQM was born on 15 September 1988, when the chief executive officers (CEOs) of 14 European businesses signed a Letter of Intent. The EFQM itself was born in October of the following year when a total of 67 companies declared their intent to follow the policy document. The European Quality Award (EQA), as it was then known, was subsequently introduced in 1991 and first awarded in 1992. In 1996, it was renamed the European Excellence Award. The model comprises a set of three integrated components:

- The Fundamental Concepts define the underlying principles that form the foundation for achieving sustainable excellence in any organisation.
- The Criteria provide a framework to help organisations to convert the Fundamental Concepts.
- Results, Approach, Deployment, Assessment, and Review (RADAR) is a simple but powerful tool for driving systematic improvement in all areas of an organisation.

The EFQM states that following RADAR logic an organisation should

- Determine the results it is aiming to achieve as part of its strategy.
- Plan and develop an integrated set of sound approaches to deliver the required results, both now and in the future.

- Deploy the approaches in a systematic way to ensure implementation.
- Assess and refine the deployed approaches based on monitoring and analysis of the results achieved and ongoing learning activities. (EFQM 2015)

The eight fundamental concepts as described in the EFQM (2013) model are listed and defined as follows:

Adding value for customers: Excellent organisations consistently add value for customers by understanding, anticipating, and fulfilling needs, expectations, and opportunities.

Creating a sustainable future: Excellent organisations have a positive influence on the world around them, advancing the economic, environmental, and social conditions in the communities they interact with by enhancing their performance.

Developing organisational capability: Excellent organisations enhance their capabilities by effectively managing change within and beyond the organisational boundaries.

Harnessing creativity and innovation: Excellent organisations generate increased value and levels of performance through continual improvement and systematic innovation by harnessing the creativity of their stakeholders.

Leading with integrity, vision, and inspiration: Excellent organisations have leaders who shape the future and make it happen, acting as role models for its values and ethics.

Managing with agility: Excellent organisations are widely recognised for their ability to identify and respond effectively and efficiently to opportunities and threats.

Succeeding through HR talent: Excellent organisations value their people and create a culture of empowerment for the achievement of both organisational and personal goals.

Sustaining outstanding results: Excellent organisations achieve sustained outstanding results that meet both the short- and long-term needs of all their stakeholders in the context of their operating environment (EFQM 2013).

The Criterion part of the model consists of enablers and results. 'Enablers' (as expected) are those things an organisation needs to do to develop and implement, that is, to enable, its strategy. Again, the EFQM sets out clear definitions.

Leadership: The first criterion highlights ways in which leaders develop and implement the firm values that are required for organisational success. When and where changes are required, they are personally involved in the management system; they need to be flexible, dynamic, trustworthy role models who can inspire their organisation and its employees.

Policy and Strategy: An organisation's most important duty is to establish a strong trusting relationship with stakeholders at all levels. Here, systems are implemented to ensure that the strategies are incorporated to best suit the needs of the stakeholders. Excellent organisations implement their mission and vision by developing and deploying a stakeholder-focused strategy. Policies, plans, objectives, and processes are developed and deployed to deliver the strategy.

People: Systems whereby people are involved and formally recognised promote a harmonious dialogue between people and organisations, creating an environment of trust; hence, competencies are developed for the good of both parties. Excellent organisations value their people, foster their development and treat them fairly. The atmosphere thus engendered is one where both personal and organisational goals can be achieved.

Partnerships and Resources: Organisations focused on BE create systems for managing partnerships and resources by balancing the present and future needs (technology, finances, and information) of the organisation. Excellent organisations plan and manage external partnerships, suppliers, and internal resources to support strategy and policies and the effective operation of processes.

Processes: Within processes, methods are used to manage and improve products and services, as well as customers' and other stakeholders' requirements. Excellent organisations design, manage, and improve processes to generate increasing value for customers and other stakeholders.

Results: The results category includes four organisational results. Specifically, excellent organisations achieve and sustain outstanding results that meet or exceed the needs and expectations of the following groups:

- Their customers
- Their people
- Society
- Business stakeholders

Customer Results: Customers' perceptions of the organisation and other aspects of the company's performance are included in this criterion; such perceptions may foster customer loyalty, as well as the public image and reputation of the firm.

People Results: This system indicates the degree of motivation, satisfaction, and involvement of the organisation's employees.

Societal Results: Excellent organisational performance is measured by the achievement of outstanding results with respect to their social effect, which primarily includes being socially responsible.

Key Performance Results: Organisations exhaustively measure and accomplish remarkable outcomes concerning the key components of their approaches and strategies, including financial and non-financial performance indicators related to present and future results.

The EFQM excellence model uses the RADAR scoring methodology. The system is composed of policies and various procedures that support each of the nine criteria, specifying how they should be evaluated and the outcomes measured, as described here. The first element is leadership, which drives people management, policy and strategy, and resources. These, in turn, drive all the processes that affect people satisfaction, customer satisfaction, and society; these three components drive the business results (Ilieş et al. 2015).

Comparatively, both the Baldrige and EFQM models imply that through the customer focus principle a company can increase customer loyalty and attract new customers, thereby illustrating effective progress in securing customer satisfaction. Therefore, it is important to understand customer needs and expectations and the company's capabilities (Kuei and Lu 2013). It is also evident that a strong, clear leader is needed to direct a successful organisation. The objectives and goals are controlled and led by the leaders, who can effectively attract and motivate employees and ensure that the goals are achieved. The strong relationship between the company and suppliers can be recognised and maintained by the utilisation of these frameworks (Lazaros et al. 2017).

Any organisation's capabilities depend greatly on its human capital. The workforce and people criteria in the models emphasise that employees need to take responsibility for their company. The consistency and effectiveness of any organisation can be maintained using the process approach. The new opportunities, innovations, flexibilities, and improved performance of an organisation can be governed by continuous improvement (Lee and Ooi 2014). Finally, the frameworks call for a logical approach to data collection and analysis, as well as to decision-making.

The Human Capital and Excellence Models

Human capital is the most important factor in generating quality (Jagadeesh 2014) as the people working in an organisation are its most important asset and resource. Their motivation and satisfaction are key elements for the business's success in an ever-changing market. If the people working in an organisation are unsatisfied or unmotivated, there is a high chance that they will not be as productive, and they will be more likely to make errors in their work. Organisations should not only focus on short-term career development, but also on the long-term development of workers. Employees should be provided with everything they need to do their jobs in the most effective way. Work productivity mainly relies on organisations' capacity to sustain human motivation, commitment, and collective and individual renewal. The TQM approach especially emphasises the importance of employees in organisations. As a result, the various excellence frameworks (the Deming, Baldrige, and EFQM prizes) have incorporated people management as one of the crucial criteria for a successful organisation. In the EFQM model, HR is included in the People criterion. As Martín-Castilla and Rodríguez-Ruiz

(2008) point out, this criterion of the EFQM model measures what the organisation does in relation to its employees. The EFQM model makes specific reference to human capital under its people criterion. This criterion relates to several aspects of HR: career development, HR planning (HRP), selection, training, teamwork, performance appraisal, communication, social benefits, compensation, innovation, creativity, and so on (Sheffield Hallam University 2003). The emphasis on human capital is further evident in the fundamental core value of the model—succeeding through people. According to the EFQM model, organisational performance is driven by people in the organisation. Thus, the criterion has five subcategories to recognise the implementation of best HRM practices. Martín-Castilla and Rodríguez-Ruiz (2008) also established that intellectual capital is considered in the overarching framework of the EFQM model. Moreover, the intellectual capital perspective is a key element that runs horizontally across the criteria of the EFQM excellence model. In the next section, the people criterion is explored in relation to the models.

Workforce Criteria in the Baldridge Framework

Flynn and Saladin (2001) defined the Baldrige model as a guide for quality management that was developed to enable not only promoting exemplary quality management practices, but also improvement based on a world-class performance framework. The workforce or human capital is one of seven categories addressing key practices that have a strong impact on creating and maintaining a high-performance environment. Koys and Decotiis (2015) argued that the workforce criterion in the Baldrige model addresses two main practices. The first involves creating and maintaining a high-performing work environment, while the second is about engaging the workforce (Koys and Decotiis 2015). Therefore, the workforce criterion can be assessed through two factors, namely the workforce environment (how do you build an effective and supportive workforce environment?) and workforce engagement (how do you engage your workforce to achieve organisational and personal success?) (Koys and Decotiis 2015). Workforce engagement has been defined as organisational citizenship behaviour (OCB) (Podsakoff et al. 2006; Koys and Decotiis 2015). In a study by Husain et al. (2001), the authors viewed the workforce as part of the resources the organisation possesses. They argued that, in the past, organisations used to pay more attention to physical resources, such as their assets, than to non-physical ones. Nowadays, organisations realise the importance of nurturing and developing human capital. According to Husain et al. (2001), firms with qualified personnel strive to retain them through rewards and compensation systems.

Oakland and Oakland (1998) argued that the effective and efficient management of human capital has become a primary concern for companies wanting to succeed in business. They also emphasised the positive relationship between effective people management leading to satisfied customers and a high level of customer satisfaction. Moreover, they explored the people management concept and the factors that influence it. The factors they identified as leading to effective people management, also defined as best practices, are communication, employee commitment and participation encouragement, employee empowerment, training and development, and teams and teamwork.

In a study on the relationship between TQM and operational performance, Samson and Terziovski (1999) discussed the people criterion as part of the Baldrige Award. Their survey sought to determine the total effects of TQM training, communication, and involvement programmes, and they argued that the most crucial part of people management is studying how HR practices align with the firm's strategies and that quality excellence in this criterion is determined by the voice of the people.

As a benchmark, leading organisations design a three-year strategic plan for HRM that is aligned with the overall strategy of the company (Oakland and Oakland 2001). The strategy is then translated into policies covering the following areas: skills, recruitment, appraisal, remuneration, and employee benefits. An interesting concept used by leading organisations is the so-called cafeteria effect whereby the company provides a core standard package to all employees that includes the salary and a 'menu' of other benefits, from which the employees can choose the ones that best suit them (company car, health insurance, dental care, etc.). The cafeteria concept has had a positive influence on employee morale; different people have different needs, thus, when this concept is applied, employees feel that their individual needs are being addressed, which increases their motivation (Oakland and Oakland 2001).

Relating to the same topic, Schuler (1992) argued that HRM should be performed strategically—that is, all employees in an organisation should contribute to achieving the success of the business. He goes on to argue that a scholarly consensus on the definition of strategic HRM has been established and defined this concept as a composite of (1) the full integration of the HR strategy with the strategic needs of the company; (2) alignment of the HR strategy with the company policy and application of the strategy by employees across all hierarchical levels; and, (3) acceptance and application of HR policies amongst all the employees. Schuler argued that strategic HRM is a combination of values, practices, culture, and policies and went on to explain that strategic HRM should be used to link and integrate all the levels of the organisation and employ the human capital to achieve the strategic needs of the organisation.

In the scope of strategic HRM, Schuler (1992) further defined the 5-P model, which helps to elucidate how HR strategies influence different individuals and groups where HRM activities are defined as follows: philosophy, policies, programmes, practices, and processes. A workforce comprises every individual who is actively involved in accomplishing tasks, whether such individuals are employees, volunteers, team leaders, or managers. Recently, many companies have termed members of their workforce 'partners' to illustrate how important they are in driving their businesses and humanising performance. Recent work by Ishizaka and Pereira (2016) portrays an employee performance management method based on multi-criteria decision analysis and visual techniques. The model they develop for employee performance management is fair and transparent but at the same time developmental, as it identifies not only key areas that employees excel in, but also areas that they can develop in the future. Another example is that of the role of HRM practices in product development through contextual ambidexterity explored by Malik et al. (2017), wherein, through the case of an offshore US MNC subsidiary in India, they provide evidence of sustained BE.

A quality award aims to enable the workforce to engage with the organisational objectives and assist it to adapt to change and succeed accordingly.

Workforce Environment

The workforce environment mainly considers workforce capability and capacity needs, looking at how the organisation can meet those needs and accomplish the required workflow by ensuring a supportive work atmosphere. The main objective is to build the most effective work environment that will help employees and encourage them to perform well while supporting the workforce.

Important Observations

- Workforce capability and capacity

Many organisations make the mistake of hiring employees with incorrect or unrelated skills because they believe that purely by hiring limited highly skilled people, regardless of whether their skills match the organisation's needs, they can meet the capacity requirements for subject processes. They generally think that the work can be accomplished by having many workers with fewer or different skills, but this is not the case; rather, having the right number of employees with the right skills is critical for the success of any business. In addition, it is recommended that organisations develop a good prediction of future needs, that is, human resources planning, since this will allow them to engage in satisfactory training, recruitment, relocation, retention, and design for work system change.

- Work support

There are many opportunities for an organisation, regardless of its size, to support the development of its workforce. The following are some examples:

- Career and personal counselling with career development
- Cultural activities
- Formal and informal recognition

- Special leave for family responsibilities and community service
- Flexible working hours and benefits packages

Workforce Engagement

Workforce engagement mainly considers the design of the system that is managing the performance of the workforce and the way in which it develops the members and motivates them to effectively contribute to the best of their abilities. The system also promotes high performance, which can be a good asset in helping the firm to ensure sustainable success and accomplishment of the action plan designed for future success.

Important Observations

- High performance

The ability to achieve high performance records is characterised by flexibility, innovation and creativity, knowledge and skills sharing, good communication skills, alignment with organisation objectives, customer focus, and rapid responses to market changes.

- Workforce engagement and performance

Many studies have indicated that a high level of work engagement can have a positive influence on performance. Engagement can be characterised as having a cooperative working environment and clear direction from the organisation.

- Drivers of workforce engagement

Workforce engagement can be driven by maintaining a healthy supportive working climate that makes the workers feel safe and secure by ensuring effective communication and good career development.

- Factors inhibiting engagement

Factors that inhibit engagement can be clarified using surveys, focus groups, blogs, or interviews with workforce members.

- Compensation and recognition

Compensation and recognition should match the work system and be tied to demonstrated skills.

- Other indicators of workforce engagement

Indicators of a lack of workforce engagement include absenteeism, turnover, and strikes.

- Workforce development needs

The needs of the organisation may vary based on its nature, size, location, number of employees, and the nature of its competitors.

- Customer contact training

Continuous training and development for employees is important, as this encourages them to gain critical skills and knowledge for development and improvement to satisfy clients and exceed expectations.

The People Criterion in the EFQM Model

The people principle of the EFQM model is the most practical, and also crucial, concept when it comes to achieving greater BE. According to this principle, people's empowerment is the most significant factor in the management of quality aspects of the organisation. People, as internal customers of the firm, are involved in managing quality, and when they are empowered, quality management becomes an even more effective approach.

Thus, a firm's most important asset is its employees. It is their hard work that takes the company to the pinnacle of its success. An organisation cannot function without its internal customers or assets, that is, its human capital. However, the employees' level of ability determines the efficiency and success of the company. Involvement of employees in the company's activities helps to increase their understanding. It also motivates them to work harder, as they feel valued by the company. Furthermore, it increases their efficiency and effectiveness. From a BE or quality perspective, the consistency of the employees also rises, and the involvement of the employees helps in eliminating waste.

According to Sheffield Hallam University (2003, p. 23), taking higher education as an example, '[e]xcellent universities manage, develop, and release the knowledge and full potential of their staff at an individual, team-based, and university-wide level. They care for, communicate, reward, and recognise in a way that motivates staff and builds commitment to using their skills and knowledge for the benefit of the University'.

As human capital is a firm's most valuable resource, it is necessary to establish a clear plan focusing on what employees should achieve; based on this, it is possible to determine what their needs are. However, it is first necessary to identify the objectives, targets, and priorities. Another important factor that should be considered is providing employees with equal opportunities, regardless of their colour, race, or sex. Having a fair and transparent environment minimises the chances of envy and loss of motivation that may occur amongst employees. It is vital to find ways of encouraging employees to create functional teams that are mostly focused on the function rather than the end results, as this will motivate them to collaborate with each other. Employees should be properly empowered by the higher administration to give them the authority they need to conduct their daily tasks; moreover, they should be provided with a sense of motivation as they perform their assigned tasks. Communication is another fundamental element in an organisation. Some people might interpret communication purely as a way of conveying instructions within an organisation. However, it is much more complex than that; it involves carefully analysing the organisation and finding the best, most efficient way of conveying information to all parts of it. It is part of human nature to want to be recognised and rewarded for hard work. Successful organisations acknowledge the value that their employees bring through rewards, recognition, and care. In some cases, such practices can be a motivational factor that encourages employees to work harder and find new ways of improving their work process.

Conclusion

The two models, Baldrige and EFQM, have similar criteria and approaches, and they have provided a basis for many national quality awards (NQAs) that have been developed around the world. Both models are considered to suit organisations of any sector and size, and they have also been employed in the non-profit sector. However, the EFQM model is considered to have more advantages than the MBNQA model in the not-for-profit sector (Al-Tabbaa et al. 2013). Quality awards, specifically the MBNQA and EFQM, have been used as a guide to implement the TQM in several enterprises (Bou-Llusar et al. 2009). Talwar (2009) also noted that in comparative studies of NQAs, three models—the MBNQA in the United States, the European Excellence Award (EEA) or EFQM in Europe, and the DP in Japan—are being used as global reference models. Specifically, Searle reported that the NQAs of 53 countries are based on the MBNQA alone.

Some studies, such as that of Dodangeh et al. (2012), have compared the global frameworks of the EFQM and MBNQA, and noted that both approaches have merits and drawbacks in the sense of the adoption of and concentration on TQM principles; ultimately, no individual framework is complete, but both provide outstanding opportunities for BE. Knowledge of the different current frameworks can help organisations to execute the appropriate principles and realise business improvements. One study observed that a combination of all NQA and EQM criteria makes it possible to use all the dimensions to achieve TQM anywhere in the world, while the MBNQA, EFQM, and Deming prizes are heavily drawn on to develop other criteria. A major difference between the Deming Prize and the others is that certain examination criteria, such as HRM, customer satisfaction, impact on society, and operational results, are not included in the former (Bohoris 1995).

Further, the two models have similar goals and objectives, the main one being the improvement of competitiveness through excellence. However, the approaches to obtaining this objective are different. For instance, there are differences in the scoring and award processes. In contrast, both models provide extensive feedback to the companies that apply for the award, thereby helping all applicants in their pursuit of excellence. The literature review showed that throughout the years, the awards have changed somewhat; however, the core principles have stayed the same. The Baldrige framework is changing, and its emphasis seems to have shifted from a strictly business-oriented result towards people and better leadership. This notion is supported by several empirical studies showing that leadership has extensive effects on overall outcomes.

Ultimately, the EFQM contends that every person touched by a company needs to be satisfied through people management, customer support, or social responsibility. This aspect of the EFQM makes scoring harder, as the measurement of an organisation's connection with society is complicated; however, overall, the model will continue to be sustainable for the future. The MBNQA is changing its focus with its recent update, and in contrast to the literature reviewed here, future scholarly papers will probably begin to highlight the move in the focus of the Baldrige criteria and scoring.

In terms of the effects of their adoption and use in various strategic business practices, the EFQM and MBNQA criteria illustrate that the success of any organisation in today's highly competitive business environment depends heavily on customer orientation and the careful integration of the quality management models into the organisation. At the same time, the EFQM and MBNQA face similar problems and challenges. For instance, leadership in many organisations has failed and continues to fail because leaders are negligent and do not act in accordance with some of the best and readily available practices at their disposal, notwithstanding the fact that both frameworks highlight the significance of having a clear leadership role. The collapse of Enron, for example, indicated great discrepancies and lack of cohesion in the organisation, which stemmed from an inadequate management style that ignored excellence initiatives and led to the company's eventual downfall (Benston and Hartgraves 2002). Leaders without an established direction determined by the company vision may also decide to focus only on certain of the criteria, such as customer results or operations, while deliberately ignoring the others as they think that pursuing these selected components will lead to instant returns or gains; however, such leaders will fail to foresee the disastrous impact that will follow an unenlightened focus on short-term gains. A close examination of the global excellence award systems suggests that the implementation of either set of criteria should be a total effort, flowing from the top management down to the rest of the organisation; moreover, it should be done with the utmost diligence to root out any and all forms of mistakes and inertia that may lead to failure. With this in mind, it should be understood that systems are not always easily implementable as they require sustainability and constant motivational drive along with cohesiveness amongst all departments in a firm if they are to succeed.

Finally, people criteria have several theoretical implications as to understand how those people enablers can be leveraged towards sustainable performance in organisations; human capital development is an essential component in excellence models and hence organisations have to play a crucial role in planning, developing, and implementing HR strategy. People or workforce focus is an essential part of excellence. Global excellence frameworks provide guidelines to leverage this enabler in organisations; and high-performing organisations embed these criteria into practice to achieve superior performance.

References

Ahmed. (2015). *New research shows 61 countries with national business excellence awards*. Retrieved from http://blog.bpir.com/latest-news/new-research-shows-67-countries-with-national-business-excellence-awards

Al-Tabbaa, O., Gadd, K., & Ankrah, S. (2013). Excellence models in the non-profit context: Strategies for continuous improvement. *International Journal of Quality & Reliability Management, 30*(5), 590–612.

Benston, G. J., & Hartgraves, A. L. (2002). Enron: What happened and what we can learn from it. *Journal of Accounting and Public Policy, 21*(2), 105–127.

Bohoris, G. A. (1995). A comparative assessment of some major quality awards. *International Journal of Quality & Reliability Management, 12*(9), 30–43.

Bou-Llusar, J. C., Escrig-Tena, A. B., Roca-Puig, V., & Beltrán-Martín, I. (2009). An empirical assessment of the EFQM excellence model: Evaluation as a TQM framework relative to the MBNQA model. *Journal of Operations Management, 27*(1), 1–22.

Dodangeh, J., Rosnah, M. Y., Ismail, N., Ismail, Y. M., Biekzadeh, M. R., & Jassbi, J. (2012). A review on major business excellence frameworks. *Technics Technologies Education Management, 7*(3), 1386–1393.

EFQM. (2013). *Fundamental concepts.* Retrieved from http://www.efqm.org/efqm-model/fundamental-concepts

EFQM. (2015). *RADAR logic.* Retrieved from http://www.efqm.org/efqm-model/radar-logic

Fisher, C., Dauterive, J., & Barfield, J. (2001). Economic impacts of quality awards: Does offering an award bring returns to the state? *Total Quality Management, 12*(7–8), 981–987.

Flynn, B. B., & Saladin, B. (2001). Further evidence on the validity of the theoretical models underlying the Baldrige criteria. *Journal of Operations Management, 19*(6), 617–652.

Hendricks, K. B., & Singhal, V. R. (1997). Does implementing an effective TQM program actually improve operating performance? Empirical evidence from firms that have won quality awards. *Management Science, 43*(9), 1258–1274.

Husain, N., Mokhtar, A., Fazli, I., & Ridzuan, M. S. (2001). The Malaysian total performance excellence model: A conceptual framework. *Total Quality Management, 12*(7–8), 926–931.

Ilieş, L., Sălăgean, H. C., Gal, A. R., & Bâlc, B. (2015). Quality awards: An image of business excellence. *Annals of Faculty of Economics, 1*(1), 1120–1129. [University of Oradea].

Ishizaka, A., & Pereira, V. (2016). Portraying an employee performance management method based on multi-criteria decision analysis and visual techniques. *International Journal of Manpower, 37*(4), 628–659. https://doi.org/10.1108/IJM-07-2014-0149

Jacob, R., Madu, C. N., & Tang, C. (2004). An empirical assessment of the financial performance of Malcolm Baldrige award winners. *International Journal of Quality & Reliability Management, 21*(8), 897–914.

Jagadeesh, R. (2014). Emphasis on human resource management in quality improvement–A case study of quality awards' criteria. *International Journal of Economics, Commerce and Management, 1*(2), 1–12.

Koys, D. J., & DeCotiis, T. A. (2015). Does a good workforce influence restaurant performance or does good restaurant performance influence the workforce? *Journal of Human Resources in Hospitality & Tourism, 14*(4), 339–356.

Kuei, C., & Lu, M. (2013). Integrating quality management principles into sustainability management. *Total Quality Management & Business Excellence, 24*(1–2), 62–78.

Lazaros, A., Sofia, A., & George, I. (2017). Malcolm Baldrige National Quality Award (MBNQA) dimensions in Greek tertiary education system. *KnE Social Sciences, 1*(2), 436–455.

Lee, V.-H., & Ooi, K.-B. (2014). Applying the Malcolm Baldrige National Quality Award criteria: An approach to strengthen organisational memory and process innovation. *Total Quality Management & Business Excellence, 26*(11–12), 1373–1386.

Malik, A., Pereira, V., & Tarba, S. (2017). The role of HRM practices in product development through contextual ambidexterity: The case of an offshore US MNC subsidiary in India. *The International Journal of Human Resource Management*, 1–29. https://doi.org/10.1080/09585192.2017.13253880958-5192

Martín-Castilla, J. I., & Rodríguez-Ruiz, Ó. (2008). EFQM model: Knowledge governance and competitive advantage. *Journal of Intellectual Capital, 9*(1), 133–156.

NIST. (2015). *The Baldrige Criteria 101*. Retrieved from https://www.nist.gov/document-3205

Oakland, J. S., & Oakland, S. (1998). The links between people management, customer satisfaction and business results. *Total Quality Management, 9*(4–5), 185–190.

Oakland, S., & Oakland, J. S. (2001). Current people management activities in world-class organizations. *Total Quality Management, 12*(6), 773–788.

Podsakoff, P. M., MacKenzie, S. B., & Organ, D. W. (2006). *Organizational citizenship behavior: Its nature, antecedents, and consequences*. Thousand Oaks: Sage.

Samson, D., & Terziovski, M. (1999). The relationship between total quality management practices and operational performance. *Journal of Operations Management, 17*(4), 393–409.

Schuler, R. S. (1992). Strategic human resources management: Linking the people with the strategic needs of the business. *Organizational Dynamics, 21*(1), 18–32.

Sheffield Hallam University. (2003). *EFQM excellence model higher education version*. Sheffield: Sheffield Hallam University.

Talwar, B. (2009). Comparative study of core values of excellence models vis-à-vis human values. *Measuring Business Excellence, 13*(4), 34–46.

5

National Approaches to Quality Management

Introduction

Many governments around the world have supported or initiated quality performance and excellence awards to measure the business performance of organisations applying total quality management (TQM) principles in different areas. The country-level quality awards were established to recognise and reward business excellence (BE) and encourage organisations to adopt best business practices. They represent the highest recognition given by the government of a nation, as awards improve the country's business competitiveness and image worldwide. The custodians are normally government bodies that have established common evaluation criteria, such as leadership, customer orientation, people, and results (Tan 2002). With the 1951 awarding of the first Deming Prize in Japan, quality and BE began to take the spotlight in the business world. In 1988, just over 30 years later, the Malcolm Baldrige National Quality Award (MBNQA) in the United States and the Australian Business Excellence Award (ABEA) were initiated. This was the beginning of the trend towards national and global quality awards in different countries around the world (Kern Pipan et al. 2011).

F. Lasrado, V. Pereira, *Achieving Sustainable Business Excellence*,
https://doi.org/10.1007/978-3-319-73314-2_5

Quality awards provide various tangible and intangible benefits (Kern Pipan et al. 2013) to their recipients, regardless of the sector, industry, or country to which they belong. Many countries, including the United States, the United Kingdom, Australia, New Zealand, Singapore, China, Qatar, Spain, Slovenia, and Sweden, have put in place various awards to reward those that aim towards better quality. The quality award programme has become an important part of most organisations' future development, as it helps them to improve their internal business processes and compete locally and globally to maintain customer loyalty and satisfaction; moreover, they represent an opportunity to be part of the global markets (Lee 2002). Furthermore, performance excellence awards have helped organisations to structure their quality improvement efforts by using different instruments, such as benchmarking and internal self-assessment (Brown 2013; Lasrado 2017).

National Quality Awards (NQAs) provide organisations with credibility and an overall positive image. The feedback given through the award adoption can be used for future improvements (Lee 2002). Organisations that have adopted NQA principles have shown improvements in their quality outcomes. Winners have shown both internal process improvement and enhancements in their financial results, market share, and business competitiveness (Hendricks and Singhal 1997; Talwar 2011). In a study of 120 NQAs, winners were found to have achieved better results than other organisations of the same size and within the same industry. Improvements included share value, sales, and cost reduction (British Quality Foundation 2003; Talwar 2011). The awards have provided organisations with the tools and techniques to assess their existing quality practices, improve their quality, and enhance their internal and external relationships (Talwar 2011).

This chapter presents a review of quality awards around the world and the economic effects of these awards on different organisations and countries. In this chapter, we present the general framework of the quality awards for BE and highlight the role of human capital in them. Thus, we present the most important international quality awards, including the MBNQA in the United States, the Deming Prize in Japan, the EQA based on the EFQM model, the Singapore Quality Award, and the ABEA. We used the official websites of institutions and foundations organising the deployment of these awards as sources of up-to-date information.

National Quality Awards

The NQA custodians thrive on world-class quality winners that provide credibility and competitiveness to the award. This ensures that organisations are ambitious enough to achieve BE and rise to global standards (Laszlo 1996). NQAs aim to recognise organisations' development in BE and quality that allows them to engage in world-class business conduct, which, in turn, contributes to their nation's economy.

The United States

The concept of NQA has been used in the United States for almost three decades, and the MBNQA has been inspiring US companies to achieve performance excellence over this time. According to Evans et al. (2012), the MBNQA is 'one of the most powerful catalysts of quality and [organisational] performance excellence in the USA'. To affirm the benefits of the MBNQA, Allvin et al. (2008) conducted a study evaluating 28 winners in the health-care and manufacturing sectors. The results revealed that in the process of trying to achieve the MBNQA, the organisations provided training for their employees, as they were considered the most important resource for the process. This resulted in increased commitment and engagement of employees. In addition, as organisations promoted their workers' work/life balance, the employee satisfaction level increased, which motivated them to perform better. Moreover, when an organisation received the MBNQA, this resulted in increased customer satisfaction, improved organisational culture, and facilitation of the achievement of workplace excellence. The framework for this award is discussed in Chap. 3.

Canada

The Canada Awards for Excellence (CAE) were established in 1984 by the then National Quality Institute—now Excellence Canada—on behalf of the Canadian government with the aim of motivating organisations to achieve organisational excellence by implementing TQM principles; to date, more than 300 organisations from the public and private sectors have been recognised. The CAE are among the most prestigious awards in Canada and the Canadian government actively encourages organisations to apply for the award as the assessment process facilitates organisational growth (Excellence Canada n.d.). The CAE aim to recognise organisations that meet a certain standard rather than having them compete against each other (Taylor 2000), allowing them to focus on continuous improvement (Vokurka et al. 2000). They also aim at providing a holistic approach to quality. The CAE recognise organisations that have provided both quality products and services and excellent internal and external performance (Jagadeesh 2014). They also reward organisations that plan for business in Canada. Companies can apply repeatedly for the award in order to maintain and/or upgrade their recognition status by demonstrating sustainability and improvements in quality management (Excellence Canada n.d.).

The award framework consists of seven distinct categories: leadership, planning, customer focus, people focus, process management, a supplier–partner focus, and business performance. It adopts a holistic approach in evaluating the participating companies; hence, the framework involves unique aspects of good governance and healthy workplace practices and principles, such as leadership, involvement, customer focus, teamwork, cooperation, continuous improvement, and social responsibility (Ahmed 2015). Kumar et al. (2009) conducted a study to confirm the impact of TQM on companies' performance in Canada. Their findings confirmed that applying TQM principles in firms improved employee morale and participation; improvement in the quality of the products and services and the process itself were also evident. In addition, it also improved customer satisfaction, as the number of complaints decreased.

Organisations are motivated by Excellence Canada, which offers platforms for innovative ideas to be presented to different interest groups. Innovation is carried out based on the comparisons derived from the success of the best-performing groups in the world and the excellence awards act as a guide to follow and a standard to attain. Through the available standards, the organisation ensures that different firms in various industries are recognised in terms of the different required skills, making it possible for them to employ these skills to achieve their full potential.

Australia

The Australian Business Excellence Awards (ABEAs) were previously known as the Australian Quality Awards (AQA), which were first established in 1988 by the Australian Quality Council (AQC), a not-for-profit, membership-based organisation. The AQAs were based on the Australian Business Excellence Framework (ABEF), which primarily describes and provides an integrated approach for management and leadership based on proven best practices, which can help in attaining success and sustainability in a business or organisation. The ABEF interprets the best principles of BE into a group of basic criteria that can be used for assessing and improving the planning process, as well as improving the overall performance of the organisation or business. The AQC provided BE services and the awards programme recognised those organisations that excelled according to the framework criteria. Encountering financial trouble, the AQC—and the rights to the ABEF and the AQAs—were bought by the then Standards Australia International Limited (presently SAI Global) in February 2002. The objective of the AQA was to increase the awareness of quality standards amongst management and to also recognise and appreciate the accomplishments in quality and productivity improvements where organisations adopt a continuous, incremental improvement from day to day, monitor and identify improvement opportunities, prioritise opportunities carefully, and ensure that all parts of the organisation are targeting this improvement. In essence, the awards provide a tool for Australian organisations and businesses that acts as a benchmark for their achievements among their counterparts (Hasan and Hannifah 2013). As the knowledge and popularity of these awards spread, this eventually led to the pursuit of increasing quality and stimulated a global interest in it.

The most important element is that the criteria are non-prescriptive; they do not tell people how to run their businesses. Hasan and Hannifah (2013) conducted a study of the AQA winners from 1990 to 2003 that were listed on the Australian Stock Exchange, which revealed the positive effects evident in the organisations after receiving the award. These included motivated employees with enhanced performance, an increase in customer satisfaction that resulted in a rise in loyal customers, improved organisational culture with improved listening, sharing, learning, creativity and innovation, and contributions to safety along with environmental awareness that resulted in organisational and community well-being (Hasan and Hannifah 2013).

In the 1990s, the frameworks of the MBNQA and the DP were also revised, and the improvements integrated into the ABEF. This resulted in the change of name from AQA to ABEA; the vision of these awards is to increase quality consciousness among the stakeholders of businesses and organisations while sharing the best practices and various experiences. The ABEA forum provides organisations and businesses in Australia with an opportunity to celebrate their success and showcase the hard work that they put in to match business principles that are accepted around the world.

The framework offers a non-prescriptive lens to organisations, which can help each organisation in its pursuit of attaining excellence, becoming high-performing and changing its organisational culture for good. With the help of the ABEF, organisations have the opportunity not only to attain and develop resilience, but also to build the integrated focus that is necessary for sustainable performance (SPRING 2017a). Moreover, by facilitating the effective prioritisation of efforts aimed at bringing about improvements, the ABEF delivers various benefits to the organisations that integrate it into their workings.

Singapore

The Singapore National Quality Award (SQA) was established in 1993 as part of the country's national quality strategy to provide a TQM system with a framework suitable for the culture and business context of Singapore (Xie et al. 1998). As far back as 1990, the country considered TQM as an integral part of developing the culture of quality (Feng et al. 2006).

The SQA recognises Singapore's organisations for their high-quality standards and BE. It is administered by the Standards, Productivity and Innovation Board of Singapore (SPRING Singapore). SPRING Singapore operates under the Ministry of Trade and Industry of Singapore and provides the award framework to encourage TQM adoption. The SQA is the highest national recognition for excellence, quality, and conformance. It aims to improve the standards of Singaporean organisations and enhance their local and international competitiveness. It also promotes innovation by organisations of all sizes (Feng et al. 2006; SPRING 2017b), and encourages them to raise their quality standards to global levels (Tan 2002).

The framework, which is based on the MBNQA, EFQM, and DP, consists of the following seven categories: leadership, planning, information, people, process, customers, and results (Feng et al. 2006; Lee 2002).

Leadership is the key driver of organisational learning and innovation. The SQA has great potential when it comes to improving the leadership management of companies because the TQM practices established by the award are new to Singapore's organisational culture. Hence, the award promotes leadership as the main driver of quality to ensure the engagement and commitment of the senior management (Xie et al. 1998). Planning, customer focus, stakeholder management, results, and social responsibility are the core values of the framework (BPIR n.d.).

To compete with the European NQAs, the SQA focused its excellence awards on innovation excellence (Feng et al. 2006). Brah et al. (2002) conducted a case study on service and manufacturing companies in Singapore to examine the benefits of TQM on business performance. The researchers received 124 responses to their questionnaire, and their analysis showed that for TQM to be successfully implemented, it is essential for an organisation to embrace any changes required to enable effective communication that moulds the way in which people work with each other and also enhances employee satisfaction across the company. This also helps to increase the customer and quality focuses which enhance the overall performance of the organisation.

SPRING Singapore collaborates with the Singapore government to transform businesses in the country and the partnership has seen companies in Singapore benefiting immensely at various stages of business growth. SPRING Singapore has been a key partner in the empowerment of small ventures to grow into giant firms that make vital contributions to the national economy. The partnership has seen businesses in the country receiving enormous support through funding and mentoring to grow into multinational companies. The group is keen on identifying and supporting firms that are committed to excellence through the provision of high-quality goods and services to consumers. It is imperative for an organisation to meet the requirements stipulated by the agency to have a chance of winning an award. Singapore's NQA also offers educational sponsorships and internships as a prerequisite for preparing a talented workforce to make vital contributions to the growth of the national economy.

Singaporean companies are committed to continuous improvement in a bid to enhance their national and global positioning. The awards offer opportunities for corporations to identify their weaknesses and strengths in relation to their competitors and go on to make any necessary adjustments. This has resulted in many organisations addressing their deficiencies in an attempt to maximise their strengths and realise BE. It ranks businesses based on their commitment to continually improving their products and services to realise excellence in the world of business. The award offers myriad opportunities for corporations to assess their capabilities in meeting the needs of the customers. The SQA initiative aims at helping businesses in building and protecting their reputations by ensuring that they are committed to realising excellence; it seeks to help corporations in the country to learn from each other and grow together in a bid to empower them to compete with their global counterparts. The initiative has seen foreign direct investment in Singapore improving steadily, a growth that business experts say will empower its national economy.

The SQA are keen on enhancing industries in the country to spur on socio-economic development. The improved quality of industrial products and the creation of an enabling environment by the government has not only attracted foreign direct investment but has also developed domestic investors (Boys and Wilcock 2014). Companies in the same industry are competing to improve their commodities through differentiation to meet consumer needs. This enables the management of the SQA to identify and reward the best-performing businesses across the various sectors in a bid to improve the country's industries.

The SQA continues to be an inspiration to both established and upcoming firms in Singapore across different industries (Schuhmacher et al. 2017).

It is also crucial for an organisation to discharge its corporate responsibility diligently to be considered for an award. An enterprise's ability to participate in the formulation of business policies that spur on economic development is also vital. This feature has seen companies in Singapore being committed to affecting the national economy positively. An excellent business is one that is active in formulating strategies and policies aiming towards the continuous improvement of the efficiency and quality of their products.

The SQA evaluate a company's unique contributions to the national economy. While unemployment has remained a significant challenge to many nations across the world, the growth of the business sector in Singapore has led to the creation of job opportunities that have helped to address the problem. The business sector is growing steadily to the extent of employing more than 50% of Singapore's workforce. The initiative is keen on determining the commitment of a company to helping the government in addressing economic problems like unemployment and so a company's ability to contribute to the national economy and address economic challenges is highly regarded by the SQA. The criteria are used to determine the best-performing organisations to encourage others to follow suit. This makes it imperative for corporations to remain committed to making vital contributions to the growth of the national economy (Cavusgil et al. 2014). It also encourages them to participate in discussions and conferences that seek to formulate economic policies to improve the socio-economic well-being of Singapore's citizens.

Staff development, participation, and leadership are also imperative to winning the SQA. Organisations that are keen on creating an enabling environment for their members to unleash their full potential are usually recognised by the awards. This is contributing enormously to Singaporean companies' commitment to improving the welfare of the staff through training programmes. For instance, some organisations provide financial support to high-performing employees to motivate them to maintain their excellent productivity.

United Arab Emirates

The quality award in the United Arab Emirates (UAE) is the Dubai Quality Award (DQA); it was introduced in 1994 and is based on the excellence model used by the EFQM. The award acknowledges organisations that exhibit BE in the public and private sectors. A recent study by Lasrado (2017) aimed to identify the perceived benefits of DQA for its recipients. Its findings highlighted the intangible benefits as increased customer satisfaction, employee satisfaction, and career development. Moreover, the study respondents also stated that the feedback report provided by the DQA post-assessment aided their organisations in identifying their strengths and weaknesses, which assisted them in the development of an improvement plan for their processes. In addition, it also helped the organisation identify their stakeholder requirements and enable teamwork and organisational learning (Lasrado 2017).

The DQA has three categories: the Dubai Quality Golden (DQG) award, which is usually given to past winners of the DQA based on tangible improvements compared with previous performance; the DQA award, given to companies in various sectors, including tourism, finance, health care, and education; and the Dubai Quality Appreciation award, which is basically a token of appreciation given to organisations who fail to win one of the other awards, in acknowledgement of their effort and hard work; this is offered to organisations in all sectors and the hope is that recipients will be encouraged to make further improvements and reapply for the DQA.

Organisations in the Slovak Republic (SR) constantly strive to achieve the country's NQA, as acquiring the award is considered extremely prestigious. Hence, the winner is recognised as a competitor in quality management by all organisations in the country. Jurkovičová and Kašubová (2012) conducted a study by distributing questionnaires to 65 organisations that were awarded the SR NQA between 2000 and 2012. The results revealed non-financial benefits of the SR's NQA, including improved internal communication, improved employee satisfaction with the management of the organisation, improved reputation and goodwill, and greater customer communication leading to an increase in customer satisfaction.

Sweden

The Swedish Quality Award (SQA) was established in 1992 by the Swedish Institute for Quality (SIQ) to promote performance excellence among the country's companies. According to the SIQ, to catalyse the implementation of TQM in a company, it should work towards attaining quality awards. Hence, the concept of participating in the SQA or having an internal quality award is encouraged. Eriksson (2003) conducted a case study on the Swedish National Road Administration as, in 1998, they had instituted an internal quality award and continued to refine it thereafter. The results of the study revealed positive effects of working with quality awards including better customer orientation, helping the company get a comprehensive insight into the business, and increasing the involvement of employees in the company.

Japan

With the introduction of the Deming Prize in 1951, Japan was the first country to establish the quality award concept in an effort to improve the quality of its products and services and re-establish its economy after World War II. Hence, the essence of intense commitment to win the quality award is embedded in the culture of some organisations in Japan (Iaquinto 1999). The aim of the DP is to facilitate the process of achieving BE for the organisation. Some of the perceived intangible benefits of the DP are that it helps organisations to understand customer expectations, thereby aiding in the process of improving customer satisfaction. In addition, it helps organisations develop and acquire new technology to develop new products, which assists organisations in gaining a competitive edge. Furthermore, it ensures that organisations list the goals they want to achieve and share them with all employees to enable efficient operations and easy communication with management. In this way, employees are made aware of what is expected of them; this affects employee satisfaction in a positive way, as it reduces task-related surprises.

India

With the coming of modern globalisation it became essential for India to develop high-quality products and services in order to survive in the global marketplace. Subsequently, India introduced quality awards for BE, such as the Rajiv Gandhi NQA in 1999 and the Confederation of Indian Industry (CII) Award, to motivate companies to strive to achieve BE in the way they operated (Tan and Khoo 2002). Madan (2010) conducted a case study on Bharat Heavy Electrical Limited (BHEL), a public firm which won the CII Award for BE in 2006. The study highlighted the BE journey of BHEL and the effects of the award. The results of the study showed that when the company applied TQM, customer satisfaction and employee satisfaction, and emphasis on employee well-being increased, and communication between employees and management, and the collaboration level in the organisation improved (Madan 2010).

Taiwan

The first country to establish NQAs in Asia was Taiwan. The Taiwan National Quality Award (TNQA) was founded in 1990 to facilitate the process of resolving quality-related issues as the government identified quality as a major component in the dignity of the country. A study conducted by Tzeng et al. (2009) strategically evaluated the cases of IBM, Panasonic, and E.SUN Bank. The study identified the benefits of the TNQA as increased employee loyalty and improved customer satisfaction. In addition, the process of taking part in the award enables organisations to constantly innovate and improve by conducting reviews of performance and self-assessments to vie effectively with their competition.

Conclusion: The Emphasis on Human Capital in National Quality Awards

NQAs play a significant part in countries' development by enhancing organisational performance. There are some similarities in the criteria used for the various award processes. It is evident that all award programmes use continuous improvement initiatives to retain their positions as benchmarks in quality systems and as quality principles in the formation of a global quality model. However, it should not be forgotten that the role of human capital is central to each of these NQAs. Talwar (2011) conducted a comparative review of the framework, criteria, and criterion weighting of 20 excellence models and NQAs, and identified Customers, People, and Business Results as the core criteria—a must for survival in business. Moreover, he identified Process, Leadership, Strategic Planning, and Knowledge and Information Management as internal environment criteria—the differentiators in a competitive environment—and Society and Suppliers/Partners as goodwill criteria for ensuring sustainability. However, other models include quality, customer focus, and corporate responsibility in their end objectives (Talwar 2011).

Although the studies that compared the NQA models concluded that they are similar in nature, individual organisations cannot consider them as a panacea for all their problems, and competitive advantage cannot be gained simply by replicating an award programme (Miguel 2015). However, the models do provide a solid foundation for organisations to assess their performance. Individual organisations must focus on their respective key dimensions, such as human capital, to derive the best performance. As human capital has become crucial to organisational success, strategies must be adopted to complement an organisation's excellence drive.

Talwar (2011) also noted that the DP is different in its focus on 'Core Quality Systems' rather than the financial results focus evident in most of the other models.

Considering the human development perspective, in studies of the Canadian excellence programme, for instance, it was noted that Canadian award programmes promote employee participation in volunteer programmes and company support of and participation in events that build a healthier community (Angell and Corbett 2009). Human capital development must also incorporate some core human values. The excellence models with core principles deeply rooted in values like leadership, employee involvement, and customer focus require human value to be maintained; Talwar (2011) suggested that the effectiveness of a core value increases when it builds human value(s) into it. For example, the core value 'leadership and constancy of purpose' will be more effective if it emanates from certain human values, such as honesty, justice, good character, compassion and respect, self-learning and knowledge-sharing, fearlessness, integrity, and the pursuit of knowledge and self-discipline. The same is true of the core values. While practising the core values of excellence models has helped many organisations to achieve favourable business results, the practice of upholding human values leads to sustainability of these favourable results, as well as bringing additional benefits for the organisation and the society in which it is working.

Although the quality award models offer a practical approach to TQM and the concept of excellence, the way in which they have been constructed and applied has varied. These variations are due to the nature of the development of the models to reflect the needs of organisations in different geographic locations, cultures, and environments.

NQAs provide organisations with a competitive advantage when they follow TQM practices (Talwar 2011). The CAE have monitored the performance of the award winners and witnessed improvements in cost savings, customer and employee satisfaction, internal processes, trust, and leadership. In Singapore, the Centre of Organisational Excellence Research reported that the awards affected the companies' 'competitiveness and sustainability' in the long run: it is also claimed that the awards motivated the organisations to become industry world leaders (Mann et al. 2012).

Finally, in today's constantly changing market, it has become necessary for organisations to implement TQM principles to gain a competitive advantage that will allow them to compete effectively in the local and global markets. NQA criteria provide organisations with the guidelines required to implement TQM, which can facilitate the journey to excellence for the organisation. Organisations should constantly strive to participate in and win quality awards at the national and global levels. Many of the NQAs have an impact on their national economy. NQAs have also been instrumental in fostering quality movements in organisations and hence underpin the necessity to remain competitive. As globalisation and the global markets evolve, it is necessary for NQA custodians to continuously review their excellence criteria.

References

Ahmed. (2015). *New research shows 61 countries with national business excellence awards*. Retrieved from http://blog.bpir.com/latest-news/new-research-shows-67-countries-with-national-business-excellence-awards

Allvin, S., Ulmer, J. M., & Ollison, T. E. (2008). The Malcolm Baldrige award: What technology managers can learn from health care winners. *International Journal of Applied Management and Technology, 6*(3), 274–301.

Angell, L. C., & Corbett, L. M. (2009). The quest for business excellence: Evidence from New Zealand's award winners. *International Journal of Operations & Production Management, 29*(2), 170–199.

Boys, K. A., & Wilcock, A. E. (2014). Improving integration of human resources into quality management system standards. *International Journal of Quality & Reliability Management, 31*(7), 738–750.

BPIR. (n.d.). *Business excellence models*. Retrieved from http://www.bpir.com/total-quality-management-business-excellence-models-bpir.com.html

Brah, S. A., Tee, S. S. L., & Rao, B. M. (2002). Relationship between TQM and performance of Singapore companies. *International Journal of Quality and Reliability Management, 19*(4), 356–379.

British Quality Foundation. (2003). *The impact of business excellence on financial performance*. London: British Quality Foundation.

Brown, M. G. (2013). *Baldrige award winning quality – 18th edition: How to interpret the Baldrige criteria for performance excellence*. Boca Raton: CRC Press.

Cavusgil, S. T., Knight, G., Riesenberger, J. R., Rammal, H. G., & Rose, E. L. (2014). *International business*. Melbourne: Pearson Australia.

Eriksson, H. (2003). Experiences of working with in-company quality awards: A case study. *The TQM Magazine, 15*(6), 397–407.

Evans, J. R., Ford, M. W., Masterson, S. S., & Hertz, H. S. (2012). Beyond performance excellence: Research insights from Baldrige recipient feedback. *Total Quality Management and Business Excellence, 23*(5–6), 489–506.

Excellence Canada. (n.d.). *Canada awards for excellence*. Retrieved from http://excellence.ca/en/awards/

Feng, J., Prajogo, D. I., Chuan Tan, K., & Sohal, A. S. (2006). The impact of TQM practices on performance: A comparative study between Australian and Singaporean organizations. *European Journal of Innovation Management, 9*(3), 269–278.

Hasan, M., & Hannifah, H. (2013). A study of Australian business excellence award winners. *Journal of Service Science and Management, 6*(1), 31–37.

Hendricks, K. B., & Singhal, V. R. (1997). Does implementing an effective TQM program actually improve operating performance? Empirical evidence from firms that have won quality awards. *Management Science, 43*(9), 1258–1274.

Iaquinto, A. L. (1999). Can winners be losers? The case of the Deming prize for quality and performance among large Japanese manufacturing firms. *Managerial Auditing Journal, 14*(1/2), 28–35.

Jagadeesh, R. (2014). Emphasis on human resource management in quality improvement–A case study of quality awards' criteria. *International Journal of Economics, Commerce and Management, 1*(2), 1–12.

Jurkovičová, M., & Kašubová, K. (2012). 12 years of the national quality award of the Slovak Republic. *Quality Innovation Prosperity, 16*(1), 1–17.

Kern Pipan, K., Gomiscek, B., Kljajic, M., & Jesenko, M. (2011). An empirical study on comparing total quality management (TQM) items of national quality award applicants in Slovenia. *African Journal of Business Management, 5*(33), 12829–12840.

Kern Pipan, K., Gomišček, B., & Kljajić, M. (2013). *Slovenian national excellence award and TQM deployment in Slovenian companies*. Paper presented at the quality management and organizational development conference, University of Maribor, Slovania.

Kumar, V., Choisne, F., de Grosbois, D., & Kumar, U. (2009). Impact of TQM on company's performance. *International Journal of Quality and Reliability Management, 26*(1), 23–37.

Lasrado, F. (2017). Perceived benefits of national quality awards: A study of UAE's award winning organizations. *Measuring Business Excellence, 21*(1), 50–64.

Laszlo, G. P. (1996). Quality awards-recognition or model? *The TQM Magazine, 8*(5), 14–18.

Lee, P.-M. (2002). Sustaining business excellence through a framework of best practices in TQM. *The TQM Magazine, 14*(3), 142–149.

Madan, P. (2010). An award journey for business excellence: The case study of a public sector unit. *Total Quality Management, 21*(12), 1343–1364.

Mann, B., Mohammad, M., & Agustin, M. T. A. (2012). *Understanding business excellence – An awareness guidebook for SMEs*. (2017). [ebook] Asian Productivity Organization. Retrieved from http://www.apo-tokyo.org/coe/files/Understanding-Business-Excellence.pdf

Miguel, P. A. C. (2015). Receiving a national quality award three times: Recognition of excellence in quality and performance. *The TQM Journal, 27*(1), 63–78.

Schuhmacher, M. C., Kuester, S., & Flötotto, D. (2017). Idea competitions in new service development: Co-creation with a certain consumer group. In C. L. Campbell (Ed.), *The customer is NOT always right? Marketing orientations in a dynamic business world* (pp. 429–432). Cham: Springer.

SPRING. (2017a). *Business excellence framework*. Retrieved from https://www.spring.gov.sg/Building-Trust/Business-Excellence/Documents/BE_Framework.pdf

SPRING. (2017b). *Enabling transformation of Singapore's SMEs through industry development*. Retrieved from https://www.spring.gov.sg/Inspiring-Success/Enterprise-Stories/Pages/Developing-Singapore's-SMEs.aspx

Talwar, B. (2011). Business excellence models and the path ahead…. *The TQM Journal, 23*(1), 21–35.

Tan, K. C. (2002). A comparative study of 16 national quality awards. *The TQM Magazine, 14*(3), 165–171.

Tan, K. C., & Khoo, H. H. (2002). The relevance of Confucianism to national quality awards in Southeast Asia. *International Journal of Cross Cultural Management, 2*(1), 65–82.

Taylor, L. (2000). A comparison of the criteria and strategies of different awards. *The Innovation Journal: The Public Sector Innovation Journal, 5*(1), 1–3.

Tzeng, J.-R., Lin, S.-C., Chen, S.-C., Liu, K.-S., Liu, S.-C., & Fu, S.-L. (2009). The strategic study of National Quality Award through business excellence model – The IBM, Panasonic and E.SUN Bank cases in Taiwan. *Systemics, Cybernetics and Informatics, 7*(5), 95–100.

Vokurka, R. J., Stading, G. L., & Brazeal, J. (2000). A comparative analysis of national and regional quality awards. *Quality Progress, 33*(8), 41–49.

Xie, M., Tan, K. C., Puay, S. H., & Goh, T. N. (1998). A comparative study of nine national quality awards. *The TQM Magazine, 10*(1), 30–39.

6

Involvement of Human Capital: Time for Teamwork

Introduction

In this chapter we focus on how people and teamwork can be leveraged for human excellence in organisations. The business excellence (BE) maturity of an organisation depends on embedded organisational changes, which in turn affect the way human resource (HR) considerations are formed in relation to strategic quality goals. It is now evident that quality experts, researchers, academics, and practitioners have realised that human capital development should be at the core of the quality philosophy and that employee involvement and commitment is essential to the successful introduction and implementation of quality initiatives, programmes, or practices and techniques (Blackburn and Rosen 1993; Soltani et al. 2004; Soltani 2003). Thus, BE has a high HR context, and this quality movement recognises the importance of HR utilisation and states a conceptual and well-defined image concerning human behaviour and motivation (Pfeffer 1994). Research evidence also suggests that as total quality management (TQM) improvement efforts proceed, a change in the corporate culture occurs, resulting in the establishment of a work climate in which participation, trust, responsibility for goal achievement, and employee involvement take place (Lawler 1994).

F. Lasrado, V. Pereira, *Achieving Sustainable Business Excellence*,
https://doi.org/10.1007/978-3-319-73314-2_6

To best aid an organisation in its efforts to achieve BE, HR needs to be involved throughout the process. Without HR participation from start to finish, the organisation's endeavours will be hampered and more likely to fail. From the initial planning stages to the introduction and ongoing implementation of quality initiatives, the HR contribution is vital. Often, it is not just a matter of introducing new procedures; old ones will need to be revised or even retired altogether. Also, it should not be forgotten that these changes will have to take place within HR, too; HR must lead by example—it is not just a matter of imposing new policy on other departments. And, of course, there also has to be a willingness to accept that these new policies themselves will almost certainly need adjusting to circumstances over time as what works and what does not becomes apparent.

Hendricks and Triplett, writing in 1989, pointed out that in order to successfully implement total quality initiatives an organisation must be willing to make changes across the board. It is not enough to target a part or parts; the whole organisation must take the change on board. These changes may be tangible (e.g. physical changes in the working environment) or intangible (e.g. changes in the corporate culture reflecting the drive for quality), but for both the involvement of HR is needed. HR is also vital for continuity, in tracking the effect of changes brought in, and in fostering an atmosphere where all employees accept, internalise, and actively work towards achieving quality targets. A happy workforce is far more likely to both support such initiatives and stay with the company (thus retaining their valuable institutional knowledge) and so organisations should look to support their employees. This support could come in various forms including training, appraisals, and recognition. Van Donk and Sanders (1993) pointed out that the interconnectedness of changes resulting from TQM is widely accepted: as structures and values change, so do people. They reflect these changes (for the better) in their level of participation and how they work together.

Another important aspect is understanding that the relationships between the award criteria make it possible for companies to analyse the projects' effects on model criteria and to apply appropriate tools for improvement while planning and setting goals for the future direction of HR excellence. In order to achieve HR excellence, companies need to be aware of the impact of criteria on each other and also conduct analysis of and establish the relationships between the people criterion and the people results criterion. Organisations must ascertain which of the sub-criteria of the people criterion and the people results criterion have the most and the least impact on creating a meaningful relationship.

Wilkinson et al. (1997) explored the relationship between TQM and HR practices in six manufacturing companies in Britain. Their findings showed (i) the importance of employees and (ii) that employee involvement under TQM was of a multidimensional nature. Eskildsen (1998) researched the relationship between people, processes, people results, and key performance results and found that weaknesses in the management of people and processes were reflected in people results and key performance results. Safari et al. (2012) also noted that the people criterion is strongly related to the people results criterion and that all sub-criteria in both sets have a high canonical cross-loading in creating a canonical variable in their criteria. They are, therefore, very effective in creating a meaningful relationship between people and people results. Thus, a balanced approach in the development of the people sub-criteria makes it possible to maximise the correlation between people sub-criteria and people results sub-criteria and, therefore, to obtain an optimal profit from the European Foundation for Quality Management (EFQM) excellence model. This result is consistent with studies on the EFQM excellence model conducted by Eskildsen (1998), Eskildsen and Dahlgaard (2000), Prabhu et al. (2000), Dijkstra (1997), Bou-Llusar et al. (2005), and Calvo-Mora et al. (2005).

Involving People in Teamwork to Carry Out an Internal Quality Assessment

The people criterion of the EFQM assessment involves asking questions about 'how human resources are planned and improved; how people capabilities are sustained and developed; how people agree targets and continuously review performance; how people are involved, empowered and recognised; how people and the organisation have an effective dialogue; and how people are cared for' (Yang et al. 2001, p. 3790). Zaremba and Crew (1995) reported on how Royal Mail, having carried out a successful self-assessment exercise over its 17 business units, looked to find ways to get its smaller units, teams, and individual employees involved to the same extent. It did so by customising the self-assessment to the smaller units and providing support in the form of published materials and designated employees who had already undergone quality training. Having identified an 'excellent unit', its methods (where appropriate) were disseminated to other units to copy. They also took the step of trialling the approach with selected units before rolling the system out company-wide; as mentioned earlier, the materials used were constantly reviewed and revised according to the results they generated.

As José Tarí (2010) found from a study conducted on different organisations, lack of staff commitment is considered one of the most significant organisational self-assessment difficulties: training employees in how to carry out these self-assessments requires a heavy investment of time by various departments during both the planning and implementation stage. He also suggested that the lack of a quality unit role in supporting, training, and implementing the self-assessment process affects the process.

In the course of carrying out self-assessments within the organisation, employees' attitudes to changes may vary (Ritchie and Dale 2000). For TQM principles to be applied in any organisation seeking BE, the organisation needs to have a strong culture that is positive towards improvements and change. While applying for the excellence award, some organisations attempt to influence the attitudes of their employees towards change; for example, management may offer internal incentives to encourage employees' willingness to raise the organisational quality standards (Ritchie and Dale 2000).

Shergold and Reed (1996, p. 50) list a number of steps that they say all organisations need to include in their self-assessment which again emphasise the importance of commitment, inclusiveness of all employees, effective communication and use of data gathered, acknowledgement that priorities will have to be assigned, supporting new plans in practice (whether with material, people, training, or financial outlays), and ongoing willingness to review and adapt.

Research: Using the Idea Management System to Enhance Human Capital

The 'people' enabler of the excellence framework emphasises harnessing creativity and innovative capabilities of its employees. Idea Management systems are one of the ways to capture employees' innovative ideas and harness creativity in the organisation. Although implementation or usage of such systems is evidenced in high-performing organisations, there are many challenges to sustain such systems. It is important for managers to understand and foster the factors that will enable them to sustain such systems and yield their benefits. The next section thus illustrates research that was conducted to understand influential factors for fostering Idea Management systems.

Background to Idea Management Systems

An Idea Management system is a tool widely used by corporations to elicit employees' creative ideas. It elicits suggestions from employees, classifies them, and dispatches them to 'experts' for evaluation. After this, the suggestion might be adopted, in which case it may well be rewarded. 'Experts' are dedicated committees who evaluate the suggestions and propose to implement them. Idea Management systems thus create win-win situations for employers and employees alike. However, despite the many benefits of the Idea Management system, sustaining it is still a challenge for organisations. Organisations need to assess their Idea Management system to determine its sustainability and to examine whether the right conditions exist for it to flourish. After all, Idea Management systems can contribute to building organisations' innovative capability.

Most importantly, these systems play a pivotal role for organisations wishing to become more innovative (Buech et al. 2010). It is a tool widely used to encourage employees to think innovatively and creatively about their work and work environment and to produce ideas which will benefit the organisation (Du Plessis et al. 2008). It primarily consists of administrative procedures and infrastructure for collecting, judging, and compensating ideas which are conceived by the employees of the organisation (Van Dijk and Van den Ende 2002).

The following section describes research that was undertaken to develop a framework to assess the sustainability of an Idea Management system. This research explored the critical success factors and barriers to the sustainability of Idea Management systems.

Method: This research was initiated in early 2010 to develop a framework to assess the sustainability of an Idea Management system. The research was planned to be undertaken in three stages. The first stage was the planning stage, in which a literature review comprising two parts was conducted. The first included exploring the meaning of sustainability in relation to the Idea Management system, process improvements, and continuous improvement programmes; and the second focused on developing a deeper understanding of the Idea Management system and exploring the critical success factors for such a system. The research development stage comprised activities such as the development of a questionnaire to elicit the opinions and views of the Idea Management system users with respect to the indicators explored in the planning stage. The data were collected and analysed using statistical tools. The data collection and analysis were extended to elicit expert opinion on the importance of the factors and factor indicators extracted based on the results of the initial analysis. At the end of this stage, a framework to assess the sustainability of the Idea Management system was conceptualised. The validation stage included three case studies. The analysis of the case studies was used to refine the framework by including a list of prevailing practices for each of the indicators and to conceptualise a sustainability status of the Idea Management system. The case study methodology was designed to address a major question: How can an organisation pursue sustainability in an Idea Management system and what are the practices or activities that are associated with each of the factors influencing the sustainability of an Idea Management system? A key feature of the case study research is the number of cases included in a project. This research planned to study three cases, making it a multi-case study. This is necessary in order to capture the range of practices applied with respect to each of the factors. Yin (2004) confirms that the evidence created from this type of study is considered robust and reliable; hence multiple case studies can be used to predict similar results. Multiple cases are preferable when the purpose of the research is to describe phenomena, and develop and test theories. This research used the following selection criteria to choose the cases:

- Size of the company by number of employees
- Industry or industry sub-sector in which the firm operates
- Duration of the Idea Management system in the company

The size of the company is an important variable as these systems are applicable to both large and small companies. The different sizes of companies would thus not only contribute to case study research questions but also provide a lens through which to view the impact of each of the factors typical of the Idea Management system. As with company size, analysing different industries or industry sub-sectors through the case studies is likely to help respond to case study research questions and, especially, to provide insight into the relevant practices associated with each of the factors for the sustainability of the Idea Management system. Finally, as in the case of the size and industry sector, the duration of the Idea Management system is also an important element to consider. Choosing cases from small to large life spans would also provide a variety of insights into how each factor plays a role in influencing the sustainability of the Idea Management system. The researchers also considered multiple sources of data for this study, for example by gathering and studying organisational documents such as administrative reports, user manuals, minutes, and news clippings for each of the organisations.

The Findings

The aim of the research was to identify the variables that are necessary to assess the sustainability of an Idea Management system and to conceptualise an assessment framework for evaluating it. A list of 32 sustainability assessment indicators was extracted from the literature review. These are defined as follows:

1. Customer satisfaction: improvement in customer satisfaction as a result of an Idea Management system
2. Product quality: improvement in a service or product as a result of an Idea Management system
3. Improvement in process: improvement in a process as the result of an Idea Management system
4. New revenues: monitory benefit generated as a result of implementing suggestions
5. Safety and employee satisfaction: employee perception of safety and job satisfaction as a result of an Idea Management system
6. Cost saving: amount of money saved as a result of implementing a suggestion
7. Commitment and sense of accountability: employee commitment and sense of accountability to their organisation as a result of satisfaction
8. Sense of security: sense of security that employees perceive as a result of an Idea Management system
9. Employee confidence: level of confidence that the employees generate about their organisation as a result of the Idea Management system
10. Suggestion implementation: rate or number of valid suggestions being implemented
11. Empowerment: opportunity for employees to make decisions and for authorities to exercise their creativity
12. Feedback: process of providing responses to the suggestions
13. Rewarding: process of recognising and awarding employees
14. Evaluation: prompt assessment of suggestions carried out by qualified evaluators to judge the suggestion value based on fair and transparent criteria
15. Awareness: publicity of the Idea Management system
16. System features: presence of a dedicated skilled administrator and a simple, easy-to-use system with a fair and consistent set of rules for the smooth functioning of the scheme
17. Resources: availability of resources to support creativity
18. Top management support: leadership, commitment, and interest of the top management in an Idea Management system

19. Supervisor support: commitment and support of the supervisor towards employees suggestions
20. Organisational support: existence of supportive provisions that include establishing a non-rigid organisational structure, supportive climate, exercising patience with employees, and developing trust amongst employees
21. Communication and networking: effective mechanisms for sharing information, opportunity to meet with colleagues internally, and social networking for sharing ideas
22. Support for innovation: safety of the employees by avoiding obstructive behaviours or non-cooperation from co-workers as a result of implementation of new co-workers
23. Co-worker support: assistance and comfort from co-workers in submitting ideas
24. Teamwork: option to submit suggestions in teams
25. Expertise: employees experience and expertise in their work area
26. Training: providing employees with necessary training to develop creativity and other required skills
27. Employee participation: scope to participate in the Idea Management system and actual participation
28. Job control: closely monitored, isolated work environments with tight time pressures where job tasks are standardised
29. Competition: employees feel that they are judged for their performance
30. Organisational impediments: unsupportive organisational practices that hinder suggestions including inadequate resources, mistrust amongst employees, inadequate rewards, fear of ideas being misused, and isolated work environment
31. Job characteristics: jobs that present challenge, variety, and complexity
32. Individual characteristics: individual attributes such as self-efficacy, positive perceptions, and proactive behaviours

The literature review explored the critical success factors and barriers to Idea Management systems, creativity, and innovation. The 32 different indicators were then grouped into 5 main factors based on a statistical analysis, namely the factor analysis. Factor analysis is a data reduction technique that uses correlations between data variables. Factor analysis can be used to understand the structure of a set of variables: to construct a questionnaire to measure an underlying variable and to reduce a data set to a more manageable size while retaining as much of the original information as possible (Field 2005). As a result, an initial assessment framework comprising 5 main factors and 24 factor indicators was created, as shown in Table 6.1.

The descriptions of the final 5 factors and their indicators are as follows.

Factor 1: System Effectiveness

This factor emphasises the benefits of an Idea Management system. The indicators included in this factor depict the outcomes of an Idea Management system in terms of profitability, customer satisfaction, employee productivity, product quality, and process improvement. These variables increase the effectiveness of an Idea Management system. The following indicators are included in this factor:

- Customer satisfaction: The purpose of an Idea Management system is to improve customer satisfaction. An improvement in customer satisfaction increases the sustainability of the Idea Management system.
- Product quality: One of the stated goals of an Idea Management system is to improve the quality of the product or service. An improvement in product quality or service as a result of an Idea Management system increases the sustainability of the Idea Management system.
- Improvements in process: Another objective of an Idea Management system is to continuously improve the organisations processes. Meeting this objective increases the sustainability of the Idea Management system.
- Employee productivity: This indicator implies the benefit that the organisation gains in terms of employee productivity as a result of suggestion. An Idea Management system helps improve employee safety and satisfaction, thus resulting in employee productivity. An Idea

Table 6.1 Factors for idea management system sustainability

Leadership and work environment	System capability	Organisational encouragement	System effectiveness	System barriers
Factor indicators				
Top management support	Support for suggestion implementation	Teamwork	Profitability	Job control
Supervisor support	Rewards	Training	Employee productivity	Competition
Co-worker support	System features	Expertise	Product quality	
Organisational support	Feedback	Employee participation	Process improvements	
Communication and networking	Awareness		Customer satisfaction	
Support for innovation	Evaluation			
	Resources			

Management system also improves employee commitment and sense of accountability to the organisation. Another benefit is that it helps employees perceive a sense of security. An Idea Management system also helps to improve employee confidence in the organisation, resulting in employee productivity.
- Profitability: This indicator implies the cost saved or new revenue generated as a result of an Idea Management system.

Factor 2: System Capability

This factor stresses on the capability of the system. The implementation of valid ideas and existence and adoption of capability indicators improve the sustainability of an Idea Management system. Capability indicators include the following:

- Support for suggestion implementation: This is concerned with the extent to which suggestions are put into action and the support of the organisation to empower employees to make implementable ideas. Empowerment helps employees to test their creativity, thereby increasing the chances of considering implementation of the idea.
- Feedback: This is concerned with how the organisation manages to provide the feedback on its employees' suggestions. A prompt and supportive feedback motivates employees to make more suggestions and be involved in the system.
- Rewards: This implies the recognition and rewards that the organisation allocates to the suggestions. Setting up a fair number of rewards increases employee involvement in the Idea Management system.
- Awareness: This indicates the publicity that the organisation makes with regard to its scheme. Communicating the benefits and the scheme itself can help attract suggestions from its employees.
- Evaluation: This is concerned with the process of evaluating suggestions. A transparent set of procedures and effective processes increases the number of suggestions.
- System features: This implies the features of the system in terms of usability and accessibility. A user-friendly system, with dedicated

administrators and timely processing of ideas can attract more suggestions and, hence, increase the sustainability of the Idea Management system.

- Resources: This indicates the extent to which the organisation supports its employees with resources to stimulate creative ideas. Adequate and timely availability of the resources can increase the sustainability of the Idea Management system.

Factor 3: Leadership and Work Environment

This factor stresses on leadership and work environment in an Idea Management system. It indicates the importance of the commitment and involvement of the top leadership and various other supportive mechanisms that impact the sustainability of an Idea Management system. The existence and adoption of the leadership and organisational encouragement increase the sustainability of an Idea Management system. The following are the leadership and organisational encouragement indicators:

- Top management support: This indicates the commitment and the support of the top management to the Idea Management system. The involvement and active participation of the top management in an Idea Management system's activities have a positive impact on employees.
- Supervisor support: This indicates the extent to which supervisors encourage their employees to make suggestions. The guidance and encouragement from the supervisors motivate the employees to make suggestions.
- Organisational support: This indicates the provisions that the organisation can make to support the Idea Management system. A flexible organisation structure, no rigid rules, and participative management styles encourage employees to make suggestions.
- Communication and networking: This indicates the communication mechanisms and opportunities for collaborating. The free flow of communication, sharing information, and networking opportunities encourage employees to make suggestions.

- Support for innovations: This implies the provision within an organisation to protect its employees from any obstructive behaviour of colleagues, as a result of their suggestion. The existence of a mechanism to deal with these issues can decrease the employees' fear of participating in the Idea Management system.
- Co-worker's support: This is concerned with the support and guidance rendered by co-workers towards making a suggestion. Co-workers' support and guidance motivates employees to make suggestions.

Factor 4: Organisational Encouragement

This factor stresses on the supportive elements that exist within an organisation to support the Idea Management system. The existence and fostering of such elements improve the sustainability of the Idea Management system. The following are indicators for organisational encouragement:

- Teamwork: Providing an opportunity to make suggestions in groups motivates employees to make suggestions and thus impacts the sustainability of the Idea Management system.
- Expertise: The employees' domain knowledge and expertise increase their ability to make suggestions.
- Training: This implies the extent to which an organisation provides training to stimulate creativity and to use the Idea Management system effectively.
- Employee participation: This implies the extent to which employees participate in the Idea Management system. Greater involvement of the employees in the Idea Management system improves the sustainability of the Idea Management system.

Factor 5: System Barriers

This factor implies the existence of unsupportive practices that hinder an Idea Management system. These barriers have a negative impact on an Idea Management system and include job control and creating a sense of competition amongst employees.

- Job control: This implies the extent to which employees are expected to follow the standard routines within their job roles. Jobs with tight time pressures and standard routines impact the creative ability of employees and discourage employees from participating in the Idea Management system.
- Competition: This implies making the participation in an Idea Management system mandatory for employees and creating an environment of competition, which has a negative impact on the Idea Management system. A free and voluntary environment will positively impact the Idea Management system.

In summary, the framework is shown in Table 6.1

The framework was refined based on expert opinion study. At this stage, the importance of the factors was identified through the application of the Analytical Hierarchy Process (AHP) method. The importance of each factor indicator was also identified.

The AHP is a theory of measurement through pair-wise comparisons and relies on the judgements of experts to derive priority scales (Saaty 2008). This technique allows for the search of relative importance placed on product attributes and attribute levels of the analysed complex goods (Scholl et al. 2005). To make pair-wise comparisons, we need a scale of numbers that indicate how many times more important or dominant one element is over another, with respect to the criterion or property to which they are compared (Saaty 2008).

After the study and analysis of the Reciprocal matrix and AHP calculations, the following can be interpreted:

- Leadership and work environment are slightly more important than both system effectiveness and system capability, somewhat more important than organisational environment, and much more important than system barriers.
- System capability is equally important to system effectiveness and slightly more important than both organisational encouragement and system barriers. However, it is slightly less important than leadership and work environment.

- System effectiveness is equally important to both system capability and organisational environment and slightly more important than system barriers. However, it is slightly less important than leadership and work environment.
- Organisational encouragement is equally important to system barriers and system effectiveness. However, it is less important than system capability and somewhat less important than leadership and work environment.
- System barriers is equally important to organisational encouragement. However, it is slightly less important than both system capability and system effectiveness and much less important than leadership and work environment.

Table 6.2 presents the order of importance for five sustainability factors based on the previous interpretations. Leadership and work environment comprise the most important factor when compared to the other four. The system capability indicator stands at rank 2, system effectiveness at rank 3, organisational encouragement at rank 4, and system barriers at rank 5.

Importance Ranks for System Effectiveness

- Profitability is much more important than product quality and process improvements. It is somewhat more important than customer satisfaction and slightly more important than employee productivity.
- Employee productivity is much more important than product quality. It is somewhat more important than process improvement. It is equal to customer satisfaction and slightly less important than profitability.

Table 6.2 Factor importance

Indicator	Importance rank
Leadership and work environment	1
System capability	2
System effectiveness	3
Organisational encouragement	4
System barriers	5

- Customer satisfaction is equal to employee productivity, somewhat more important than product quality, slightly more important than process improvement, but less important than profitability.
- Process improvement is slightly more important than product quality but slightly less important than customer satisfaction, somewhat less important than employee productivity, and much less important than profitability.
- Product quality is slightly less important than process improvements and less important than customer satisfaction. It is much less important than profitability and employee productivity.

Table 6.3 depicts the order of importance for five system effectiveness indicators based on previous interpretations. Profitability is the most important indicator when compared to the other four. Employee productivity is placed at rank 2, process improvement at rank 3, customer satisfaction at rank 4, and product quality at rank 5.

Importance Ranks for System Capability

- Rewards are equally important to support for suggestion implementation and somewhat more important than resources, awareness, and system failures. It is slightly more important than evaluation and feedback.
- Support for suggestion implementation is equally important to rewards, slightly more important than evaluation, feedback, system features, and awareness, and somewhat more important than resources.
- Feedback is slightly more important than evaluation and system features, somewhat more important than awareness and resources, but slightly less important than rewards and support for suggestion implementation.

Table 6.3 Importance ranks—system effectiveness

Indicator	Importance rank
Profitability	1
Employee productivity	2
Process improvement	3
Customer satisfaction	4
Product quality	5

- Evaluation is slightly more important than system features, somewhat more important than resources and awareness. It is slightly less important than support for suggestion implementation and rewards and feedback.
- System features is equally important to awareness and slightly more important than resources. It is slightly less important than evaluation and feedback and rewards and somewhat less important than suggestion implementation.
- Awareness is equally important to system features, slightly more important than resources, somewhat less important than evaluation, feedback, support for suggestion implementation and rewards.
- Resources are equally important to awareness, slightly less important than system features, and somewhat less important than evaluation, feedback, support for suggestion implementation, and much less important than rewards.

Table 6.4 depicts the order of importance for seven factor indicators based on previous interpretations: rewards at rank 1, support for suggestion implementation at rank 2, feedback at rank 3, evaluation at rank 4, system features at 5, awareness at rank 6, and resources at rank 7.

Importance Ranks for Leadership and Work Environment

- Top management support is much more important than co-worker support (5), moderately more important than communication (4), somewhat more important than support for innovation, and slightly more important than organisational support and supervisor support.

Table 6.4 Importance ranks for system capability

Indicators	Importance rank
Rewards	1
Support for suggestion implementation	2
Feedback	3
Evaluation	4
System features	5
Awareness	6
Resources	7

- Supervisor support is moderately more important than co-worker support (4) and somewhat more important than communication and support for innovation. It is slightly more important than organisational support but slightly less important than top management support.
- Organisational support is slightly more important than support for innovation and communication, somewhat more important than co-worker support, but slightly less important than top management support and supervisor support.
- Communication is slightly somewhat more important than co-worker support and slightly more important than support for innovation. It is much less important than top management support and moderately less important than supervisor support.
- Support for innovation is slightly more important than co-worker support, slightly less important than communication and organisational support, and somewhat less important than supervisor support and top management support.
- Co-worker support is slightly less important than support for innovation and somewhat less important than organisational support and communication. It is much less important than top management support and moderately less important than supervisor support.

Table 6.5 presents the order of importance for six indicators of the leadership and work environment factor. Top management support is assigned the highest rank in importance, followed by supervisor support at rank 2, organisational support at rank 3, communication at rank 4, support for innovation at rank 5, and co-worker support at rank 6.

Table 6.5 Importance rank leadership and work environment

Indicator	Importance rank
Top management support	1
Supervisor support	2
Organisation support	3
Communication	4
Support for innovation	5
Co-worker support	6

Importance Ranks for Organisational Encouragement

- Employee participation is somewhat more important than teamwork, moderately more important than training, and much more important than expertise.
- Teamwork is somewhat more important than training and moderately more important than expertise. However, it is slightly less important than employee participation. Training is slightly more important than expertise. However, it is somewhat less important than teamwork and moderately less important than employee participation. Expertise is slightly less important than training, moderately less important than teamwork, and much less important than employee participation.

Table 6.6 depicts the order of importance for four indicators on organisational encouragement based on previous interpretations. Employee participation is placed at rank 1, teamwork at rank 2, training at rank 3, and expertise at rank 4.

The research framework to assess the sustainability of an Idea Management system was created on the basis of data analysis as discussed. The Fig. 6.1 depicts the importance of the factors on the framework. The centre circle represents the five factors and the connected circles represent indicators within each factor. The factors and factor indicators are arranged according to their importance. The innermost layer represents the most important and the outermost layers represent the least important factors. Tables 6.7, 6.8, 6.9, 6.10, and 6.11 explain how each of these indicators is to be assessed.

The first factor on the assessment framework is leadership and work environment. It consists of indicators such as top management support, supervisor support, organisation support, communication, support for

Table 6.6 Factor importance organisational encouragement

Indicator	Importance rank
Employee participation	1
Team work	2
Training	3
Expertise	4

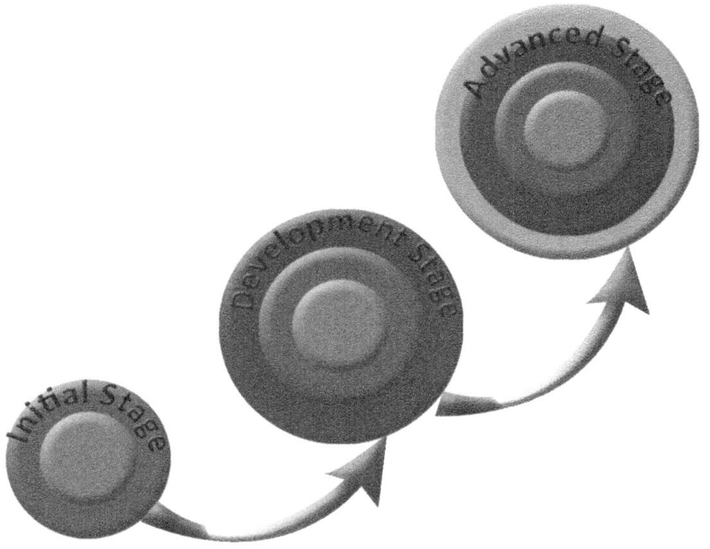

Fig. 6.1 Sustainability stages (Own)

innovation and co-worker support. The main questions to be addressed in assessing the leadership and work environment factor are given in Table 6.7.

Table 6.8 explains the questions needed to evaluate system capability.

Table 6.9 explains the questions needed to evaluate system effectiveness.

Table 6.10 explains the questions needed to evaluate organisational encouragement.

Table 6.11 explains the questions needed to evaluate system barriers.

Finally, the framework was refined in light of the three case studies conducted. Robson defines a case study as 'a strategy for doing research which involves an empirical investigation of a particular contemporary phenomenon within its real life context using multiple sources of evidence'. Yin (2004) proposes that case studies can be used for validation to check if certain theories are correct—the exact objective of the testing phase. According to Yin (2004), a case study design should be considered when (a) the focus of the study is to answer 'how' and 'why' questions;

Table 6.7 Assessing leadership and work environment

Indicators	Descriptions
Top management support What evidence is available to demonstrate top management support?	Top management support implies the commitment and the involvement of the top management in their Idea Management system. This is usually exhibited through their daily actions in a range of ways. These include formulating vision, mission for the Idea Management system. They also form strategies and procedures in support of the Idea Management system and engage in awarding the employees.
Supervisory support What evidence is available to demonstrate supervisor support to Idea Management system?	Supervisor support refers to the assistance of the supervisor or managers to promote the Idea Management system. Supervisors encourage and guide their subordinates to make suggestions.
Organisational support What evidence is available to demonstrate organisational support for the Idea Management system?	Organisational support refers to the facilitation of the organisation to promote the Idea Management system. The organisation facilitates its employees to take part in the Idea Management system by organising creativity-related workshops, establishing non-rigid structures, and creating a supportive organisation culture.
Communication Explain how communications and networking impacts the Idea Management system in your organisation.	Communication refers to the mechanism that the organisation has in place to support the Idea Management system. Organisations facilitate formal meetings amongst employees, create networking opportunities for such participation in conferences, and organise creativity-related activities. They may also establish an in-house newsletter and website to communicate and share information.
Support for innovation What mechanism exists in your organisation to protect your employees in case of disputes due to the Idea Management system?	Support for innovation implies how an organisation can protect it employees from disputes as a result of suggestions from co-workers. Organisations establish supportive HR polices and direct the suggestions to the supervisors for their initial evaluations. They empower supervisors to make decisions and also establish a central suggestion evaluation team.
Co-worker support How would you describe the work relationships amongst the employees in relation to the Idea Management system?	Co-worker support refers to the guidance from colleagues to make suggestions. Co-workers help nurture the initial idea or help in formulating a joint suggestion. They may collaborate together to find solutions to issues and even provide support to promote colleagues' recommendations.

Table 6.8 Assessing factor 2 system capability

Variable	Description
Suggestion implementation What evidence can be used to demonstrate the actualisation of the suggestion?	Suggestion implementation refers to the actual implementation of suggestions in the organisations. Organisations keep a record of the suggestions received from their employees and the number of suggestions implemented after evaluation. They also keep a record of revenues generated as a result of suggestion implementation. They create success stories of their Idea Management system and publish them for internal or external knowledge.
Empowerment How do you describe empowerment in relation to the Idea Management system in your organisation?	Empowerment refers to the extent to which employees are given an opportunity in decision-making and job autonomy. Organisations involve their employees in departmental meetings and provide them the opportunity to apply their creativity to their work-related problems.
Awareness How does your organisation create awareness of the Idea Management system?	Awareness refers to the publicity that an organisation makes to promote the Idea Management system. Organisations hold promotional campaigns and make use of their bulletin boards, websites, and newsletters. They hold induction programmes as well.
Feedback Explain the feedback process in your organisation.	Feedback refers to the facilitation of the timely response with regard to the suggestions of employees. Organisations usually have policies to process the suggestions within a stipulated date and provide feedback to the employer. The form of the feedback should be encouraging and if a suggestion is rejected, the reasons for rejection are explained.
Rewards Explain the reward scheme for the Idea Management system in your organisation.	Rewards refer to the recognition facilitation that exists in the organisation. Recognition may be handled through a well-defined reward scheme to include tangible or non-tangible benefits. The monetary benefits are established based on the value of the suggestion. Rewards are fair and rewarding procedures are transparent.
Evaluation Explain the evaluation procedure for the Idea Management system in your organisation.	Evaluation refers to the assessment of a suggestion. The organisation will have an evaluation team to assess suggestions from employees. It establishes an evaluation procedure and rules for the evaluation process. The process of evaluation is made transparent to all employees.
Resources Explain the resource availability of the Idea Management system in your organisation.	Resources refers to the allocation of budgets to implement suggestions. Organisations set aside financial budgets and establish procedures for its employees to revert if any physical resources are need to facilitate the suggestion-making or suggestion implementation.

Table 6.9 Assessing system effectiveness

Variable	Description
Profitability Does your system generate new revenue or save cost?	Profitability refers to the monetary benefits that the organisation gains as a result of the Idea Management system. Organisations report their profitability as a result of the Idea Management system annually
Employee productivity Describe how employee productivity is improved as a result of the Idea Management system.	Employee productivity refers to the improvement in employees' perceptions with regard to job satisfaction, sense of security, employee confidence, organisational commitment, and accountability. Organisations see improvements in these parameters as a result of their Idea Management system and compare the employee participation rates across the years.
Process improvements Does the Idea Management system trigger improvements in the processes? Give examples.	Process improvements refer to the revisions made to processes as a result of an Idea Management system. Organisations keep a record of these improvements as a result of the Idea Management system.
Customer satisfaction Does the Idea Management system impact customer satisfaction? Give examples.	Customer satisfaction refers to the improvement in customer satisfaction as a result of the Idea Management system. Organisations keep a record of improvements in customer satisfaction as a result of their Idea Management system and also state the objective of their Idea Management system for improving customer satisfaction.
Product quality Does the Idea Management system impact the quality of the product? Give evidence.	Product quality refers to the adjustment or revisions to services or products due to the Idea Management system. Organisations provide a record of such revisions and display their commitment to quality improvement.

Table 6.10 Assessment of organisational encouragement

Variable	Description
Teamwork Is there a provision to make suggestions in teams for which rewards are given for teams?	Teamwork implies the possibility for employees to collaborate and make joint submissions. Organisations encourage collaborations and provide facilities to make joint suggestions. Awards are given to the entire team. Employees can team up with colleagues from other departments as well.
Training What training do you provide to employees?	Training implies facilitation of training to employees with regard to the Idea Management system or to stimulate creativity. Organisations conduct training programmes to use their Idea Management system. They also organise events and workshops to stimulate creativity.
Expertise How do you describe employee expertise in your organisation?	Expertise refers to the extent to which employees' domain knowledge, skills, and experience impact their suggestions. It can be noted from an organisation's Idea Management system's record which category of employees generally makes suggestions.
Employee participation What evidence is available to demonstrate employee participation in the Idea Management system?	Employee participation refers to the scope of the system and actual participation in suggestion-making. Organisations make their Idea Management system open to all employees and keep a record of suggestions received annually.

Table 6.11 Assessing system barriers

Variable	Description
Job control Describe the job environment in your organisation?	Job control refers to tight schedules, rigid job roles, and work pressures. Organisations that don't give opportunities to think out of the box and exercise task routines hinder creativity.
Competition Do your employees consider the Idea Management system as a competition to test their ability in any way?	Competition refers to creating a sense of competing amongst employees to test their abilities. Organisations don't run the scheme as a competition but make participation optional and at employees' will.

(b) you cannot manipulate the behaviour of those involved in the study; (c) you want to cover contextual conditions because you believe they are relevant to the phenomenon under study; or (d) the boundaries are not clear between the phenomenon and the context. The purpose of using case studies for this research is to determine how the factors in an evaluative framework are to be used to assess the sustainability of Idea Management systems. It would not be possible to develop assessment criteria without having a true picture of how the necessary factors influence the sustainability of Idea Management systems without considering the context within which it occurs. Therefore, the case study method is applied here because it can be used to examine what might be the practices that influence the sustainability in Idea Management systems. The analysis of the case study was used to understand the sustainability stages and to identify a list of practices associated with each of the factor indicators on the initial, developmental, and advanced stages.

Case A

Organisation A is categorised as a large-scale organisation with about 3000 employees. The main function of this organisation is manufacturing aluminium, and its Idea Management system has been active since 1981.

The Idea Management system of this organisation has three main objectives:

- To encourage creative thinking and ideas
- To give personal rewards and recognition
- To encourage a culture of continuous improvement

The organisation demonstrates how its Idea Management system 'has achieved audited, cumulative savings amounting to $ 31.85 million from a total of 137,543 implemented and awarded suggestions. During 2011 alone, the company implemented more than 20,000 suggestions, resulting in audited savings worth almost $4.36 million and 100 per cent participation from eligible employees'.

Good evidence is available in Organisation A to demonstrate leadership and organisational encouragement. The top management of the organisation is proud that their system has become a benchmark for many other organisations in the United Arab Emirates (UAE) and they have affirmed a vision and mission for their system. The support of the management is visible as it recognises its employees and hosts conference such as Ideas Arabia. The supervisor is the heart of their system. It has an open communication format and networking opportunities to share and mingle with their colleagues as required and the organisation arranges creativity workshops to stimulate creativity amongst its employees. Moreover, the high-value suggestions are considered a result of cooperation and collaboration amongst colleagues.

Good evidence and support is also demonstrated for system capability. The organisation has a policy to consider a suggestion for awards only if it is implemented and Organisation A has a good record of suggestion implementations. The top management strongly believes in empowerment of their employees and states that it is empowerment that has resulted in the success of their system. The technical expertise and experience of their employees have resulted in making award-winning suggestions at the international level. The suggestion-tracking and feedback system of the organisation is so encouraging that there is no rejection of a suggestion as such but it is noted as 'not feasible to implement at this time' and stored on the database. The employees can monitor the progress of their suggestion online. The best part of their Idea Management system is their awareness campaigns, which also won a prize at international level in 2010. Their Idea Management system is simple to use, and since its inception it has gone through an evolution from a paper-based system to a highly sophisticated online system.

An important factor is the organisational encouragement, which is also well demonstrated within Organisation A. The organisation recognises the importance of team work and facilitates team suggestions. It may also be noted that high-value suggestions are mostly team-based suggestions. Organisation A also provides training to its employees in using the Idea Management system and organises creativity-related workshops; on average, each employee underwent 4.2 man-days of training in 2011 (9.13 man-days in the case of UAE nationals). All employees are eligible to participate in the Idea Management system and it was noted that for the sixth consecutive year it received 100% participation from its employees. The top management reiterated that the success of their Idea Management system is purely due to the involvement of its employees.

The outcomes of the Idea Management system are highly satisfactory in Organisation A. The organisation demonstrated how it has maintained customer satisfaction and competitive advantages over its competitors due to their Idea Management system. It is their employees' creativity that has resulted in enhancing the processes significantly and improving their product quality. Over the course of their tenure, A's production capacity has expanded from approximately 150,000 metric tonnes a year to more than 1 million tonnes a year.

Finally, the Idea Management system barriers, namely job control or environment of competition, are barely visible within the organisation. Employees are given job autonomy so that if an employee's suggestion does not carry a solution it will not be considered a valid suggestion. Moreover, the success of the Idea Management system is attributed to empowerment and no task reutilisation or standard practices are to be followed strictly. The free flow of communication and creativity-related workshops mainly demonstrate a supportive culture within the organisation rather than a controlling environment. Employees are expected to participate in the system at their will and participation is not mandatory.

Case B

Organisation B is categorised as a medium-scale organisation with about 1000 employees. The main function of this organisation is to facilitate the completion of all customs transactions for the people in Dubai. It is an entity of the UAE government and was established in 2001. The Idea Management system was initially introduced in this organisation in 2004.

The organisation demonstrates that its Idea Management system has achieved audited, cumulative savings amounting to $490 K since its inception in 2004.

Good evidence is available in Organisation B to demonstrate factor 1, namely leadership and organisational encouragement. The top management of the organisation is very supportive towards the scheme as they are directly involved in awarding and personally handing over the prizes to the employees. The next rung of the management also sets an example by making suggestions themselves. They further sponsor and organise events relating to creativity and innovation. The supervisor is also an important component of the Idea Management system. He plays a role in the success of the Idea Management system by creating an encouraging culture within the organisation. The organisation observes an open-door policy and nominates its employees to participate in local, regional, or international creativity-related events.

Good evidence and support is also demonstrated for system capability. Organisation B has a good record of suggestion implementations. It was noted that suggestions are mainly received from the medium-skilled and high-skilled employees and less from the low-skilled employees due to their domain knowledge and less technical expertise. The suggestion-tracking and feedback system of the organisation is also encouraging as it has a policy to revert to the suggestion within 15 days of its submission. The organisation has different awareness campaigns that include the use of monthly themes, bulletin boards, and banners.

The organisational encouragement factor is also well demonstrated within Organisation B. First, the organisation recognises the importance of teamwork and facilitates team suggestions. Organisation B also provides training to its employees in using the Idea Management system and organises creativity-related workshops. It was noted that about eight workshops were conducted in 2014. All employees are eligible to participate in the Idea Management system, and it was noted that participation increased from the 2004 to 2012.

The outcomes of the Idea Management system are satisfactory in Organisation B. Finally, the Idea Management system barrier, namely job control, is barely visible within the organisation. Employees are given job autonomy so that if an employee's suggestion does not carry a solution it will not be considered a valid suggestion. Moreover, the success of the Idea Management system is attributed to empowerment and no task reutilisation or standard practices are to be followed strictly. The free flow of communication and creativity-related workshops mainly demonstrate a supportive culture within the organisation rather than a controlling environment.

In conclusion, it can be said that, overall, Organisation B demonstrates good practices with respect to most of the sustainability indicators. There is good scope for improving employee involvement. It has well-set and high-value rewards to motivate employees towards the scheme. The expertise of employees is also lacking, and the culture of suggestion-making could be further improved.

Case C

Organisation C is categorised as a small-scale organisation with about 250 employees. The main function of this organisation is to provide services to residents with respect to constructions such as roads, buildings, and communications, electricity, water, and sewerage.

Good evidence is available in the organisation to demonstrate leadership and work environment. The top management of the organisation is very supportive towards the scheme as they have documented decisions supporting the Idea Management system. They sponsor and organise conferences relating to creativity and innovation. The supervisors play an important role in the Idea Management system by encouraging and guiding their subordinates to make suggestions to the Idea Management system.

The system capability factor is also well demonstrated in Organisation C. The suggestion-tracking and feedback system of the organisation is also encouraging as it has a policy to revert to the suggestion within 15 days of its submission. The organisation has different awareness programmes to publicise their scheme and they have a brand name for their Idea Management system.

Organisational encouragement is also fairly demonstrated within the Organisation C. The organisation recognises the importance of teamwork and facilitates team suggestions. It also provides training to its employees in using the Idea Management system and organises creativity-related workshops. The Idea Management system is open for all employees and customers to participate. However, the employee participation rate was not mentioned.

This organisation has many stated objectives. Accordingly, it demonstrates that the Idea Management system brings customer satisfaction and improves employee productivity. It was also stated that the Idea Management system contributes to saving cost and generates new revenue.

Finally, the Idea Management system barrier, namely job control, is barely visible within the organisation. Employees are given job autonomy. Moreover, the success of the Idea Management system is attributed to empowerment and no task reutilisation or standard practices are to be followed strictly. The free flow of communication and creativity-related workshops mainly demonstrate a supportive culture within the organisation rather than a controlling environment.

In conclusion, it can be said that, overall, Organisation C demonstrates good practices with respect to most of the sustainability indicators. It has well-set and high-value rewards to motivate employees towards the scheme.

The following are examples of good practices found by the research across the three organisations:

- Top management's direct involvement in programmes, such as best suggestions award, review of Idea Management system, performance report, involvement in making suggestions related to work and setting up a vision and mission for the Idea Management system, and an 'audit system' to monitor system activities.
- Making the supervisor responsible for reviewing employee ideas and providing subordinates with input and assistance in refining the ideas; recognising the supervisor for his/her contributions.
- Centrally storing the suggestions and fostering a supportive organisation culture and giving clear guidelines and awareness to formulate suggestions.
- Sharing information regarding the Idea Management system through an in-house monthly newsletter, encouraging staff to participate at national- and international-level conferences, and setting up an active website detailing the status of the Idea Management system.

- Provision to dissolve any disputes amongst employees and support to forward their suggestions fearlessly.
- Facilitating collaboration and options to upload colleagues' suggestions.
- Providing encouraging feedback and setting up realistic deadlines for processing the suggestions.
- Setting up financial and other rewards.
- A skilled evaluation team, evaluation criteria, and prompt evaluation of the suggestions.
- Establishing a brand name for Idea Management systems and conducting promotional campaigns.
- An efficient system to elicit ideas with user-friendly features.
- Availability of financial resources and procedures to seek resource support.
- Provision to submit ideas in teams and making the scheme open to all for participation.
- Flexibility in working environment, innovation-supportive practices, and job autonomy.
- Avoiding the feeling amongst employees that they are judged for their performance through competition.

The initial framework conceptualised earlier was applied to three cases identified as Organisation A, Organisation B, and Organisation C. All three organisations demonstrated the influence of factors and factor indicators in their Idea Management system. The analysis of the three cases shows that there is a variation in the way these indicators are fostered in each organisation. The practices associated with an indicator range from the lowest form to the highest level. These practices, as discussed earlier, can be improved or developed beyond the initial stage to the advanced stage. Thus, the sustainability of an Idea Management system in a particular organisation can be understood to be at its initial stage, a developmental stage, or an advanced stage.

The initial stage is conceptualised as the beginning stage where there are few or often an absence of practices relating to the factor indicators. It is also possible that some adverse practices are present, negating the impact of an indicator at this stage. The developmental stage could be conceptualised as exhibiting adequate evidence for each of the indicators. The good set of practices for each of the indicators implies an advanced status. At this stage, each of these indicators can demonstrate good evidence of the practices relating to each of the indicators.

The analysis of the three cases helped to conceptualise the sustainability status in three forms as depicted in Fig. 6.1.

The following section explains the associated practices with each of the stages, that is, the initial, developmental, and advanced stages.

An Idea Management system exhibits robust evidence for the top management's support in established organisations. The commitment and involvement are exhibited in a number of formats. Although at the initial stage this commitment and form of support are not very visible, they gradually develop. On the other hand, there might be some adverse actions that can hinder the success of an Idea Management system. For example, an Idea Management system is implemented in isolation and employees are not at all motivated to participate. The supervisor support is crucial for the success of an Idea Management system. The supervisor's guidance and encouragement are the basic requirements for the success of an Idea Management system. To develop this support, it is then necessary that organisations formalise this facilitation by making the supervisors responsible for the success of the suggestions system and this could be further moved to an advanced level by empowering and recognising them too on awarded suggestions. At the same time, supervisor support could be undermined if the organisation does not recognise the role of the supervisor in the success of the Idea Management system. At the initial stage, organisations provide guidance on the type of suggestions and how to make a suggestion. They develop centralised or decentralised systems to review the ideas. Organisations move beyond their initial stage to the developmental stage to create a supportive organisation culture. At an advanced level, they organise creativity simulation workshops and options to replicate the ideas across the organisations and develop central repositories. Organisations can hinder the creative ability of employees, and the success of an Idea Management system may be put in danger if the organisation's basic culture is not innovation-supportive. For example, the rigid rules and organisational structure fostering a pressurised work environment can have negative impacts. Organisations encourage open communication and provide opportunities to meet and share ideas through formal or informal meetings. This facilitation is further developed by strengthening the communications through usage of in-house newsletters or websites and avoiding the barriers for communication amongst the departments. Organisations further create opportunities for networking with external and internal parties to share ideas and stimulate creativity.

Employees need to be protected from co-workers' disruptive behaviours. Organisations provide support to resolve disputes arising as a result of suggestions. If employees are to sort the disputes on their own, it would have a negative impact on the Idea Management system.

Organisations demonstrate that the comfort and guidance of workers motivate employees to make suggestions. But, of course, such support is visible in organisations that demonstrate a long tenure of the Idea Management system, and where advanced facilities such as options to submit suggestions for colleagues are given. The practices that instil negative impact here occur when employees hinder success by simply not supporting their colleagues' initiative.

The success of an Idea Management system depends on evaluating and implementing valid suggestions. An organisation should demonstrate that it implements the suggestions. The implementation rate should gradually improve. Advanced organisations further ensure that they award only implemented suggestions. The performance status report is shared amongst all stakeholders. Organisations may sometimes invite ideas and not implement them at all. The managers take the ideas of their subordinates and act as if they are their own, giving employees a free ride. It is necessary that employees be given job autonomy to exhibit their creative ability. Organisations further demonstrate that they value their employees and encourage participation by giving an opportunity to take part in decision-making. Tight work routines and pressurised work environments greatly hinder creativity.

Feedback is one of the most important components of an Idea Management system. Organisations therefore set deadlines for processing the suggestions. It is not sufficient to only process the suggestions within the deadlines; feedback needs to be supportive and cooperative. Organisations therefore guarantee that the system is organised to ensure that encouraging feedback is given. On the other hand, organisations may provide discouraging feedback and demotivate employees. Rewards are key components of Idea Management systems. Organisations therefore set up financial benefits or some recognition mechanism. Organisations at a developmental stage ensure that there is a transparent process of rewards and recognition. At an established state, the rewards are also calculated in proportion to the value of the suggestions, as depicted later.

At an initial stage, it is necessary that an effective evaluation process is in place to assess the suggestions. Organisations depending only on teams or managers to validate the ideas may have adverse impact. Evaluation could be developed by making this process transparent to employees or by creating more awareness of the evaluation process, and upon completion of the evaluation process employees should be given a fair chance to appeal if needed. At an advanced stage, organisations even provide feedback on rejected suggestions as depicted in Table 6.12.

Organisations create awareness of their scheme using common communication mechanisms. At the developmental stage, the campaigns are more focused and use advanced mechanisms for promotions. Organisations have a system to receive employees' ideas and process them on time. This is improved by implementing electronic and user-friendly systems. Established organisations then install dedicated administrators and central systems and develop clear roles and responsibilities.

Organisations set side financial resources to support the Idea Management system. They build mechanisms to distribute resources support to stimulate employee creativity.

Customer satisfaction would be evidenced in the established schemes, and if there is no evidence of this benefit the scheme is at the initial stage. The improvement in product quality would be evidenced in the established schemes, and if there is no evidence of this benefit the scheme is at the initial stage.

The improvement in processes would be evidenced in the established schemes, and if there is no evidence of this benefit the scheme is at the initial stage. Moreover, the objectives of the scheme would be to elicit suggestions for improving the processes.

Established Idea Management systems exhibit good savings. If there is no evidence of this benefit the scheme is at the initial stage.

Table 6.12 Possible evidence for the guidelines to use the framework

Factors and factor indicators		Evidence available? Yes	No	Place where available
Sustainability stages	Factor 1—leadership and work environment			
	Top management support			
Initial	The involvement of top management in the Idea Management system is not very visible			
Developmental	Establish vision and mission for the system			
	Set up robust policies and procedures for the smooth functioning of the Idea Management system			
Advanced	Direct involvement of the top management in programmes for awarding the best suggestions			
	Participation of the top management in the events relating to the Idea Management system			
	Review the Idea Management system performance monthly			
	Host events and sponsoring events relating to creativity			
	Give strategic directives to improve the performance			
	Set up examples by involving themselves in making suggestions			
	Supervisor support			
Initial	Supervisors provide their guidance and encouragement to submit ideas but are not directly responsible or not made accountable			
Developmental	Supervisors are responsible for Idea Management systems by setting up targets			
	Supervisors encourage their team members to discuss any work-related issues prior to submitting a suggestion to the system			
Advanced	Supervisors provide guidance to subordinates, and are responsible for reviewing employee ideas and providing suggestions with input and assistance in refining the ideas. They are empowered and taken into confidence			
	Supervisors and their line managers are recognised on winning suggestions			
	Supervisors review monthly or quarterly reports of the Idea Management system performance			
	Organisational support			

Initial	Clear suggestion guidelines and awareness to formulate suggestions
Developmental	Supportive organisation culture
	Employees are given a suggestion target and are recognised on their performance review
	Hosts events to honour the winning suggestion
Advanced	Organising creativity simulation workshops
	Organisation supports if an implemented suggestion needs to be replicated in other departments
	Employees can also avail the support of the central Idea Management system team should they need any help
	Employee suggestions are centrally stored
	Communication
Initial	Little evidence of open communication within the organisation (e.g. formal or informal meetings)
	Minimum or no opportunity for networking internally and externally
Developmental	Good evidence of open communication within the organisation
Advanced	Constant flow of information through websites, newsletters, and so on
	There are opportunities for networking internally and externally
	Support for innovation
Initial	No evidence or support to control disruptive behaviour of co-workers
Developmental	*Provision to dissolve any disputes amongst employees*
Advanced	Provision and good support to dissolve any disputes amongst employees
	Co-worker support
Initial	Employee collaboration and support for each other is not very visible
Developmental	Employees usually collaborate to make suggestions
Advanced	Employees collaborate and submit suggestions for their colleagues

(*continued*)

Table 6.12 (continued)

Factors and factor indicators		Evidence available? Yes	No	Place where available
	Factor 2—system capability			
	Rewards			
Initial	Financial rewards are set up			
	Other rewards such as certificate of appreciation/ nominating distinguished suggestion owners for taking part in local, regional, and international suggestion contests			
Developmental	Financial and other types of rewards are set up and the reward scheme is transparent			
Advanced	Rewards are fairly calculated as per their savings			
	Established special annual award categories			
	Support for suggestion implementation			
Initial	Organisations usually implement suggestions			
Developmental	There is improvement in the rate of suggestion implementation			
	Provision to replicate an implemented solution elsewhere in the organisation			
Advanced	Awarding only implemented suggestions			
	Monitoring the system performance with regard to suggestion implementation			
	Employees are empowered to test their creativity			
	Feedback			
Initial	Set up reminders to evaluators and implementers on pending suggestions			
	Set up realistic deadlines for processing the suggestions			
Developmental	Provide encouraging feedback			
Advanced	Provision to submit the suggestion to central administrator if needed			
	Evaluation			

Initial	Dedicated schedule to evaluate the suggestions
	Dedicated evaluation team
	Evaluation criteria
Developmental	Making the evaluation procedures and team members transparent
Advanced	A chance to appeal the decision at least once
	Providing reasons for rejected suggestion
	System features
Initial	Multiple mechanisms to submit suggestions
Developmental	A user-friendly electronic system to receive and timely process the suggestion
Advanced	A user-friendly electronic system and dedicated Idea Management system administrator
	Established roles and responsibilities for all stakeholders with regard to the Idea Management system
	Awareness
Initial	There are some promotional campaigns and notification about the scheme
Developmental	There are frequent promotional campaigns
Advanced	There are regular promotional campaigns and the scheme has a brand name
	Resources
Initial	Availability of financial resources is limited
Developmental	Adequate availability of financial resources and procedure to avail physical resources
Advanced	Additional management support to source resources as required
	Factor 3—system effectiveness
	Profitability
Initial	There is no evidence of new revenue generation or cost savings
Developmental	There is adequate evidence of new revenue generation or cost savings

(*continued*)

Table 6.12 (continued)

Factors and factor indicators		Evidence available? Yes	Evidence available? No	Place where available
Advanced	There is good evidence of new revenue generation or cost savings			
	Employee productivity			
Initial	There is little improvement in employees' sense of accountability and commitment to the organisation			
	There is little improvement in employees' job satisfaction			
	There is little improvement in employees' confidence in the organisation			
Developmental	There is adequate improvement in employees' sense of accountability and commitment to the organisation			
	There is adequate improvement in employees' job satisfaction			
	There is adequate improvement in employees' confidence in the organisation			
Advanced	There is general improvement in suggestion numbers from the past years			
	There is good improvement in employees' job satisfaction, sense of security, confidence in, and commitment to the organisation			
	Suggestions aimed at morale improvements have a reward scheme			
	Process improvements			
Initial	Very few process improvements take place as a result of suggestions			
Developmental	There is adequate evidence of process improvements taking place as a result of suggestions			
Advanced	There is good evidence of process improvements taking place as a result of the Idea Management system			
	Customer satisfaction			
Initial	No evidence of improvement in customer satisfaction			
Developmental	Adequate evidence of improvement in customer satisfaction			
Advanced	Good evidence of improvement in customer satisfaction			
	Product quality			

Initial	There is no evidence of product quality improvement as a result of the Idea Management system
Developmental	There is adequate evidence of product quality as a result of the Idea Management system
Advanced	There is good evidence of product quality improvement as a result of the Idea Management system
	Factor 4—organisational encouragement
	Employee participation
Initial	Employee participation is limited to a few employees
	Number of suggestions received is not known or made public
Developmental	Making the scheme open for all to participate
	Evidence available to demonstrate the actual participation (number of suggestions)
Advanced	Organisations or employees win awards for their suggestions
	Setting participation targets (minimum number of suggestions per year)
	Encourages suggestions for any area and not necessarily for cost savings
	No strict boundary between job role and creativity
	Team work
Initial	No mention of team suggestions
Developmental	Team suggestions are encouraged
	Team rewards are established
Advanced	Teams make high-value suggestions
	Training
Initial	No formal training is offered
Developmental	Training programmes are offered in using the Idea Management system
Advanced	Creativity-related workshops and training
	Expertise
Initial	Organisation has a few talented employees

(continued)

Table 6.12 (continued)

Factors and factor indicators		Evidence available?		Place where available
		Yes	No	
Developmental	Organisation has talented and experienced employees who make more suggestions when compared to others			
Advanced	High-value suggestions are elicited from experienced employees			
	Suggestions get awarded in local or international competitions			
	Factor 5—system barriers			
	Job control			
Initial	Little flexibility in working environment			
	Usually standard work routines and work under pressure mostly			
Developmental	Moderate flexibility in working environment			
	Usually no standard work routines and work under pressure			
Advanced	Good flexibility in working environment			
	No standard work routines or work pressures			
	Competition			
Initial	Employees feel pressured to make suggestions as they believe that they are judged for their performance through the Idea Management system			
Developmental	Employees are somewhat informed that participation is not mandatory but are tied indirectly for its success through different target setting			
Advanced	Employees are well informed that they can participate in the Idea Management system of their own free will and they are not judged for their performance and therefore not tied to any targets			

In an established scheme, suggestions aimed at employee morale and resulting in employee productivity would reward the employee with an appropriate reward scheme. Employees would feel safe and satisfied with their jobs. Their confidence in the organisation would improve. Thus, they would make more suggestions.

For the success of Idea Management systems, it is necessary that there are no barriers to creativity, and as such employees should be free to carry out their tasks and not work under pressure at all times. The more support there is from organisations on these parameters, the better the result of the Idea Management system.

Employees' domain knowledge and experience is also instrumental in the success of the Idea Management system. Organisations demonstrate that due to their talented employees, their systems are successful. They also note that, over periods, it is skilled employees who make more suggestions and established schemes that attract rewards at local or international level.

Organisations support their employees through training related to Idea Management system usage, but established organisations further provide creativity-stimulating training, whereas such training is not very common at the initial stage.

Established schemes ensure that they receive suggestions relating to any improvement and not necessarily relating to saving costs. Established schemes also demonstrate that they participate in local and international competitions and, moreover, they do not draw a strict line between the job description and creativity. At a developmental level, schemes would be made open to all and the status of employee participation is made public. Organisations also limit participation for certain employees, and this might result in low sustainability of the Idea Management system. The variations in employee participation are presented in Table 6.12.

Competition is a major barrier for the success of an Idea Management system. The existence of such a practice lowers the sustainability of an Idea Management system. Established organisations therefore ensure that employees participate of their own free will and make it clear to the employees that they are not judged for their performance. This may not be well stated at the initial stages.

The results also showed that these practices varied across the organisations, demonstrating the transition from an initial stage to an advanced stage. The analysis of the three cases also yields that sustainability is not just a binary stage of 'sustaining' or 'not sustaining'. The sustainability factors and indictors demonstrate varied influence on the Idea Management system. These influences vary from initial stage to advanced stage. Therefore, sustainability is conceptualised as changing status from the initial stage to the advanced stage. The initial stage means that there is no or very little evidence to demonstrate the existence of practices associated with that indicator. At this stage, it is also possible that each indicator exhibits adverse practices. The developmental stage demonstrates that there is adequate evidence of the existence of supporting practices; however, these could be further developed for improvements. The advanced stage implies that there are various good practices in the organisation to demonstrate the influence of the indicators on the Idea Management system. The case analysis thus helped to develop the practices associated with each of these indicators and to map these practices to each of the sustainability stages. The results of this analysis thus helped to refine the initial framework and propose a final assessment framework as shown in Table 6.12. The outcome of this research is to propose a framework to assess the sustainability of an Idea Management system. The results of qualitative and quantitative analyses discussed earlier facilitated the creation and refinement of the assessment framework. The resulting proposed framework is depicted in Table 6.12.

This framework is to be applied to determine the sustainability of the Idea Management system.

So the sustainability of the Idea Management system is not just a binary state of 'sustaining' or 'not sustaining'. The sustainability factors and indictors demonstrate varied influence on an Idea Management system. These influences vary from initial stage to advanced stage. Therefore, sustainability is conceptualised as changing status from an initial stage to the advanced stage. The initial stage means that there is no or very little evidence for demonstration of the existence of practices associated with that indicator. At this stage, it is also possible that each indicator exhibits adverse practices. The developmental stage demonstrates that there is adequate evidence of the existence of supporting practices; however, these could be further developed for improvement. The advanced stage implies that there are various good practices in the organisation to demonstrate the influence of the indicators on the Idea Management system. Organisations can assess the sustainability of their Idea Management system by applying this assessment framework and determining the sustainability status. Sustainability of an Idea Management system can be understood as a model comprising three stages:

The initial stage
The developmental stage
The advanced stage

So there are many key practices associated with each of the stages. Sustainability of the Idea Management system should be understood from the perspective of its key success factors. The sustainability indicators have varied influence on the success of the system. Sustainability can be understood as a three-stage model from initial to the advanced stage. There are various good and bad practices associated with each of these indicators.

The following are key practices that are associated with the initial stage:

- There is little visibility of the top management's involvement in Idea Management system activities.
- Supervisors provide guidance and encouragement to submit ideas but are not directly responsible or not made accountable for the success of the Idea Management system.
- Clear suggestion guidelines and awareness to formulate suggestions is available.
- There is little evidence of open communication within the organisation (e.g. formal or informal meetings) and minimum opportunity for networking internally and externally
- There is no evidence or support to control the disruptive behaviour of co-workers.
- Employee collaboration and support for each other is not very visible.
- There are limited types of financial rewards and they are not linked to the value of the suggestions.

- There is feedback to the employees on their suggestions.
- There is a dedicated schedule to evaluate the suggestions, dedicated evaluation team, and evaluation criteria.
- There is a system to elicit the employees' creative ideas.
- The cost savings or new revenues are minimal.
- There is little improvement in employees' sense of accountability and commitment to their organisation, employees' job satisfaction, or employees' confidence in the organisation.
- There is no evidence of customer satisfaction or product quality improvement as a result of the Idea Management system.
- Employee participation is limited to a few employees.
- The organisation has limited talented employees.
- Employees usually have standard work routines and work under pressure, mostly.
- Employees feel pressured to make suggestions as they believe that they are judged for their performance through the Idea Management system.

The following are key practices for the developmental stage:

- Top management establishes a vision, mission, and robust policies and procedures for the smooth functioning of the Idea Management system.
- Supervisors are made responsible for the Idea Management system by setting up targets.
- There is good evidence of open communication within the organisation.
- There is a provision to dissolve any disputes amongst employees and employees collaborate to make suggestions.
- The reward scheme is transparent and there is usually an improvement in the rate of suggestion implementations.
- It has a provision to replicate an implemented solution elsewhere in the organisation and the organisation often creates success stories.
- Provides encouraging feedback to the employees on their suggestions.
- The evaluation procedures and names of the evaluation team are transparent.
- There is a user-friendly electronic system to receive and timely process the suggestion.

- Adequate resources are available and there is a procedure to avail physical resources as required to support creativity.
- A moderate amount of new revenue generation or cost savings is evidenced.
- Adequate evidence of improvement in employees' sense of accountability and commitment to their organisation, job satisfaction, and employees' confidence in the organisation.
- There is adequate evidence of process improvements taking place and of customer satisfaction as a result of suggestions.
- Team suggestions are encouraged and creativity-related training is provided.
- There is moderate flexibility in the working environment, there are usually no standard work routines, and employees don't work under pressure.
- Employees are informed that participation is not mandatory but they are tied indirectly to its success through different target setting measures.

The following are key practices for the advanced stage:

- Top management is directly involved in suggestion-making and Idea Management system-related activities.
- Supervisors guide their subordinates and are empowered to make decisions.
- Creativity simulation workshops are often facilitated.
- There is a constant flow of information through websites, newsletters, and so on, and employees can submit suggestions for their colleagues.
- Rewards are fairly calculated as per their savings and have numerous special annual award categories.
- There is a provision to submit the suggestion to the central administrator if needed and a chance to appeal the decision at least once.
- Reasons should be provided for rejected suggestions and dedicated Idea Management system administrator to monitor the system is available; the roles and responsibilities for all the stakeholders are well stated.
- There is good evidence of new revenue generation or cost savings.

- Suggestion are encouraged for any area and not necessarily for cost savings; no strict boundary between job role and creativity.
- Suggestions get awarded in local or international competitions.
- There are no standard work routines or work pressures.
- Employees are well informed that they can participate in the Idea Management system of their own free will and they are not judged for their performance and therefore are not tied to any targets.

The following are bad practices that can hinder the success of the Idea Management system:

- Implementing an Idea Management system in isolation without the support of the middle management
- Absences of participative management style and organisations structures are not very flexible
- Paying little attention to suggestion implementation
- Suggestions are sought but no rewards are given for employees contribution
- Restricting the participation to certain categories of employees only
- Making employees responsible for the effectiveness of the idea

The sustainability of Idea Management systems can be improved from initial to developmental or advanced stages by raising the practices for indicators that are at the lowest level. An improvement roadmap can guide the progress.

The framework is useful for Idea Management systems that have goals or objectives such as profitability, customer satisfaction, workplace process improvement, improvement in product quality, and improvement in employee productivity.

The following guidelines are to be used to assess and interpret the sustainability of an Idea Management system:

- The assessor should identify the key informants, preferably the Idea Management system administrator, who can provide evidence and explain their Idea Management system. It must be ensured that the informant has a good understanding of their Idea Management system and is able to provide the evidence of practices as required.

- The assessment framework shown in the appendix is to be applied. Table A shows a corresponding assessment question for each of the indicators and Table B shows possible practices for an indicator.
- Upon completion of Table B, the assessor should identify the indicators that have been marked with 'Yes'. These are to be examined to appreciate the evidence.
- The indicators that exhibit the 'initial status' and that are marked with 'no evidence' are to be identified for improvement. The improvement roadmap should be developed by choosing possible solutions shown under developmental stages.
- The previous exercise is to be repeated to note the 'developmental status' and the mark of 'no evidence'.
- An improvement roadmap is to be developed by proposing the possible solutions shown under established stages.
- A graphical presentation to indicate the overall status of factor indicators is to be produced for a quick glance at the sustainability status.

Conclusion

Teamwork is an important element for quality to flourish in organisations. The key task of conducting an assessment on quality involves building a team to carry out the project or exercise within the organisation by gathering the required evidence for a chosen model. The assessment of the drivers of the excellence model then requires a team to build consensus and agree on future action points. Human capital is truly essential to these important tasks and it is interlinked with various other drivers of excellence. Hence, teamwork should not only be encouraged but systematic approaches for forming and grooming teams for excellence are of great importance in achieving human excellence in various quality-related activities.

Finally, teamwork is crucial when it comes to the actual implementation of quality programmes in organisations. Teams need to be fostered in order to carry out an effective quality self-assessment in organisations. Hence, teamwork should not only be encouraged but systematic approaches for forming and grooming teams for excellence are of great importance for achieving human excellence in various quality-related activities—and such signals should be clearly sent out by management in organisations that strive to achieve overall BE.

The research on the sustainability of idea systems extends the knowledge on sustaining creativity and innovation programmes, particularly the Idea Management systems. The key findings of this research suggest five factors for assessing the sustainability of an Idea Management system. These include leadership and work environment, system capability, system effectiveness, organisational encouragement, and system barriers. Sustainability of an Idea Management system can be understood as a three-stage model comprising the initial stage, the developmental stage, and the advanced stage. The evaluative framework could provide a basis for further research in this field and generate new knowledge in terms of assessing the sustainability of Idea Management systems. The research presented here considers critical success factors and barriers which have emerged in previous studies to develop the assessment framework. This research thus provides a base for future studies in the sustainability field of creativity and innovation which is crucial in harnessing the human capital of an organisation.

References

Blackburn, R., & Rosen, B. (1993). Total quality and human resources management: Lessons learned from Baldrige award-winning companies. *The Academy of Management Executive, 7*(3), 49–66.

Bou-Llusar, J. C., Escrig-Tena, A. B., Roca-Puig, V., & Beltrán-Martín, I. (2005). To what extent do enablers explain results in the EFQM excellence model? An empirical study. *International Journal of Quality and Reliability Management, 22*(4), 337–353.

Buech, V. I. D., Michel, A., & Sonntag, K. (2010). Suggestion systems in organizations: What motivates employees to submit suggestions? *European Journal of Innovation Management, 13*(4), 507–525.

Calvo-Mora, A., Leal, A., & Roldán, J. L. (2005). Relationships between the EFQM model criteria: A study in Spanish universities. *Total Quality Management & Business Excellence, 16*(6), 741–770.

Dijkstra, L. (1997). An empirical interpretation of the EFQM framework. *European Journal of Work and Organizational Psychology, 6*(3), 321–341.

Du Plessis, A. J., Marx, A. E., & Wilson, G. (2008). Generating ideas and managing suggestion systems in organisations: Some empirical evidence. *International Journal of Knowledge, Culture and Change Management, 8*(4), 133–140.

Eskildsen, J. K. (1998). Identifying the vital few using the European Foundation for Quality Management Model. *Total Quality Management, 9*(4–5), 92–94.

Eskildsen, J. K., & Dahlgaard, J. J. (2000). A causal model for employee satisfaction. *Total Quality Management, 11*(8), 1081–1094.

Field, A. (2005). *Discovering statistics using SPSS* (2nd ed.). London: Sage.

Lawler, E. E. (1994). Total quality management and employee involvement: Are they compatible? *The Academy of Management Executive, 8*(1), 68–76.

Pfeffer, J. (1994). Competitive advantage through people. *California Management Review, 36*(2), 9–28.

Prabhu, V., Appleby, A., Yarrow, D., & Mitchell, E. (2000). The impact of ISO 9000 and TQM on best practice/performance. *The TQM Magazine, 12*(2), 84–92.

Ritchie, L., & Dale, B. G. (2000). Self-assessment using the business excellence model: A study of practice and process. *International Journal of Production Economics, 66*(3), 241–254.

Saaty, T. L. (2008). Decision making with the analytic hierarchy process. *International Journal of Services Sciences, 1*(1), 83–98.

Safari, H., Abdollahi, B., & Ghasemi, R. (2012). Canonical correlation analysis between people criterion and people results criterion in EFQM model. *Total Quality Management and Business Excellence, 23*(5–6), 541–555.

Scholl, A., Manthey, L., Helm, R., & Steiner, M. (2005). Solving multiattribute design problems with analytic hierarchy process and conjoint analysis: An empirical comparison. *European Journal of Operational Research, 164*(3), 760–777.

Shergold, K., & Reed, D. M. (1996). Striving for excellence: How self-assessment using the business excellence model can result in step improvements in all areas of business activities. *The TQM Magazine, 8*(6), 48–52.

Soltani, E. (2003). Towards a TQM-driven HR performance evaluation: An empirical study. *Employee Relations, 25*(4), 347–370.

Soltani, E., Gennard, J., Van der Meer, R. B., & Williams, T. (2004). HR performance evaluation in the context of TQM: A review of the literature. *International Journal of Quality & Reliability Management, 21*(4), 377–396.

Tarí, J. J. (2010). Self-assessment processes: The importance of follow-up for success. *Quality Assurance in Education, 18*(1), 19–33.

Van Dijk, C., & Van Den Ende, J. (2002). Suggestion systems: Transferring employee creativity into practicable ideas. *R&D Management, 32*(5), 387–395.

van Donk, D. P., & Sanders, G. (1993). Organizational culture as a missing link in quality management. *International Journal of Quality & Reliability Management, 10*(5), 5–15.

Wilkinson, A., Godfrey, G., & Marchington, M. (1997). Bouquets, brickbats and blinkers: Total quality management and employee involvement in practice. *Organization Studies, 18*(5), 799–819.

Yang, J. B., Dale, B. G., & Siow, C. H. R. (2001). Self-assessment of excellence: An application of the evidential reasoning approach. *International Journal of Production Research, 39*(16), 3789–3812.

Yin, R. R. (2004). *Case study research: Design and methods* (3rd ed.). London: Sage Publications.

Zaremba, D., & Crew, T. (1995). Increasing involvement in self-assessment: The royal mail approach. *The TQM Magazine, 7*(2), 29–32.

7

Cases of Business Excellence: Emphasis on Human Capital

Introduction

This chapter introduces four cases of excellence where the emphasis is on the role and importance of human capital. These four organisations represent the retail, construction, and service sectors. The main aim of this chapter is to highlight the importance and relevance of human capital and people management in high-performing organisations. The chapter illustrates the various strategies that have helped these organisations in achieving high employee engagement. The best practices of these organisations mainly stem from excellence models and total quality management (TQM) foundations.

The first case is Apparel Group. Apparel embarked on its journey of excellence from its early days, and its growth from 1 to 1700+ stores with an average annual sales growth of 18% and gross profit of 55% is testimony to its adoption of the best practices of world-class companies, the brand principles, and local business groups of the United Arab Emirates (UAE) and Gulf Cooperation Council (GCC) region. The case illustrates various best practices of people management. It highlights the importance and role of leadership in achieving excellence in addition to emphasising 'knowing your customers' and striving to be a responsible organisation

F. Lasrado, V. Pereira, *Achieving Sustainable Business Excellence*,
https://doi.org/10.1007/978-3-319-73314-2_7

through various corporate social responsibility (CSR) initiatives that are necessary to achieve a level of excellence. 'People' are an important asset to this organisation whose slogan is 'Where dreams come alive'.

The second case is Abela & Co, a leading food services management company based in the UAE. Founded in 1967, Abela & Co was a pioneer of the catering industry in the region. Headquartered in Dubai, it serves over 120 local and international clients, across an array of industries including but not limited to hospitality, education, construction, health care, pharmaceutical, power, manufacturing, shipbuilding, petroleum, aviation, information technology (IT), oil & gas. The case is developed based on inputs received from Nancy Nouaimeh, vice president for Quality, Safety, and Performance Excellence, and demonstrates the best practices of workforce and people management at Abela. Strategies such as voice of customer/employees, employee engagement, empowerment, and development of excellence culture through learning and development are themes demonstrated in the case, which is thus useful for understanding the quality strategies, tools, and techniques used to successfully implement and maintain quality standards and accreditations.

The third case study is Khansaheb, LLC. Khansaheb Civil Engineering L.L.C. has been operating in the UAE for more than 80 years, during which time it has completed numerous building and civil engineering projects. Khansaheb, founded in 1935 by Khansaheb Hussain bin Hassan Amad, was the first contractor in the then called Trucial States and undertook projects of great importance to the overall development of the region in difficult conditions. Two of its most significant contracts were the construction of the first motor track between Ras Al Khaimah and Sharjah in 1935 and the first causeway between Mugtta and Abu Dhabi in 1952. Ravi Prakash, the Group QA Manager, successfully implemented the ISO 9001 standard across the company and attributes the company's success to its people.

The fourth case is Oasis Investments, the holding company of the Al Shirawi Group of Companies, founded in 1971. With a conglomerate of 34 companies, their operations span the GCC. In this Group, the General Manager for Quality and Business Excellence explains the best practices of quality management that have led to successful quality management systems across its companies.

The fifth case is on Jumeirah Emirates Towers. Opened in 2000, Jumeirah Emirates Towers is one of the most stunning architectural highlights on the Dubai skyline and a significant landmark of the UAE. One of the first skyscrapers to rise on Sheikh Zayed Road, Jumeirah Emirates Towers translates Dubai's ambition, pride, and modernity.

This chapter helps in understanding the various triggers that pull the performance excellence of organisations, particularly keeping in mind the most important asset of the organisations—their human capital.

CASE A

'Where Dreams Come Alive': Apparel Groups *Excellence*

Introduction

Apparel Group (AG) is a global fashion and lifestyle retail conglomerate with leading international brands and a diversified business portfolio of footwear, apparel, accessories, cosmetics, fragrances, watches, health care, and food and beverages.

Founded in 1999, over the last 18 years AG has expanded its brand portfolio to 75 brands with over 1700 retail stores across 17 countries and has a diverse workforce of over 13,000 employees consisting of 93 nationalities. Popular brands in the Apparel portfolio include Nine West, Tommy Hilfiger, Kenneth Cole, Aldo, Dune, Charles & Keith, Tim Hortons, and Cold Stone. AG also has its own concept stores in the kids, apparel, and footwear categories and is expanding their portfolio through the acquisition of luxury and bridge fashion brands. AG's strategy is to make conveniently available an array of brands and innovative customer experiences to aspirational and lifestyle consumers by leveraging brand-building expertise, real estate relationships, and an omni-channel distribution approach. They intend to achieve this by delivering 100% customer satisfaction to two million customers and enhancing their lifestyles. AG has recently acquired brands like Juicy Couture, Levis, Crocs, and plans to scale them up within the GCC over the next four years. This growth proves that AG has been succeeding and has achieved their mission despite fierce competition from other fashion and F&B retailers in the UAE such as Alshaya Retail, Al Tayer Retail, Jashanmal Group, Al Futtaim Group, Costa Coffee, McDonalds, and Starbucks.

AG says its success is due to its management capabilities, culture, and people's unparalleled execution. They select, train, and follow young talent's careers from the store-level onwards.

AG leaders are motivated by an aggressive variable compensation system that stimulates high performance, accountability, and entrepreneurship. Everyone at AG is focused on reaching both their short- and long-term sustainable goals. Strict financial discipline is intrinsic to their culture. They react swiftly to the external market environment and, utilising 'SPEED' as their quality policy, changes by management are quick, deft, and successful. They have had failures, but have learnt from their mistakes and ensure that they are not repeated. 'We are a young company, with an average age of 30. Nonetheless Apparel also has very capable leadership and management teams' says Chief Human Capital Officer (CHO) at AG. The CHO confirms that leaders take an active part in recruiting the best talent, carefully selecting the company's next generation of leaders. These basic principles are supported by employees, by proprietary processes, and by the unique way they make things happen.

> AG's Vision is 'to be the No. 1 Retailer Globally'. In line with this vision, AG aspires to be the 'Best Place to Work For' for its employees. AG has built an entrepreneurship driven environment which allows innovation, collaboration and partnership, empowerment, and respect where people openly discuss issues to achieve a level of excellence that is a benchmark for best practice locally and internationally. This was achieved with the understanding and confidence that expectations of both leadership team and employees were clear and transparent within the company.

AG has expanded their footprint to Egypt, Pakistan, Jordan, and South Africa and is looking for more regions to grow their business. The strategy is to scale up the business of each brand, while keeping an eye out for opportunistic acquisitions that have the capability of scaling up. The mission of AG is to operate 2000 profitable stores by 2020.

Leadership, at its core, is about making other people better because of your presence and making sure **that impact lasts in your absence**. The AG leaders create the conditions for their team members to perform and do what it takes to sustain those conditions, even when they are not present. Designing good systems is part of this 'absentee leadership' but the most powerful tool we have, by far, is culture. Culture not only guides individual decision-making, but also provides the foundation for all other organisational behaviour and action. In other words, culture doesn't tell you what to do—it shows you how to think and implement. It is all about ownership mindset. AG's core values are integrity, working together, passion for excellence, respect, and recognition. These values are not a matter of training, but deal breakers.

The AG leadership team expects its employees to have a 'can do' attitude as part of their culture to make it a high-performing company. The leaders want their employees to take ownership of their job roles and responsibilities and encourage teamwork in their projects and assignments. To achieve this, employees must be engaged. Their aspirations should be nurtured and fulfilled.

AG's vision, mission, and values are developed by the senior managers and reviewed annually by the leaders and managers. These are displayed on the premises of the company, and at all stores. They are also set as the standard wallpaper of all desktops and laptops of employees. The vision, mission, values, and daily purpose form a part of the induction programme for new employees. These are also printed in the induction material and given to all new employees for quick reference. The chairman and the leaders personally communicate AG's achievements, objectives, and future goals to all employees during trainings, events, and meetings. They also visit the stores on a weekly basis to connect with the mall, area, and store managers to solicit feedback on product sales and customer preferences. This direct interaction with the leaders inspires the sales employees and they feel respected, important, and valued. Sales employees are encouraged to come up with innovative ideas to improve the business and enhance sales and are rewarded appropriately. Employee satisfaction surveys include questions related to vision, mission, and values and have received high scores.

They continuously seek to bring diversity into their workforce by hiring different nationalities to serve the multicultural customers in the UAE. To be able to do this, candidates are recruited locally and overseas through various recruitment sources. They have changed their recruitment styles and have adopted social media to recruit the new generation of employees—millennials as full-time and part-time employees within AG.

Their commitment to recruiting, training, and retaining the best people is the key element of their strategic initiatives. AG employees are their greatest competitive advantage and the company knows how to leverage them. AG recruits people who have talent, skills, and a desire to grow, and actively encourages their development. To make this possible the following actions are adopted:

- They foster an environment where great people feel great. Their new office premises has breakout areas and open floor plans—no doors, standing meeting rooms; Amphitheatre and Tim Hortons canteen are some examples. They also have flexible HR policies, CSR activities, employee engagement activities, meritocracy, informality, and candour.
- Great people get great compensation; performance is rewarded. The best people move up from base quickly, being constantly rewarded for their top-notch performance. Many sales employees earn 12–15 times their gross salaries every month in performance bonuses. Non-performers are either coached to improve or are let go to look out for opportunities externally.
- Career development pathway. In the meritocracy system that exists at AG, focused, skilled, and talented employees are promoted on the basis of their achievements, so that they can assume higher roles in the organisation in future. Approximately 25–30% of AG's workforce is promoted in any one year. The backbone of the meritocracy is a variable compensation plan backed by individualised goals and performance reviews. Variable compensation at AG comes in two forms: money and promotions coupled with added responsibility and accountability.

In 2016, AG partnered with Tech Mahindra and Oracle to get on board Oracle Fusion Retail, Oracle Human Capital Management, and Oracle Finance—a cloud-based system that integrates all the functions of

AG business in one system. This enables speed, transparency, and real-time data to be available to the stakeholders at any time, in any place.

Approachability with open office setup: AG has recently changed their open-door policy to a no-door policy wherein employees can meet their manager or any senior officer to discuss their issues or concerns at any given time with no hindrances at all. Other employee feedback routes include a monthly employees satisfaction survey (ESS), quarterly human capital forums with the vice chairperson, regular meetings, feedback on emails and/or intranet, feedback on training programmes, performance appraisals, exit interviews, and informal discussions based on employees' needs and requests for meetings with his manager or supervisor or human capital department personnel.

As part of the fashion retail industry, the AG management decided to implement a 'smart casual' dress code in the office, even sanctioning denim jeans on Thursdays. This allows employees the flexibility to express their personal taste in fashion by still looking neat and professional but not as formal as the business attire.

AG has a horizontal organisational structure, wherein each department consists of several functional areas overseen by a head of department (HOD) or general manager who reports to top management. It has an employee-centred approach, which emphasises teamwork and collaboration amongst employees. The absence of multiple structural layers provides streamlined communication and reporting processes, making the company more nimble and adaptable to change. This also allows employees to attain greater satisfaction due to freedom and autonomy, which encourages innovation and bright ideas, keeping AG ahead of the competition.

Growth (up or out). Salary is often not the driver for retention; there are various other reasons why employees leave the organisation. AG management believes in a high performance culture and provides growth opportunities cognizant of the value an employee brings; they work to retain valuable employees, but wish them well if they decide to further their careers outside the company. New employees are welcomed and integrated into the company's culture through a five-day induction, which covers an introduction both to the company and the country, as well as more mundane matters such as the employment contract, bank account enrolment, employee information sheet, ID card, SIM card, and cash advances. Employee engagement activities like role-playing and games take place to create bonds both between the new employees as individuals and between them and the company.

On the last day of induction, new retail store employees are taken for a tour of different brand stores in the prominent shopping malls to introduce them to the UAE's retail environment. On the same day, to ensure that the employees are completely acquainted with the store and products of their assigned brand, they also receive a post-induction booklet covering what is expected of them over their first four weeks. The respective store manager and area sales manager train the new employees on the job and work with them on their weekly and monthly plan so they will be ready for the post-induction follow-up test. A 'buddy' is nominated to each new employee to help them settle in the country, city (where applicable), and new role within AG. The new associate is also scheduled on the same shift as the buddy. At the end of the fourth week, a follow-up test is administered to the new employee. The objective of this test is to ensure that the employees continue to learn on the shop floor, assimilating their brand standard operating procedures (SOPs), customers, and the AG. Their job descriptions with key performance indicators (KPIs) and other important details and documents are handed over to them. Each employee is given their weekly and monthly targets as a part of their KPIs. New employees who score above 80% in the post-induction follow-up test receive their store name badges and are allocated to work in a particular store: those who score over 90% are placed in stores located in prominent or AAA malls, while those who score less than 80% have to retake the test until they pass.

Customer Service

'All the Answers Are in the Store'

Talent growth: In the past, stores hired mediocre talent and made them heroes. AG management believes that attitude is more important than aptitude, and has set out to deliver the best attitude in all its 1700+ retail stores. Recruitment focuses on AG values, which are the right attitude, enthusiasm, communication, and interpersonal skills.

They also believe that in order to create a great experience for their customers, they need an engaged and energised workforce. To enable this, any gaps in competencies required for the job role are identified and employees are trained to improve their skills and competencies. Training covering products, customer service, selling skills, behaviours, and so on is provided to all employees as part of the induction and ongoing training.

'Know Your Customers'

AG believes in listening to the voice of the customer (VOC) and has put in place various channels of communications: a toll free number, website, customer feedback form, customer focus groups, email, Twitter, and Facebook. Club Apparel (CA), the customer loyalty department of the company, manages and monitors customer feedback by having feedback forms available in all stores and is responsible for ensuring resolution of customer complaints. AG has clear policies and procedures for speedy and impartial complaint resolution. These policies and procedures are documented and communicated to all stores emphasising the accountability and responsibility of individual employees to resolve complaints courteously and fairly. All customer queries/complaints are resolved within seven days. This process is applied to all complaints and reviewed at monthly meetings. This enables top management to monitor efficiency and effectiveness of complaint resolution and facilitate analysis, thus enabling continuous improvement in customer satisfaction.

To enhance its people's approach to customers, the top management has strategically developed and deployed their customer touchpoint strategy, the '360° approach', which is comprised of participation strategy, authentication strategy, and copy strategy. The 360° approach helps the company to identify different customer groups and create targeted marketing strategies. At the end of every season, the top management, in a post-mortem meeting, analyses the results along with the principles. This informs future strategies and goals which are developed and cascaded down to the operations team for deployment, for example the starting of a biker service to deliver products to customers within 3 hours.

CA is a cardless loyalty programme which is designed as a platform to build long-term relationships with its customers and open new avenues of communication with them. The benefits offered to customers include hassle-free on-the-move rewards collected by mobile phone and instant rewards which can be redeemed immediately after earning them. Customer data are segmented into demographics such as age group, nationality mix, location, and buying behaviour to allow targeted marketing and promotional campaigns via newsletters, the website, SMS, and emails. The top management reviews CA data to determine company performance and customer trends, and these data, along with market intelligence, are used to develop strategies to enhance customer relationships.

AG brands are also members of Dubai Service Excellence Scheme (DSES) and the company uses the DSES mystery shopping parameters to benchmark service levels against other retail organisations in the UAE.

Giving Back to the Community

Meritocracy, intense employee training, and the need to give employees more growth opportunities remain strong traits of AG's culture. They also believe in giving back to the community, country, and people through their 'Educate Engage Enable' programme, the purpose and underlying philosophy behind their CSR.

Educate: Educate people (internal and external stakeholders) and create awareness of various key social issues through knowledge sharing and communication.

Engage: Engage people in various social activities and encourage them to take productive and responsible actions towards society (people).

Enable: Enable people by providing an empowering and healthy environment to be independent and support the surrounding community (planet).

Charity partners supported include the Red Crescent, Big Heart Foundation, Friends of Cancer Patients, and many more. Examples include the AG's organising of the United Nations International Day of Yoga 2016, Dubai, in which more than 14,000 people participated and learned yoga from Yogrishi Swami Ramdev and working with more than 7000 customers to raise awareness and funds (approximately AED 1,357,980) for the Beat Breast Cancer Project.

As a part of the 'Reading Nation' campaign launched by His Highness Sheikh Mohammad Bin Rashid Al Maktoum, Vice-President and Prime Minister of the UAE and Ruler of Dubai, AG donated 60,620 books worth AED 3,331,563 to Sharjah City for humanitarian services. AG also recycled more than 320 tons of packaging waste to reduce its carbon footprint, successfully engaged more than 1208 employees for 24,658 man-hours in social service and reached out to more than 54,524 beneficiaries through its various community initiatives.

Table 7.1 summarises AG's CSR activities since its inception.

Table 7.1 CSR activities

CSR activities		Achievements as of 2016	Unit of measurement
Internal and external communication			
1	Creating companies brand in CSR initiatives	80	No. of events attended/ organised for Apparel Group representation
2	Media coverage of CSR	126	No. of news coverage
Employee engagement			
1	Activities conducted	164	No. of activities
2	Employees engaged	7652	No. of employees
3	Man-hours contributed	48,362	No. of man-hours
Brand-specific CSR			
1	Brands involved in CSR	50	No. of brands
2	Product donation/GV	184,283	No. of units
3	Retail value of products donated	11,243,113	AED
4	Funds donated	13,396,816	AED
Customer's engagement			
1	Funds donated/raised	672,909	AED
2	Customers engaged	17,999	No.
Suppliers and vendors engagement			
1	Staff engaged	105	No. of staff
Environment			
1	Plastic bales recycled	13.09	Tons
2	Carton bales recycled	838.34	Tons
Community			
1	Beneficiaries	76,452	No. of people

Internships

AG started its internship programme as one of the company's ways of giving back to the community. It helps students to gain experience, develop their skills, make connections, strengthen their CVs, learn about a field, and assess their interest and abilities in the retail world. As the internship is paid, it also enables economically disadvantaged youth to participate, especially those who need money to fund their own education.

Apparel Group Awards

To date, AG has received 215 awards since 2003 in various categories as shown in Table 7.2.

Conclusion

Clearly, AG has a history of receiving accolades. Their performance record highlights leadership and people management, and leaders take an active part in recruiting the best talent, carefully breeding the company's next generation of employees. They take pride in making things happen in unique ways. With 'Educate Engage Enable', AG believes not only in training its people but giving back to community. The internship programmes are in place to pursue this goal. Employee growth is a matter of concern for AG and it addresses this with its open-door policy and supportive organisational structure.

Table 7.2 Awards received by Apparel Group

Year	Award	Category
2003	Sahara Centre Awards 2003 for Marketing – Aldo	Other
2003	First International Lifestyle Retailer to be member of Dubai Service Excellence Scheme	DSES
2004	Excellence in Advertising – Seef Mall	Other
2004	Excellence in Customer Service & Visual Presentation – Seef Mall	Customer service
2004	Sahara Centre awards for Retailer of the Year – Aldo	Other
2005	Best High Street Retailer of the Year Awarded by 'Emirates Women' – Nine West	Other
2005	Deira City Centre Awards 2005 for Top Footwear Store – Sport Aldo	Other
2005	Retail City Award 2005 nominated for Best Corporate Social Responsibility Apparel Group	CSR
2005	Retail ME Award 2005 for Best Customer Service Initiative of the Year – Jennyfer	RetailME Awards
2005	Retail ME Award 2005 for Best International Retailer of the Year – Jennyfer	RetailME Awards
2006	Best Sales Per Square Meter Fall 2006 Aldo Accessories – Seef Mall	Other
2006	Best Sales Per Square Meter Fall 2006 Aldo – Deira City Centre	Other
2006	Best Sales Per Square Meter Fall 2006 Aldo: Mall of the Emirates	Other
2006	Best Sales Per Square Meter Fall 2006 Spring: Mall of the Emirates	Other
2006	Best Sales Performance Fall 2006 Aldo Accessories: Mall of the Emirates	Other
2006	Certificate of Appreciation for Dubai Quality Appreciation Program: Apparel Group	Business Excellence
2006	Dubai Human Development Appreciation Award: Apparel Group	Business Excellence
2006	Dubai Service Excellence Scheme Awards 2006 for Best Service Performance Brand: Aldo	Customer service
2006	Retail ME Awards for Business Excellence of the Year: Aldo	RetailME Awards
2006	Retail ME Awards for Rising Star of the Year: Dune	RetailME Awards
2006	Retail ME Business Excellence: Aldo	RetailME Awards
2006	Sharjah City Centre Award for Best Accessory Retailer of the Mall: Strandbags	Other
2007	Best Percentage Increase over Last year Fall 2007 Aldo Accessories: JIMI Mall	Other
2007	Best Percentage Increase over Last year Fall 2007 Aldo: Atria Mall	Other
2007	Best Percentage Increase over Last year Fall 2007 Spring: Seef Mall	Other
2007	Best Sales Per Square Meter Fall 2007 Aldo Accessories: Mall of the Emirates	Other
2007	Best Sales Per Square Meter Fall 2007 Aldo: Deira City Centre	Other
2007	Best Sales Per Square Meter Fall 2007 Spring: Mall of the Emirates	Other

(continued)

Table 7.2 (continued)

Year	Award	Category
2007	Best Sales Performance Fall 2007 Aldo Accessories: Mall of the Emirates	Other
2007	Best Sales Performance Fall 2007 Aldo: Avenue Mall	Other
2007	Best Sales Performance Fall 2007 Aldo: Deira City Centre	Other
2007	Best Sales Performance Fall 2007 Aldo: Mall of the Emirates	Other
2007	Deira City Centre Awards 2007 for Top Shoes/Sports Store: Aldo	Other
2007	Dubai Human Resource Development Appreciation Award: Apparel Group	Business Excellence
2007	Dubai Quality Appreciation Award: Apparel Group	Business Excellence
2008	Best Community Founded Charity Program – 2008 Gulf Cooperative Council Autism Charity Program: Cold Stone Creamery	CSR
2008	Best Market X Factor – 2008 Gulf Cooperative council: Cold Stone Creamery	Other
2008	Best Percentage Increase over last year sales Fall 2008 Aldo: Dubai Festival City	Other
2008	Best percentage increase over last year sales Fall 2008 Spring: Dubai Festival City	Other
2008	Best Sale Per Square Meter Fall 2008 Spring: Mall of the Emirates	Other
2008	Best Sales Per Square Meter Fall 2008 Aldo Accessories	Other
2008	Best Sales Performance Fall 2008 Aldo Accessories: Mall of the Emirates	Other
2008	Best Sales Performance Fall 2008 Aldo: Mall of the Emirates	Other
2008	Best Sales Performance Fall 2008 Spring: Mall of the Emirates	Other
2008	Golden Spade – 2008 Lamcy Plaza Gulf Cooperative Council: Cold Stone Creamery	Other
2008	Mohammed Bin Rashid Al Maktoum Business Award in the Re-Exporting Category: Apparel Group	Other
2008	Retail ME Award: Kenneth Cole	RetailME Awards
2008	Retailer Awards – Best Footwear Store/Sports store Awards: Mall of the Emirates	Other
2008	Top Dollar Club – 2008 Airport Gulf Cooperative Council: Cold Stone Creamery	Other
2008	Top Footwear Store/Sports store Awards: Deira City Centre	Other
2009	Best Footwear Store/Sports store Awards: Deira City Centre	Other
2009	Best Innovative Campaign 2009 Gulf Cooperative Council: Cold Stone Creamery	Other
2009	Dubai Service Excellence Awards: Dune	Customer service
2010	Dubai Quality Award Programme, certification for Business Excellence – 2009	Business Excellence

2010	Dubai Service Excellence Award for Best Customer Service Store: Charles & Keith	Customer service
2010	Franchise Operator of the Year at the Retail City Awards: Cold Stone Creamery	Other
2010	Best Service Performance Brand – 2010 cycle – Department of Economic Development: Cold Stone Creamery	Customer service
2010	Best Service Performance Brand in Medium Business Category: TAF	Customer service
2010	Best Footwear & Sports store: Deira City Centre	Other
2010	Highest Performing Store: Mall of the Emirates	Other
2010	Highest Sales Per Square Meter Sales: Deira City Centre	Other
2011	Dubai Service Excellence Scheme – Best Service Performance Outlet Inglot: Bawadi Mall Al Ain	Customer service
2011	Dubai Service Excellence Scheme – Best Service Performance Outlet Naturalizer:Town Centre Jumeirah	Customer service
2011	Dubai Service Excellence Scheme – Best Service Performance Outlet Cold Stone Creamery: Ajman City Centre	Customer service
2011	Most Admired Retailer of the Year – CRM Initiative Retail ME Awards: Club Apparel	RetailME Awards
2011	Most Admired Retailer of the Year – Food Service – Retail ME Awards: Cold Stone Creamery	RetailME Awards
2011	Top Dollar Club – Mall of Emirates/Dubai Mall 2 and Villagio: Cold Stone Creamery	Other
2011	Million Dollar Club – Atlantis: Cold Stone Creamery	Other
2011	Highly Commended For the Category of Innovation in Retail – Retail City Awards: Club Apparel	Customer service
2011	Golden Spade – Hyatt Plaza/Ajman City Centre and Mall of Emirates: Cold Stone Creamery	Other
2011	Grazia Award	Other
2011	Best Footwear & Sports Store: Sharjah City Centre	Other
2011	Highest Performing Store: Aldo Dubai Mall	Other
2011	Highest Sales Per Square Meter Sales: Dubai Mall	Other
2011	10th Anniversary recognition – Celebrating Year of Collaboration and Outstanding Partner Support	Other
2012	TIM HORTONS for Most Admired Marketing Campaign of the Year	RetailME Awards
2012	CLUB APPAREL for Most Admired Retailer of the Year – CRM Initiatives	RetailME Awards
2012	TIM HORTONS for Most Admired Retail Launch of the Year	RetailME Awards

(continued)

Table 7.2 (continued)

Year	Award	Category
2012	TOMMY HILFIGER for Most Admired International Retailer of the Year	RetailME Awards
2012	Grazia Style Awards 2012 – Best Shoe Brand – Budget Category – Aldo	Other
2012	Grazia Style Awards 2012 – Best Shoe Brand – Budget Category – Aldo	Other
2012	Sharjah Retailers Award – Best Fashion Store – Aeropostale	Other
2012	Sharjah Retailers Award – Best Footwear and Sports Store – Charles & Keith	Other
2012	Mall of the Emirates-Retailers Award – The Best Footwear & Sports Store –Birkenstock	Other
2012	UAE Superbrands 2012 – Nine West	UAE Super brands
2012	UAE Superbrands 2012 – Aldo	UAE Super brands
2012	UAE Superbrands 2012 – Kenneth Cole	UAE Super brands
2012	UAE Super brands 2012 – Skechers	UAE Super brands
2012	Nine West – Best Service Performance Brand 2012 in the Large Business Category	Customer service
2012	Nine West – Best Outlet (Al Ain) in the Footwear Category	Customer service
2012	Naturalizer – Best Outlet (Mall of Emirates) in the Footwear Category	Customer service
2012	Aldo Business Concepts – Dubai Quality Appreciation Award in the Retail Category	Business Excellence
2013	MENA Customer Delight Award for Exceptional and Fantastic Customer Service & Customer Experience from ISMM	Customer service
2013	MENA Customer Delight Award for Speed of Service Delivery, Quality of Service & Products, Customer Satisfaction and Customer Experience from ISMM	Customer service
2013	Excellence in Customer Service Award from American Liberty University	Customer service
2013	UAE Super brands 2013 – Aldo	UAE Super brands
2013	UAE Super brands 2013 – Nine West	UAE Super brands
2013	UAE Super brands 2013 – Skechers	UAE Super brands
2013	UAE Super brands 2013 – Tim Hortons	UAE Super brands
2013	UAE Super brands 2013 – Tommy Hilfiger	UAE Super brands
2013	Tommy Hilfiger – Most Admired Retailer of the Year – Fashion	RetailME Awards
2013	Nine West – Most Admired Retailer of the Year – Footwear & Accessories	RetailME Awards
2013	Tommy Hilfiger – Most Admired Retailer of the Year – Children's Wear	RetailME Awards
2013	Tim Hortons – Most Admired Retailer of the Year – Food Service	RetailME Awards

2013	Garage – Most Admired Marketing Campaign of the Year	RetailME Awards
2013	Garage – Most Admired Rising Star Retailer of the Year	RetailME Awards
2013	Club Apparel – Most Admired Retailer of the Year – CRM Initiative	RetailME Awards
2013	Aeropostal – Most Admired International Retailer of the Year	RetailME Awards
2013	Sheikh Khalifa Excellence Award 2013 is bestowed on Aldo Business Concept	Business Excellence
2013	Apparel Group was awarded the Dubai Chamber CSR Label	CSR
2013	'Dubai Award for Sustainable Transport' under the category of 'Mobility Management: Transport Safety'	CSR
2013	Grazia ME Style Awards 2013 – Aldo Best Budget Shoe Designer	Other
2013	Apparel Qatar was awarded the most 'Successful business partner for the year 2013' from Doha Bank	Other
2013	Skechers Distributor of the Year 2013	Other
2013	Nine West – Dubai Quality Appreciation Award in the Retail Category	Business Excellence
2013	Dubai Service Excellence Awards – Nine West – Best Service Performance Brand 2012 in the Large Business Category	Customer service
2013	Dubai Service Excellence Awards – Nine West – Best Outlet (Al Ain) in the Footwear Category	Customer service
2013	Dubai Service Excellence Awards – Naturalizer – Best Outlet (Mall of Emirates) in the Footwear Category	Customer service
2013	Aldo Business Concepts – Dubai Quality Appreciation Program award in the Retail Category	Business Excellence
2014	Sheikh Khalifa Excellence Award (SKEA) 2014 – Apparel Group – Gold Winner 2014	Business Excellence
2014	Sheikh Khalifa Excellence Award (SKEA) 2014 – Nine West – Silver Winner 2014	Business Excellence
2014	Cortefiel Sales Performance and Operational Excellence Award	Other
2014	'Supply Chain & Transport Awards 2014' has awarded Apparel Group	CSR
2014	Dune – Best Service Performance Outlet (Bawadi Mall) in the Footwear Category	Customer service
2014	Apparel Group was awarded the Dubai Chamber CSR Label	CSR
2014	UAE Super brands 2014 – Aldo	UAE Super brands
2014	UAE Super brands 2014 – Nine West	UAE Super brands
2014	UAE Super brands 2014 – Skechers	UAE Super brands
2014	UAE Super brands 2014 – Tim Hortons	UAE Super brands
2014	UAE Super brands 2014 – Tommy Hilfiger	UAE Super brands

(continued)

Table 7.2 (continued)

Year	Award	Category
2014	UAE Super brands 2014 – Cold Stone Creamery	UAE Super brands
2014	UAE Super brands 2014 – Kenneth Cole	UAE Super brands
2014	Most Admired Retailer of the Year Fast Fashion – Aeropostale	RetailME Awards
2014	Most Admired Retailer of the Year Footwear & Accessories – Nine West	RetailME Awards
2014	Most Admired Retailer of the Year Beauty & Wellness – Inglot	RetailME Awards
2014	Most Admired Retailer of the Year Food Service (Casual Dining) – Tim Hortons	RetailME Awards
2014	Most Admired Store Design of the Year Sportswear Retail – Athlete's Co	RetailME Awards
2014	Most Admired Store Design of the Year Footwear Retail – Charles & Keith	RetailME Awards
2014	Most Admired Store Design of the Year Lifestyle Retail – Le Chateau	RetailME Awards
2014	Most Admired Retailer of the Year CRM Initiatives – Club Apparel	RetailME Awards
2014	Most Admired International Retailer of the Year – Aldo	RetailME Awards
2015	Employer of the Year at the Middle East – HR Excellence Awards 2015	Business Excellence
2015	VIP Category Rating – DED's Self-Inspector Programme	Business Excellence
2015	Most Admired International Retailer of the Year Footwear – Aldo	RetailME Awards
2015	Most Admired Store Manager of the Year – Call It Spring	RetailME Awards
2015	Most Admired Retailer of the Year – Food Service [QSR] – Tim Hortons	RetailME Awards
2015	Most Admired Store Design of the Year – Aeropostale	RetailME Awards
2015	Most Admired Store Design of the Year – TOMS	RetailME Awards
2015	Most Admired Retailer of the Year CRM Initiatives – Club Apparel	RetailME Awards
2015	Most Admired Rising Star of the Year – Pedro	RetailME Awards
2015	UAE Superbrands 2015 – Aeropostale	UAE Super brands
2015	UAE Superbrands 2015 – Aldo	UAE Super brands
2015	UAE Superbrands 2015 – All About Watches	UAE Super brands
2015	UAE Superbrands 2015 – Call It Spring	UAE Super brands
2015	UAE Superbrands 2015 – Cold Stone Creamery	UAE Super brands
2015	UAE Superbrands 2015 – Tim Hortons	UAE Super brands
2015	UAE Superbrands 2015 – Inglot	UAE Super brands
2015	UAE Superbrands 2015 – Nine West	UAE Super brands

2015	UAE Superbrands 2015 – Skechers	UAE Super brands
2015	UAE Superbrands 2015 – The Children's Place	UAE Super brands
2015	UAE Superbrands 2015 – Tommy Hilfiger	UAE Super brands
2015	UAE Superbrands 2015 – Kenneth Cole	UAE Super brands
2015	International Business Excellence Award – Retail	Business Excellence
2015	International Business Excellence Award – Customer Loyalty	Business Excellence
2015	International Business Excellence Award – Employee Engagement	Business Excellence
2015	International Business Excellence Award – Corporate Social Responsibility	Business Excellence
2015	Key of Hope – Award from HH Sheikh Ahmed Bin Saeed Al Maktoum	Other
2015	UAE Excellence Awards – Gold award for Best Fashion Website	Business Excellence
2015	Dubai Quality Appreciation Award – Apparel Group	Business Excellence
2015	Dubai Service Excellence Scheme – Best Service Performance Brand – Le Chateau (Clothing)	Customer service
2015	Dubai Service Excellence Scheme – Best Service Performance Brand – Skechers (Footwear)	Customer service
2015	Princess Haya Award for Special Education in the CSR Excellence Category	CSR
2015	Great Place to Work – Apparel Group	Business Excellence
2015	Golden Medal for Quality & Service Award – Apparel Group	Business Excellence
2015	Dubai Service Excellence Scheme – Best Service Performance Outlet – Cold Stone Creamery	Customer service
2015	Dubai Service Excellence Scheme – Best Service Performance Outlet – Bikenstock	Customer service
2015	Dubai Service Excellence Scheme – Best Service Performance Outlet – Nine West	Customer service
2016	Most Admired International Retailer of the Year Footwear and Accessories: Aldo	RetailME Awards
2016	Most Admired Retailer of the Year Beauty and Personal Care – Inglot	RetailME Awards
2016	Most Admired Retailer of the Year Fashion (Premium) – Tommy Hilfiger	RetailME Awards
2016	Most Admired Store Design of the Year – Rituals	RetailME Awards
2016	Most Admired Retailer of the Year CRM Initiatives – Club Apparel to have 6 consecutive wins	RetailME Awards
2016	UAE Superbrands 2016 – Aeropostale	UAE Super brands
2016	UAE Superbrands 2016 – Aldo	UAE Super brands
2016	UAE Superbrands 2016 – All About Watches	UAE Super brands
2016	UAE Superbrands 2016 – Beverly Hills Polo Club	UAE Super brands
2016	UAE Superbrands 2016 – Birkenstock	UAE Super brands
2016	UAE Superbrands 2016 – Calvin Klein	UAE Super brands

(*continued*)

Table 7.2 (continued)

Year	Award	Category
2016	UAE Superbrands 2016 – Call It Spring	UAE Super brands
2016	UAE Superbrands 2016 – Cold Stone	UAE Super brands
2016	UAE Superbrands 2016 – Inglot	UAE Super brands
2016	UAE Superbrands 2016 – Kenneth Cole	UAE Super brands
2016	UAE Superbrands 2016 – Levis	UAE Super brands
2016	UAE Superbrands 2016 – Nine West	UAE Super brands
2016	UAE Superbrands 2016 – Skechers	UAE Super brands
2016	UAE Superbrands 2016 – The Children's Place	UAE Super brands
2016	UAE Superbrands 2016 – Tim Hortons	UAE Super brands
2016	UAE Superbrands 2016 – Tommy Hilfiger	UAE Super brands
2016	New Balance – Preferred Sports Brand of the Year Award – The Filipino Times Awards	Customer service
2016	Inglot – Preferred Make Up Brand of the Year Award – The Filipino Times Awards	Customer service
2016	UAE Excellence Awards – Gold award for Best Fashion Website	Business Excellence
2016	18th rank for GREAT PLACE TO WORK (GPTW) for the year 2015–2016 in the GCC	Business Excellence
2016	Dubai Quality Appreciation Awards – Tim Hortons	Business Excellence
2016	Dubai Quality Appreciation Awards – Cold Stone Creamery	Business Excellence
2016	Dubai Service Excellence Scheme – Cold Stone Creamery	Customer service
2016	Dubai Service Excellence Scheme – MBT	Customer service
2016	Dubai Chamber CSR Label Award 2016	CSR
2016	Commitment to CSR by the World Confederation of Business	CSR
2016	The Apparel Group – Recognition for outstanding Results in Exemplifying Respect by Aeropostale	Other
2017	The Apparel Group – Most Implementation of Happiness Meter Service Centres	Other
2017	Cold Stone Creamery – Best Performing Brand for 2016 cycle – Café	Customer service
2017	La Vie en Rose – Best Performing Brand for 2016 cycle – Clothing	Customer service
2017	TOMS wins Responsible Retailer of the Year Award at World Retail Congress	Customer service
2017	Best High Street Shoe Brand: Aldo	Customer service
2017	Winner of the 2017 Grazia Middle East Style Awards	Other

CASE B

Case of Quality and People Management at Abela & Co with Nancy Nouaimeh, AVP Quality, Safety, and Performance Excellence

Introduction

This case about Abela & Co is developed based on inputs received from Nancy Nouaimeh, vice president for Quality, Safety, and Performance Excellence, and demonstrates the best practices of workforce and people management at Abela.

Nancy Nouaimeh has been the AVP for Quality, Safety, and Performance Excellence at Abela & Co for the past ten years. She also serves as a country counsellor of the UAE Chapter of the American Society for Quality. Under her leadership several initiatives are currently running in the country.

Abela & Co

Founded in 1967, Abela & Co is one of the leading food services management companies in the UAE and was a pioneer of the catering industry in the region. Headquartered in Dubai, it serves over 120 local and international clients, across an array of industries including but not limited to hospitality, education, construction, health care, pharmaceutical, power, manufacturing, shipbuilding, petroleum, aviation, IT, oil & gas, and fast-moving consumer goods (FMCG).

With an extensive network of four production units, strategically located across the UAE, combined with its business in Qatar and Egypt, Abela & Co produces over 120,000 meals each day and employs more than 3000 employees, who are responsible for delivering exceptional customer service every single day. Integrity, equal opportunity, customer focus, service excellence, creativity, flexibility, and CSR are just a few of the ingredients that make it the company of choice for businesses and employees. The company has grown from around 2000 employees in

2007 to its current 3200, in addition to the opening of various franchised outlets which include Sandella's, a US-based flatbread cafe (acquired in 2008, currently with 17 operational outlets in the UAE), and many home-grown franchises including Zaatar w'Aktar (Manakish), One2Three (juice bar), Red Apron and Bean There (coffee shops and bistros).

Food safety has always been, and still is, the company's number one priority. Nancy pointed out that Abela & Co was amongst the first to be certified in Hazard Analysis Critical Control Point (HACCP) in the country. The company, under the leadership of Nancy, decided to work on being certified for one of the ISO standards (ISO 22000:2005), the food safety management system, HACCP at its core and around 40% resemblance with the management elements of ISO 9001:2008 (quality management systems).

Nancy built on the success of her previous initiatives that she had achieved so far; she used many of the quality concepts and tools and Deming's 14 points for management, in addition to team-building activities, to break the barriers between the departments involved and move forward with the project. She needed to modify the culture and mindset as focusing on 'measurement', a key element to make a drastic change in the way work is done was very difficult in the creative environment in which chefs work. The project began with lengthy brainstorming sessions to establish clear accountabilities, align the team, and prepare a detailed project charter and timeline as well as an intensive training programme on the ISO standard requirements. The cross-functional team from food safety, quality, purchasing, culinary, and operations, focusing on reducing non-added value activities and transforming the company processes to match world-class catering companies, was ready to apply for certification after eight months. In 2013, two years after certification, a third-party audit rated the company at a compliance score of 92/100, the best in the UAE catering industry.

The ISO team continued to hold regular meetings and initiate further improvement projects, which also achieved excellent results:

- Food Safety Excellence Culture Assessment (TSI, 2015, score 81)
- Food Safety & Quality Excellence Culture Assessment (TSI, 2016, score 82, Grade A, the highest in the industry group) (Quality 81.4, Food Safety 82.6)

- Improved suppliers' performance
- Reduced clients' complaints related to quality and food safety
- High grades in municipality inspections

It should be noted that Nancy also has to lead the Quality Department in a multicultural environment and multisite organisation with a workforce of over 3000. In this respect, the alignment of each department and employee is crucial to sustaining quality standards and systems. Understanding the purpose of the quality initiatives, how they link together, interact, and integrate with the other systems in place is crucial to success, as is an equal focus on both 'internal' and 'external' customers; the first is often less considered. Acknowledging employees, the internal users of the company process as customers, leads to looking at each of the touch points and identifying their requirements, added and non-added value activities, and best practices to implement, and this knowledge can then be used to ensure that the company processes are efficient.

Departments, and their respective employees, by default naturally focus on their areas of work, failing to commit, unintentionally in most cases, to improvement projects called for by other departments, especially in the absence of a strong commitment from the leadership of the organisation to quality, excellence, and continuous improvement. As quality touches all areas of business and their processes, a collective understanding of the need for quality tools and mindset should be made evident to all. Support from top management in the form of providing the necessary resources for a strong training and learning programme is a cornerstone in building quality.

The following are some of the best practices observed at Abela & Co:

One of the key focus areas of their Food Safety Management System was to improve communication and knowledge of food safety amongst junior and middle management staff to ensure their full involvement in implementing and maintaining the system. This included the transfer of required knowledge from the food safety team to them and capturing the lessons learnt from the field back to the team.

Over two years the company implemented several projects to support this operation:

- Specific Job Duties Matrix: captured all specific assignments related to food safety, quality, occupational health and safety (OHS), environment, and operations of the key staff in each production unit with an assigned and trained person and recorded all documents needed to accomplish the work as per the established standard.
- Standard manuals: organised all necessary information needed for operational staff in specific manuals (cleaning, emergency response, food & beverages best practices, safe work instructions) using multiple illustrations as visual aids to facilitate understanding and bridge any language barriers. Material was translated into staff native languages when possible.
- Quality workshops: special quality workshops were conducted in the production units with practical demonstrations.
- Lean waste identification posters: with examples from each and every operation and production area, departmental workshops were designed to discuss all forms of waste, with junior staff using posters and games.
- Recognition: a scoring system and sheet were used to record positive and negative observation points related to safe practices of the team. This record was used to encourage staff to improve their scores and motivate the teams.

This resulted in an improved engagement in Quality & Food Safety and better decision-making with improved safety levels.

Perspectives on Managing People

According to Nancy, one of the hardest things to achieve is leading people because it is important to understand their mindset and expectations, and tailor your message in a way that will get their buy-in and alignment. In other words, you need to 'talk their language' while remaining loyal to the message you need to convey. Communication is one of the key soft skills that a leader should have and the use of efficient communication tools to reach out to all employees in the organisation is the responsibility of an organisation's leadership. No one should be left ignorant of the organisation's direction and progress. If you can explain and convince the staff why it is necessary to cut costs, they might own it better and surprise you with amazing ideas.

She then iterates that with challenges related to people comes the challenge of building efficient teams, utilising the strength of the individuals in finding the right amalgam of required internal competences. Competent teams need empowerment; if they are not empowered they should not be expected to deliver effectively and efficiently. They also need appropriate recognition, in whatever form, for the achieved outcome to maintain motivation and improvement pace.

She believes that the strength of a good leader comes from the strength of his/her team. Good leaders coach their people, provide the right direction, and establish a culture in which each feels safe and empowered to think and contribute to the decision-making process, and improvement of the day-to-day operations and long-term development of the organisation. One of the best practices established within their organisation is the involvement of the senior leaders at various levels in coaching and mentoring junior staff, through different programmes established through the years. Effective communication and freedom to act within established boundaries are crucial for empowering people.

Nancy also recollects that working in quality, interacting regularly with all functions in the organisation, in a multicultural environment such as the UAE, one tends to value the diverse knowledge, expertise, and national cultures of people, understanding the areas of strengths and improvements. Moreover, developing high emotional intelligence is necessary to manage sensitive and conflicting relations. Valuing differences in behaviours and areas of interest (millennials, for example) and understanding specific cultural traits is a must for a quality leader to help establish effective projects and efficient teams.

Abela & Co further believes in 'emphasis on internal customers'. Hence, as quality leader, Nancy gave special attention during the trainings provided to this notion, promoting the idea that the company's 'internal' customers were just as deserving of good service as its external ones and that this was a way in which improvements could be made. One of the ways to identify areas for improvements, if not made explicit by the concerned parties, is a 'pain-storming session' where the pains of the internal customer can be identified in a structured manner and prioritised for further improvement actions.

The VOICE of the employee is another crucial aspect for the organisation. They believe that employees are assets of the organisation who deliver the products and services. Nancy affirms that the VOICE of the employee can be a valuable tool to identify improvements needed in the business and people processes. Employees close to the process and customers have access to accurate and significant information that is captured through regular interactions. If captured and utilised well, it can be very useful. Meetings, reports, and internal surveys can be used for this purpose. To capture the VOICE of their supervisors, the feedback they receive from external customers, and the issues they encounter, Abela & Co designed an internal survey where employees can freely and transparently share their concerns with the internal teams and contribute by suggesting improvements needed to enhance customers' satisfaction with the services and products served. Nancy went on to explain that one of the challenges she had faced as a quality leader in the organisation was to establish a culture of quality that is not only beneficial to the continuous improvement process needed to drive performance, but, most importantly, works towards adding value and in harmony with the food safety culture in place. They began, she said, by identifying the common areas of action, and all plans were articulated around what they believed to be the base for both cultures:

- Joint quality and food safety team for leading ISO certification and continuous improvement
- Focus on people development and alignment:
  - Accredited in-house training centre and Learning and Development Academy were established to tailor training that responds to our needs and the needs of our multicultural workforce (three main languages, visual aids)
  - Cross-functional committees for improvement projects, which helped the alignment of different sites, business sectors, and departments
  - Balance between decentralised and centralised quality-related activities

The quality department led internal improvement projects for key areas that impact quality, such as suppliers' performance, with a special consideration given to the following:

- Managing cultural sensitivity due to the multicultural workforce
- Well-managed processes with clear process map and a set of KPIs
- Top-down drive, with constant involvement and bottom-up feedback
- Reducing waste and costs
- Improving processes efficiency

In 2015, it was then decided to measure the culture in place in a structured manner, through a third-party provider; the food safety culture achieved a score of 79%. In 2016, both cultures—quality and food safety—were measured in an attempt to understand the impact of one on the other and the barriers, if any, considering different groups of the workforce. A total score of 82% (A Grade) was achieved; the industry average during the same period was 69%. Efforts deployed to create a positive quality culture were beneficial not only for quality but also for food safety.

The exercise also enabled the company to understand the different perceptions and definitions of quality held by operators, supervisors, and managers, and the barriers to higher levels of quality and food safety culture excellence as perceived and ranked by the same workforce groups. For example, for managers, one of the important barriers was the company's multicultural workforce; operators, however, listed 'time' as the worst barrier to implementation of safe practices and quality, which highlighted a problem with time management skills and workloads. In this context, designing actions to tackle the barriers from both points of view was needed to further enhance the excellence culture score in future years. Surveys conducted by a third-party in 2013 and 2015 reported that 94% and 97% respectively of the top two tiers of staff were proud to be part of the company.

Finally, reflecting upon her role, Nancy explained that being a leader is about developing people and supporting each member of the team to reach their maximum potential. Respecting limitations is a key to developing learning programmes that, as far as possible, work at all levels. A competent and happy workforce is needed to ensure the sustainability of the business, and, as Simon Sinek said, 'Happy employees ensure happy customers. Happy customers ensure happy shareholders – in that order'. Not every individual wishes, or is able, to undertake continuous learning outside of the workplace; structured programmes developed in-house and tailor-made to the needs of employees and the business that employees can attend during working hours in areas other than their job area, aiming at developing their skills, and preparing them for higher accountabilities are thus of great benefit to both the company and the employees. At the Abela Learning & Development Academy, their in-house education centre, the chief executive officer (CEO) and senior management conduct courses in marketing, finance for non-finance people, nutrition, storekeeping, and quality, all of which are open to any employee, some of whom have discovered hidden talents.

Nancy also strongly recommends involvement and performance evaluation. She noted that when teaching and implementing kaizen (improvement) principles we always tell people to go to the gemba (the place where value is created). A good leader cannot lead effectively if he/she is not involved in one way or another with the gemba and does not have sufficient knowledge of his workforce, business, and of the perception the team has of his/her leadership style. People are less prone to follow a leader who dictates actions that are perceived as not aligned with the reality of operations and business. Getting involved in high-level projects with the team, paying visits to the gemba and interacting with staff, partaking in major staff events and talking to staff are effective ways in which a leader can get knowledge of and proximity to his/her workforce. When a leader evaluates his/her team performance and calls for improvement, he/she should be open to the same, seeking honest and transparent feedback from his/her team and direct subordinates on their perception of and satisfaction with his/her leadership. Feedback, if objective and constructive, can have a very positive return on building relations.

Building knowledge alone is good but never enough; once your competent employee leaves, if the knowledge gained through structured training and lessons learnt while performing the job are not captured and transferred to the others in the team, it is lost knowledge. A good leader will coach and mentor direct team members, and establish structured programmes within the organisation which guarantee that mentoring and coaching is a methodology followed by all so that knowledge is retained rather than lost. The leader being a role model himself/herself is much needed in this context.

In Nancy's narration, the only way for quality to succeed in any organisation is when it is integrated within the other functions and partially performed by each of the departments, which in return would demonstrate a self-sustained motivation and acquired skills to measure current performance, identify areas for improvements, and design improvement projects that are best suited to the organisation and its clients.

Conclusion

Abela clearly exhibits the role of human capital, particularly through its strategies of voice of customer/employees, employee engagement, empowerment, and development of excellence culture through learning and development, which are the themes demonstrated in the case. The case is thus useful for understanding the quality strategies, tools, and techniques used to successfully implement and maintain quality standards and accreditations.

CASE C

Journey of Excellence with Ravi Prakash, Khansaheb Civil Engineering L.L.C

Introduction

This case details Khansaheb Civil Engineering, which has been operating in the UAE for over 80 years, during which time it has completed many prestigious building and civil engineering projects.

Ravi Prakash has been the Group QA Manager for over 20 years and is in charge of best practices of managing human resources and involving people in the company's quality drive. Having successfully implemented the ISO 9001 standard across the Khansaheb Civil Engineering business, Ravi explains that an organisation's success is purely based on its people.

Khansaheb, founded in 1935 by Khansaheb Hussain bin Hassan Amad, was the first contractor in the Trucial States, the name by which the UAE was known at the time. Projects were undertaken in difficult conditions which were of great importance to the overall development of the region. Two of the most significant contracts were the construction of the first motor track between Ras Al Khaimah and Sharjah in 1935 and the first causeway between Mugtta and Abu Dhabi in 1952.

In 1948, the founder retired and the business was taken over by Hussain Abdul Rahman, the present chairman. Over time, Khansaheb has built both a large fleet of construction plant and equipment and a professional, technical team, the combination of which has led to Khansaheb's position amongst the few leading, quality contractors in the Emirates.

In 1981, in order to maintain momentum and ensure continued access to new and modern developments in construction methods and techniques, an association was made with Douglas International Limited, the offshore arm of Robert M. Douglas Holdings PLC, a Birmingham-based UK construction group. In 1991, this association was further strengthened when Tilbury PLC merged with Douglas Holdings to form Tilbury Douglas PLC. In 2002, Tilbury Douglas PLC changed its name to Interserve PLC and is publicly quoted on the UK Stock Exchange.

Khansaheb, which is renowned for its quality products, has over the years adopted a policy of diversification into various activities all relating directly to the construction industry.

While the construction division remains at its heart and accounts for some 85% of the annual 1.5 billion Dirhams turnover, the company now operates several separate divisions including joinery, interiors, architectural metals, and building services, which altogether employ over 1300 members of staff with a labour force of 6000 and is certified by ISO 9001, ISO 14001, and OHSAS 18001.

Espousing the fundamentals of the TQM approach, Ravi shared the company's success in people management. Employees are the pillars of the organisation. Delivering projects on time and within budget by doing the job right the first time is one of the key cornerstones of organisational success. Training employees adds value to the business as it contributes to a professional approach combining competence, confidence, and belief, leading to customer satisfaction and repeat orders for the company. Ravi joined Khansaheb in 1996, when the company's turnover was approximately 450 million AED. The main construction division was supported by specialist divisions, all of which had competent divisional managers who were responsible for the profit and loss results. Since then each division has grown fourfold in terms of securing business to meet its individual set target through efficient business plans put in place and currently the organisation has a turnover of approximately 1.2 billion UAE Dirhams. This success was a result of putting user-friendly systems in place by effectively monitoring the performance of the process through measurable objectives at various functions and levels as a part of continual improvement.

With the belief that everyone is important in an organisation, the Group QA manager explained that the involvement of open-minded people is a healthy sign for any company's success. Reward and recognition will also motivate the employee to do better. Organisations must, however, strongly discourage the blame culture. Ravi explained that when he joined the organisation, the majority of the staff had been with the company for over 15 years and some followed old schools of thought. He said that it was a big challenge to get the process owners to understand the eight quality management principles' potential benefits. He began by holding one-to-one discussions with members of the project team and then established a small quality team to coordinate with the relevant team members. Looking into customer/project requirements, he had to design relevant documents and put them on a trial basis for the creation of records. These records proved to be a very powerful tool in dealing with day-to-day activities with consultants and sub-contractors. This exercise established a solid platform for involving people at various levels: end results were achieved with facts and figures resulting in fewer customer complaints and excellent customer satisfaction scores. Further, the introduction of KPIs allowed results to be measured with a powerful dashboard for reviewing things at planned intervals. A drastic improvement was seen on taking necessary corrective actions, thus resulting in the proper delivery of items as defined in the Quality Policy.

Applying the simple plan-do-check-act (PDCA) process to business, people involvement is a strong characteristic of the organisation. Ravi further explained that one of the eight quality management principles is 'involvement of people' during all steps of the improvement process. People, at whatever level, are the most important resource within any organisation and their involvement is crucial to allow their abilities to be used for the excellent performance of the organisation:

> I would strongly say that people are the fuel that drives the setup and a solid workforce relies mainly on the involvement from the beginning of employees who put in place the strategies all the way through to the management levels who set goals and ensure that processes are implemented correctly.

He went on to say that quality management relies on the involvement of people for the success of all processes and strategies at various functions and levels and the best way to encourage their involvement with respect to the quality management system is by allowing them to take ownership of and have the responsibility to resolve obstacles. One should make use of tools available—such as the fishbone diagram—and/or utilise performance analysis to get accurate data on requirements. Overall, one should continually seek out ways to make improvements and improve competences, knowledge, and experience.

Ravi is also a proponent of sharing knowledge and experience in groups: this dispersal of knowledge allows the organisation to strengthen the departments by ensuring that they are able to operate smoothly and correctly in a professional manner.

Each employee should focus on the formation of value for the customer, thus promoting the organisation's goals. Innovation plays a strong role in fielding new work to monitor and achieve an organisation's objectives.

The involvement of people improves the organisation's reputation with all its stakeholders, from customer to local communities and other audiences.

People's involvement also allows them to get satisfaction from their work, finding ways to address any concerns they have with the workload or assigned task. It also makes them feel proud to be a part of the organisation. The final aspect determining how people are able to contribute and influence improvement is that they should feel proud of and excited to be involved in the systems and procedures they have put in place. This ensures personal interest in the quality management system, thereby motivating them to adhere to the processes on their own accord and contribute to the organisation's achieving its objectives. People at all levels are the essence of an organisation and their full involvement enables their objectives to be used to the organisation's benefit.

The Khansaheb Employees Foundation (KEF) is another best practice of the organisation, showcasing staff involvement. Established in 2014, many KEF initiatives have been undertaken through the involvement of people at various levels from different departments/divisions of the organisation across the business.

The KEF supports local charity organisations such as 'Dubai Cares'. In an effort to make a difference in society, KEF is associating itself with Manzil (www.manzil.ae), which means 'destination' in Urdu or 'home' in Arabic. Manzil is an institution which caters to children of different nationalities with mental challenges. The non-profit centre was inaugurated in 2005.

Another area identified by KEF is to help in refurbishment of facilities. As usual with charity initiatives, this is over and above daily schedules and commitments, but guarantees a sense of personal fulfilment. Without people's support it would not be possible and this highlights the basic requirements, that is, the funds and manpower, and is another best practice at Khansaheb.

Apart from these specifically measurable parameters, the organisation has received numerous comments and suggestions for making the workplace more effective and rewarding. A quick analysis of the categories of comments/suggestions received from employees revealed their priorities and Khansaheb then worked to incorporate them throughout the business where possible through KPIs. The following are examples of the good practices that they observe:

- They set financial and non-financial targets required to meet strategic objectives and satisfy stakeholder critical success factors.

- They measure past and current performance trends.
- They learn from and take action based on performance trends.
- They have leading performance indicators that provide an early warning of deviation from business targets.
- They regularly review performance to identify deviation from targets.
- Information regarding performance indicators can be easily accessed.
- They have a clear understanding of performance outcomes (results) relative to plans, objectives, and targets.

Ravi also pointed out the importance of having regular performance appraisals as a stepping stone towards development. All line managers are encouraged to ensure eligible staff are appraised on their performance and career aspirations discussed. New staff undergo a formal performance review at the end of their probation period which allows the company to better understand the alignment of new staff joining the business. At the end of a successful completion, a letter of confirmation is issued to the staff, and line managers are required to discuss the team and annual objectives. An annual training calendar is used to keep track of staff development requirements. To date, the organisation has conducted 2944 man-hours of soft skills training and 11,697 man-hours of technical training. Riding on the success of workers training at the Training Centre they formalised training modules for front-line supervisors, which have been well received.

Finally, Khansaheb believes that getting their employees to adopt a quality mindset is the real key to producing high-quality products and services. Employees must feel a sense of ownership. That is, they must feel responsible for the outcome of anything connected with the product or service. One always takes better care of something that they own as opposed to something that they do not. With ownership, employees will feel a sense of pride when hearing that their product or service has the highest reputation in the marketplace. To instil a sense of ownership, employees must feel that they play an important role in the success of the product and this is achieved through teamwork. A team is defined as a collection of individuals who rely on group collaboration in order to achieve specific goals and objectives. Team members contribute their individual thoughts and expertise to the team and have different responsibilities in the fulfilment of the team's objectives.

The real experts in any process are almost always the ones actually doing the job, not the ones who write about it in theory. A well-run team makes experts out of everyone and takes advantage of the experience and knowledge possessed by its members, thus allowing everyone to 'own' a part of the product or service. Once employees feel attached to the outcome of the process, they will have achieved the quality mindset necessary in order to meet or exceed the expectations of the customer.

The following are some of the success factors of teamwork:

- Open to feedback
- Accepts responsibility for members' behaviour
- Provides feedback to other team members
- Takes initiative
- Concerned about winning
- Willing to let others win occasionally
- Willing to confront and stand up on important issues
- Attacks problems, not people
- Is a good listener
- Willing to change
- Willing to lead when necessary
- Eager to learn new things

Khansaheb has built a reputation within the construction industry of fostering excellence. This reputation is based on a number of initiatives established by the current group general manager with the active cooperation of his/her top management team. These initiatives are based on his/her determination to bring to life the Khansaheb vision of 'Redefining the Future for People and Places'.

This vision has been enshrined in the company's values:

- Do the right thing
- Everyone has a voice
- Bring better value to life
- Take pride in what you do

Khansaheb's management believes that these values need to be translated into tangible, measurable actions which will be reflected in the quality of the work done by the company. In an effort to establish best practices and proactive employee development, Khansaheb has instituted several systems and practices to help improve the capabilities of its people.

Initiative # 1 → Training Centre—Jebel Ali

Soon after joining Khansaheb, the group general manager realised that the general quality of the workforce coming from developing countries was sadly lacking in some of the basic trade skills required in the UAE. This not only had an impact on safety and productivity on site but also limited the earning potential of these people. One of the 'out of the box' initiatives has been the Khansaheb Training Facility, established in 2014. Bucking the usual trend of classroom training for staff and managers, this training school was purpose-built for operative training, imparting the necessary skills and confidence to do the job right the first time.

Initiative # 2 → Middle Managers Programme (MMP)

Once the organisation saw the benefits of training, the next group identified for development was middle management, which included senior site agents, senior engineers, works managers, and senior quantity surveyors as well as construction managers, project managers, and facility managers. The content of this modular programme (thus allowing participants flexibility in attendance) was developed internally and the programme was delivered by senior management.

Initiative # 3 → Front-line Supervisors Training (FLST)

In the course of designing the MMP, senior managers recognised the direct impact of improving front-line supervision; this was the genesis of the FLST. FLST is aimed at foremen, senior foremen, junior site agents, and site agents. This group is a bridge between the operatives and middle management. The content for this training was also developed in-house. Initially it was delivered by an external provider but management is currently working to take this in-house as they feel this would be better for both the company and the staff.

Initiative # 4 → SustainAbilities

Sustainability is Khansaheb's plan for managing the increasing environmental issues, social challenges, and economic pressures that are rapidly changing the business landscape in the UAE.

Sustainability is redefining the company and how it will meet the needs of its customers in the coming years. It is part of Interserve's global **Sustainability** agenda, and provides an action plan from today to 2020 and beyond.

It manages business risks for the company and its customers through sustainable business management, performance reporting, supply chain management, and involvement in the communities in which Khansaheb operates. In short, it puts the issue of sustainability at the forefront of decision-making. **SustainAbilities** guides the company to work with customers who care about sustainability and puts energy and operating costs at the centre of the company's actions.

What's It All About?

- Khansaheb has put in place a health and well-being programme for employees that includes providing better quality accommodation and recreational amenities, healthier food & health monitoring.
- Implementation of sustainable supply chain management and work with suppliers and subcontractors to reduce waste and carbon, and to procure all timber from sustainable sources.
- In Khansaheb, developing talent is part of the SustainAbility agenda. The company's Graduate Training Scheme (GTS) is training the next generation of construction professionals.

- Fuel and water consumption has steadily reduced from 2010 through better management of vehicles, plant and equipment and the use of renewable energy, which has reduced CO_2 emissions by 40%.
- Khansaheb works with the **ABSHER** Initiative to encourage UAE nationals into the workforce and build the country's skill base. National recruitment is already up by 20% and the company is working hard to increase this further. One of the initiatives is the GET Programme.
- The Khansaheb Employee Foundation is now up and running as part of the **SustainAbilities** plan, and is tasked with getting employees involved in the communities in which the company operates and with charitable causes. It is managed by the employees who are passionate about this and donate their time on a voluntary basis.

Initiative # 5 → Rewards and Recognition

Khansaheb believes in recognising and rewarding exceptional contributions and people who have demonstrated inspirational performance across the business.

Khansaheb also encourages employees to share their ideas about how to do things better in the following areas:

- How to encourage better communication with our teams?
- How to improve tools, materials, or processes?
- How to better care for the environment?

Conclusion

Involvement of people has been a huge success for Khansaheb. The group QA is proud of the company's approach, which has upheld the engagement with various initiatives that include its training centre, middle management development programme, frontline supervisors training, and sustainability. Using reward and recognition will also motivate employees to do better. The 'blame culture' is strongly discouraged and the company has established a strong vision with clear dedication to workforce development. These values clearly exhibit the care for its people. Communication and sharing of experiences is of clear importance in Khansaheb's work culture and a systematic process is followed to stimulate ideas and share experiences.

CASE D

People Management Best Practice with Oasis Investment LLC

Introduction

This case illustrates the quality management practices at Oasis Investment and highlights the key results achieved in terms of 'people' criteria.

About the Company

Oasis Investment Company, the holding company of the Al Shirawi Group of Companies, was founded in 1971. From the beginning, the founders, Abdullah Al Shirawi and Mohan Valrani, embedded a sense of pragmatism into the culture of the group. It is this pragmatism that has not only seen the company through the most difficult of times but has also allowed it to capitalise on opportunities during favourable times.

Oasis began as a trading house, growing to an industrial complex and then on to a conglomerate of 34 companies spanning the trading, industrial, distribution, contracting, and service industries across the GCC. Today all their companies see the world as their marketplace and they continue to grow at a steady pace.

Speed is a virtue that they have stood by at all times. The successful induction of the next generation into the business has allowed them to retain the advantages of remaining a family concern but at the same time has enabled them to act with speed in the hiring of top-grade professionals.

The group has been built on the premise of sheer hard work. They have progressed this far by believing in their values and never shying away from putting in the effort needed to grow. For them the journey has been a long one but they see it as just the beginning of bigger things to come. The next generation is now fully equipped to take the group forward.

We want everyone who deals with us to see, understand and experience that we provide high-quality solutions – and to reap the full benefits of working with a company where innovation, unrivalled quality and the pursuit of excellence are day-to-day realities.

Vision, Mission, Goals, and Values

Vision: To become the most respected company in the industry by exemplifying professionalism, efficiency, and ethical values. To ensure customer satisfaction and maximise stakeholders' value through sustained profitability.

Mission: Through investment in advanced technology, equipment, and people, they hope to create a dynamic and techno-savvy work environment that will result in products and services of the highest standards.

Values: Excellence, transparency, compassion, honesty, empowerment, and discipline are inculcated in every employee.

Culture: A culture of openness runs through all their organisations. This transparency combined with a passion for excellence gives them the power to deliver a superior product and service to their customers.

Goals: Sustaining profitability, upholding reputation through excellence in people, process, and technology.

Transmission: The company understands the need to transmit their core values, vision, mission, and culture through periodical events such as

- Induction training
- Discussions about case studies on core values
- Sharing of success stories by following core values and culture
- Promoting people who follow core values
- A CEO blog to promote core values and culture

The vision and mission are indispensable parts of each and every presentation and corporate communication events.

- Employee orientation
- Prequalification documents
- Website and brochures

Best Practices

Al Shirawi Engineering Services group has a meticulous way of setting strategic objectives. Every quarter of the financial year, the company conducts strategy review meetings to understand the current strengths and weaknesses in the management (internal) and socio-economic challenges prevailing in the market that need to be addressed for better performance. Through this opportunities and threats review, the company identifies the value stream for future growth. The techniques to identify the areas of concern and opportunities are selected carefully and workshop sessions are held by the CEO in an informal manner to encourage the top management team to air their views on the various challenges and opportunities.

1. Porter's Five Forces Model

The CEO through Q&A sessions summarises the environment in which the organisation is working by critically evaluating the company's strength with respect to its bargaining power with the suppliers, threats from new entrants, bargaining power of buyers (customers), and whether the product can be substituted with others. These discussions are held to understand the following:

1. The company's position in the market
2. Key areas of improvement required to make the business lucrative
3. Resources and competency requirements
4. Merger/acquisition decisions
5. Sustainability for a better future

6. Cost–benefit analysis (CBA)

Various business priorities and challenges related to customer retention, business re-engineering requirements, diversification of operations, and resources planning are discussed during strategy review meetings. The management team is asked to vote for the most pressing assignments where added attention is required and identify the best opportunities for the company to invest its resources, time, and attention to make it one of the best in the industry.

At the end of the session, a strategy statement is developed to ensure management has agreed on three core issues to work upon which may result in the following:

1. Selection of critical product line(s) based upon the key customer requirements on which the organisation should focus
2. Vertical expansion of operations from sales to service and after-sales service based upon customer feedback
3. Employee engagement and motivation through certification programmes such as 'Great Place to Work', rewards and recognition programmes
4. Participation in MEP/climate control or similar industry-relevant awards for brand promotion and better market visibility

After each strategy review meeting, the minutes and action plan and its accomplishment are continually reviewed during subsequent review meetings.

2. Risk-based Thinking

With the adoption of ISO 9001:2015 standards, fundamental risk-based thinking methodology is being inculcated while reviewing any business proposals as well as opportunities. All business risks are identified in advance through risk and opportunities probing sessions with the top management team. Risk mitigation is then undertaken to make the risk acceptable with controls. A detailed risk and opportunities register is created, which will undergo periodical scrutiny in the following circumstances:

- Changes in the previously agreed-upon scope
- Risk/opportunities due to changes in the legal and legislative requirements
- Risk/opportunities due to diversification of resources, time, and cost
- Risk/opportunities due to volatilities in the market

3. People Management

In order to accomplish critical tasks discussed during the review meeting, an action committee is set up under the close supervision of the CEO to undertake various tasks as decided and narrated in the strategy statement:

- Individual KPIs are centred against this critical task and during performance appraisals additional weight is given to key task fulfilment.
- Employee recognition and appreciation programmes are also made available to motivate people to work towards the task.
- The relevant working committee is given absolute freedom to take the decision and escalate the matter to the top management for any impediments faced during the process of performing the task.
- Milestone reviews of the assignments are done during KPI review meetings with the core committee members.

4. Contribution Towards Sustainability

The Al Shirawi Engineering Services group of companies understands the requirements of sustainability in the region and with that objective in mind, the company has created a sustainability initiative committee under the supervision of the CEO.

The committee works to safeguard the most important natural resources through the following initiatives at the group level:

- Changing traditional refrigerant-operated heating, ventilation, and air-conditioning (HVAC) equipment to environment-friendly R410A energy star-certified units, which enabled energy savings of 12–15%.

- Changing traditional florescent lamps to light-emitting diode (LED) lamps, resulting in a reduction in unit consumption of 22%.
- Carbon footprint reduction campaign through reduction in paper consumption by embracing technology. The use of online portals for approvals and attachment of documents in the enterprise resource planning (ERP) portal for vendor registration and management resulted in a 50% reduction in paper consumption.
- The introduction of waterless urinals resulted in a 38% reduction in water consumption.

People Management Strategies, Systems, and Processes

The Al Shirawi Group of Companies is commonly managed by its holding company, Oasis Investments, which has a wider market reputation in the areas of its expertise ranging from trading, construction, facilities management, utility management, and logistics to the educational sector.

The company is professionally managed by sector-specific experts handpicked for their expertise in people management, processes, and systems.

The company's core competencies are always revamped based upon the changes in customer requirement and market conditions.

During recruitment special care is taken to identify candidates who will support the core values of the organisation in terms of the following:

- Excellence
- Honesty
- Compassion
- Transparency
- Empowerment
- Discipline

Top management spends a significant amount of time to inculcate these values across all the function levels, and line managers are trained to undertake induction training and develop a culture that supports the core values.

To support the core value of 'Compassion', the company assigns mentors to support and collect feedback from candidates during the initial phase of their joining period (three months).

The company has an ethics policy and ethics champion who has easy access to the top management to report any unfair practices reported by any employees.

All the group companies have been certified to meet ISO 9001 standard requirements, which help to follow the 'PDCA' philosophy on processes with a critical eye on continuous improvement. Employees are inducted on process and systems with the help of well-defined procedures, guidelines, and sector-specific training.

As a customer-focused, proactive organisation, monthly management review meetings are conducted to review the processes and performance related to the following:

- Customer satisfaction and complaint management
- Results of audits
- Process performance improvement areas
- Changes that could affect management system
- Quality policy and its adherence
- Resources management

In order to ensure compliance in processes, a dedicated internal quality audit team has been established with specific skills to undertake audits that can pinpoint compliance and deviations related to the following:

- Contractual compliances
- Customer satisfaction
- Adherence to procedures
- Legal requirements
- Action plan on strategy

All deviations from process and system are specially recorded as non-conformance, and the respective department and employee are asked to comply with the requirements by taking corrective action within the stipulated time through a non-conformity report (NCR). Reported deviations undergo regress probing where remedial, root cause, and corrective actions are recorded to ensure complete closure of deviations. NCRs thus closed are discussed in the review meetings.

The company places special emphasis on evidence-based decision-making and quality tools used to conclude various management actions.

Some of the tools used for the statistical evaluation of results for effective decision-making include (but are not limited to) the following:

- Pareto Chart
- Control Chart
- Fishbone Diagram
- Swim line Diagram to vindicate the processes

The company values transparency while taking decisions. To support this requirement a business excellence (BE) department has been floated with a clear objective to make unbiased decisions on people performance. During performance appraisals, individual KPIs are reviewed which are then audited by a third party who has been given authority to access any document related to individual performance, scoring data for reasons for any shortfall in achieving objectives. Complete transparency is maintained while submitting the KPIs and final increment is planned based upon the achievements of the KPI.

The BE department also conducts comprehensive surveys to understand the internal and external customers' and service providers' requirements. Customer/employee satisfaction survey results are discussed on a half-yearly basis and the following actions are taken:

- A low score ($\leq$5) is considered as a customer complaint and corrective action has to be taken.
- Employees' satisfaction results are discussed during the management review meeting and specific concerns and grievances are addressed with action plans.
- An HR Bulletin is issued as a corrective action for founded grievances.

- Customer satisfaction re-surveys are conducted for low-score clients.
- The organisation is devoted to customer satisfaction and complaint resolution.
- Employee, stock, and debtor turnover is measured to arrive at decisions on people, process, and profitability on a regular basis.

The company pays specific attention to enhancing the knowledge of its employees. This is done through knowledge transfer initiatives and training needs identification process under the training and development department.

Specific training requirements are identified according to the contractual competency requirements, employee appraisal outcomes, changes in the system, technology, and a well-defined training calendar, which is prepared based upon identified training needs. Training is imparted by approved tutors both internally and externally.

The knowledge enhancement programme is also conducted through the following:

- Project closed out meetings and lessons learned sharing
- Sharing of best practices during management review meetings
- Implementation of best practices to improve the system
- On and off the job training

People Results and Some Overall Organisation Results

The company conducts periodical review meetings to compare its objectives with actual performance and the following results were observed:

- Overall business growth from the new revenue stream increased by 25%.
- Diversified into more lucrative business portfolios such as education and infrastructure utility management.
- Employee satisfaction increased by 3% from 88% to 91% as a result of acquiring the 'Great Place To Work' (Group Company – Leminar Airconditioning Company) title continuously for three years.

- Employee recognition programme and reward system encouraged better employee retention.
- Training and development of employees conducted to make sure their competency was enhanced in various areas.
- Empowerment survey conducted to ensure proper transparency in deals and relationships. Overall improvement of 8% from 81% to 89% reported during last survey.
- Employee engagement programme resulted in better employee relationships, teamwork, and communication between departments.
- HR conducts the following employees' engagement programmes to ensure people are motivated in the workplace:
    - Birthday celebrations
    - Annual sports fest
    - Annual cricket tournaments
    - Celebrating big wins
    - Annual picnic
    - Star of the quarter
    - Employee of the month/year
    - Long-service awards
- Social events organised to support CSR activities include the following:
    - Breast cancer awareness
    - International Women's Day celebration
    - Earth Hour celebration
    - World Environment Day celebration
    - Triple R (reduce, reuse, and recycle campaign) to support the environmental management programme

Conclusion

This case has illustrated the quality journey for Oasis Investments. The company is characterised by strategy review meetings, risk-based thinking, contributions to sustainability, and people management, recognised as a 'Great Place to Work', and engages in various best practices for employee engagement.

CASE E

Good Practices of 'People' Enabler at JET

Opened in 2000, *Jumeirah Emirates Towers* is one of the most stunning architectural highlights on the Dubai skyline and a significant landmark of the UAE. One of the first skyscrapers to rise on Sheikh Zayed Road, Jumeirah Emirates Towers translates Dubai's ambition, pride, and modernity. Boasting a triangular design inspiration that stemmed from themes pertaining to Islamic and regional cosmology, the structure was designed and constructed between 1996 and 2000. A total of 133,000 cubic metres of concrete, 22,000 tons of reinforced steel, 1,800,000 metres of cables, and 27,000 sprinkler heads were used in creating this landmark building.

Jumeirah Emirates Towers' dedication to excellence and continuous improvement is demonstrated through the commitment of innovation and learning. Through their Business Management System, they deliver benefits to customers, colleagues, business partners, owners, and society by listening, building loyalty, and developing mutually beneficial relationships. Success and sustainability are also achieved by considering guests as first priority and striving constantly to exceed expectations by applying hallmarks, guiding principles, and core standards in their day-to-day activity. They follow a culture of excellence by leading by example and role modelling in everything they do.

They have various systems to measure their customer performance indicators and their main mechanism is their Quarterly Mystery Guest Assessments, which provide us quantitative and qualitative data on customer experiences against their Jumeirah and International Luxury Standards. The administration of mystery guest's assessments is done by the highly prestigious Leading Quality Assurance Company, which provides this service to most of the best-in-class luxury hospitality organisations. Their mechanism to acquire customer perceptions data and intelligence are their guest questionnaires, which are administered by JD Power and Associates. The questionnaire follows an international standard of set statements for organisations of the hospitality sector, which are presented on a Likert scale ranging from 1 to 10. Each set of questions is organised within an index, which assigns appropriate importance to weights and encompasses all relevant areas of their business. As it is a standardised questionnaire, it allows us to benchmark against similar organisations for most of the questions in order to assess performance and prioritise improvements.

Their Guest Feedback Management system plays an important role in understanding their guests' needs and expectations, and all guest feedback received is logged into their guest feedback system. Feedback is assigned for corrective action and response to relevant department heads and closure monitored on a daily basis. Top recurring comments are analysed at the end of each month and through sentiment analysis in their Medallia portal. They also review the effectiveness of the feedback system by regularly examining response time, quality of responses, and reoccurrence. An example of a recent refinement was the empowerment of assistant managers to act on and respond to customer queries, which has enhanced the speed and resolution of recurring issues. Once a month, the hotel manager leads a review and discussion on the various customer perceptions and performance indicators to identify areas for improvement and lessons learned. Further analyses were conducted by the hotel manager and BE manager periodically during one-to-one meetings for any improvements that can be made. An example is the recent inclusion of front-line colleagues as attendees of this forum to gather further operational input on causes for trends. Their team efforts were reflected in their guests' happiness and loyalty and their customer satisfaction level consistently increased from 799 in 2010 to 869 in 2016 (Fig. 7.1).

Good Examples—Never Been Done Before (NBDB)

This approach is initiated to encourage leaders to continuously seek new emerging technologies within networks and areas of expertise to help the organisation achieve its vision and also to bring the latest software and innovative products which assist the organisation in driving the agility of its core processes. All ExCom members are encouraged to bring innovative initiatives in respective areas for review of the general manager, the

Fig. 7.1 Customer satisfaction trends (Source: Jumeirah Emirates Towers)

hotel manager, and the IT manager. Relevance and funds are studied and prioritised, and initiatives are implemented following their IT and financial processes. Their Excom innovation board is reviewed periodically, and an example of recent innovations brought through this initiative was their Newspaper Direct and their Room Expeditor System (REX).

Lobster Ink

This approach was developed to create training programmes in their core customer processes to ensure their colleagues have the necessary encouragement to deliver their mission. The Lobster Ink training videos were tailor-made to suit the needs and brand promise of the Jumeirah group. The videos focus on their core customer process: manage arrivals, deliver personalised service, and manage departures. All front-line colleagues have student IDs and have targets for training completion and exam scores.

The colleagues are encouraged to use the tool and the trends on colleague scores are monitored on a monthly basis as well as their performance against targets. A recent refinement was the introduction of the Lobster Ink awards to motivate their colleagues to strive for excellence in performance. There has been considerable increase in CSI score since the launch of the programme in 2013.

The following section describes JET's BE policy: vision, mission, and values.

Our dedication to excellence and continuous improvement is demonstrated through our commitment of resources to innovation and learning. Through our Business Management System, we deliver benefits to our customer, colleagues, business partners, owners and society by listening, building loyalty and developing mutually beneficial relationships.

Vision

To be a world-class luxury international hotel and hospitality management company, we are committed to being the industry leader in all of our activities through dedication to our stakeholders: colleagues, customers, business partners, and owners.

Mission

An iconic hotel and commercial complex where our engaged and efficient colleagues deliver consistent quality and services to our valued customers.

Culture

JET's culture of excellence comprises the following sections, –which have **Our Hallmarks** at their core:

1. I will always smile and greet our guests before they greet me.
2. My first response to a guest request will never be No.
3. I will treat all colleagues with respect and integrity.

Guiding Principles (Core Values)

Integrity – We act with honesty and sincerity in everything we do. We say what we mean, do what we say, and build confidence in our team.

Teamwork – We work towards common goals through open communication, mutual support, and win-win attitudes. We respect our differences and build upon our strengths.

Recognition – We ensure that people's individual needs and successes are supported and recognised.

Innovation – We are open-minded, challenging conventional thinking, improving our processes, and implementing new ideas faster than our competitors.

Continuous growth – We provide an environment where our colleagues and our business can flourish and grow.

People focus – We focus on our colleagues, customers, and business associates and they acknowledge us as preferred partners.

Our Guests

The guests at JET are from local and international markets and coming for both leisure and business purposes. They include those staying in the rooms, dining in our restaurants or bars, and members of our sports and leisure facilities. The key markets are the United States, the United Kingdom, Germany, the GCC, and the new markets India and China.

Our People

Our colleagues make the success of JET possible and ensure the consistency of excellence. Our senior leadership team represents all areas of the hotel and, in collaboration with our company's leadership, is the forum for agreement for our overall policies and strategy.

Our Competitive Market

Comparable luxury corporate hotels within Dubai define our competitive market. We have a primary competitive set of six corporate hotels within the city side of Dubai against whom we benchmark our performance.

Our Community

We are committed to conducting our business in a responsible and transparent manner, balanced economically, socially, and environmentally. Our practices and related policies come together under our company's strategic CSR model. Jumeirah Emirates Towers is proud to have become Jumeirah's first hotel to be certified by Green Globe, and our commitment to our community and CSR practices is attested by the highest Green Globe audit score within the Middle East across all industries.

Our Approaches

Leadership

1. **Vision, mission, hallmarks, and guiding principles** – The objective for this approach is to define and embed a clear core purpose and aspirational vision to align the organisation's people and strategy. Communicated to all colleagues during their induction and through intranet, notice boards, and quarterly communication forums. The reformulation of JET's (Jumeirah Emirates Tower) mission in 2013 followed a structured process which involved all colleagues in the organisation. Hallmarks and guiding principles is a dimension within our appraisal system which all colleagues go through twice each year.
2. **Delegation of authority and empowerment** – To align the focus on efficiency of our mission with a culture of quick and responsive colleagues who make fact-based decisions, we have documented the delegation of authority document, which establishes levels of empowerment for various levels of the organisation. Empowerment grid is implemented to all departments dealing with guests.
3. **Afkar** – To create a channel to collect, review, and prioritise improvement and innovation ideas submitted by colleagues and leaders. We have an online portal accessible to all colleagues for submission of ideas. Submitted ideas reviewed and approved by the executive committee for implementation, which is followed up by deadlines in the departments. Leaders are encouraged to submit ideas during their structured one-to-ones instead.

Strategy

1. **Big Engagement Workshop** – The aim of this workshop is to communicate the review of the strategy to all colleagues in the organisation, enabling them to understand and support the delivery and become ambassadors of the mission and vision. Following the approval of the balanced scorecard (BSC) targets and actions by our CEO in Q1, JET organises a four-hour workshop to communicate the strategy to colleagues. Design and communication are done in a way to suit the communication needs of the audience.
2. **Political, Economic, Social, Technological, Environmental, Legal (PESTEL) Analysis** – To study the external environment and identify risks and opportunities to consolidate the strategy.

   Study developed and reviewed each year during our Progressive Strategy Planning process based on a review of available industry and geopolitical reports. This is used to formulate our yearly Commercial Plan and BSC.
3. **Business Excellence Policy** – Established in 1998, our Business Excellence Policy was created in alignment with our vision and following the European Foundation for Quality Management (EFQM) model. It is communicated through all our stakeholders through posters and our website. The objective for this policy is to define and communicate the organisation's commitment to deliver the mission and the vision.

People

1. **Manpower Planning** – Each year Heads of the Departments (HODs) are involved in their headcount budget and recommend headcount required based on the operation needs. This is reviewed by HR, Finance, GM, and Corporate Office based on the property strategy and financial objectives.
2. **Organisational Structure** – The HRD together with HODs and Finance monitor the movements within the organisation in terms of manning. This is done through regular updates of the organisational

charts as well as comparisons of positions in other properties so as to better understand what positions are no longer required (redundancy). These unplanned changes require departments to rapidly adapt to new organisational structures and the continuing efforts to deliver results.

3. **Colleague Needs** – The objective of this approach is to assess and refine processes within the business through the use of different surveys and forums. We have various mechanisms that are being used to collect colleague feedback. Results of annual Colleague Opinion Survey (COS) are systematically analysed and shared with colleagues and HODs, who implement action plans which are part of their BSCs. The Careline is in place so as to address any grievances. Exit Interviews Focus groups are also used to gather feedback.
4. **Place to Start and Place to Grow** – The aim of this approach is to manage the recruitment and selection of colleagues in all grades through defined and set procedures. JET utilises an applicant-tracking system called Sniper Hire which compiles applications from various sources such as our career site Jumeirah.com or Global Caterer. We also utilise our internal database to identify potentials within our existing colleagues through talent reviews and our HiPo programme.
5. **Colleague Consultative Committee (CCC)** – This practice involves colleagues in the formulation of strategic goals and actions. The CCC is formed by the colleagues in each department voting for their representative. Meetings are held every quarter and it is minuted. CCC is further complemented by 'Talk of the Towers' when we invite a guest speaker to talk to colleagues about their welfare issues in medical, payroll, and accommodation.
6. **Job Profiles and Jumeirah Competencies** – This approach is to set tasks for each position to ensure department goals are achieved and performance measured on competencies. Job profiles are used in the recruitment process so as to define the performance levels required for each position within the business. All job profiles are updated prior to posting a new position. Jumeirah has a defined competency framework for leaders and colleagues which is used during the recruitment process, appraisal process, and performance management process.

7. **Appraisal Process and Performance Management** – The objective for this approach is to have a continuous process of assessing and documenting progress and providing ongoing and constructive feedback to ensure that all colleagues are meeting their career goals and objectives. Our colleagues undergo appraisal training and managers also undertake training to acquire skills to conduct appraisals. Managers are then audited on the quality of appraisals conducted by them and areas for improvement (AFIs) are addressed. There are different cycles for colleagues on probation (every two months) and colleagues who have passed probation (every 6 months).
8. **Learning Needs Analysis (LNA)** – Yearly LNA is conducted to identify the needs that serve as an input to the annual learning and development (L&D) budget. Feedback collected from COS, interview, and Focus Groups is compiled in the LNA report. A training plan is then produced for the following year and recommendations are knitted into the training budget.
9. **Learning and Development Activities** – This approach is to have a set of qualified team trainers who will provide necessary and consistent training to all colleagues. The L&D activities are divided into sections, Jumeirah Way, Supervisory Development, Managerial Development, Health & Safety, and Leadership Development. These modules are delivered to the colleagues across JET by the L&D team and complemented by departmental training through qualified trainers. In addition, the cross-training tool is used to develop colleagues to fulfil various roles within the organisation.
10. **HiPo Project/Leadership Pathway** – In 2013, JET introduced a programme known as High Potential (HiPo), which focused on the talent review of all JET colleagues through their performance (appraisal scores) and their potential. The leadership pathway includes five training modules that were offered first to the HiPo colleagues and then introduced to all the colleagues in the business.
11. **Training and Development of Colleagues** – The objective for this approach to provide the business with quality and skilled training for colleagues at all levels. External training is also provided to colleagues as a part of career development after verifying the requirement for the course and the benefit for the business.

12. **Key Performance Indicators, Business Objectives, and Bonus process** – This approach is to ensure that colleagues are accountable for the business results and are aware of the impact they have on their quarterly bonus and KPI figures. Bonus KPI targets are set quarterly in alignment with the departmental BSCs and following an approach of continuous improvement. Each quarter HODs and colleague representatives present their proposed targets, which are assessed and approved by the Colleague KPI Bonus Committee.
13. **Interdepartmental Activities** – Every quarter, various engagement activities such as internal departmental competitions are carried out so as to encourage departments to showcase their creativity and innovation. These competitions are linked to the HR BSC projects and focus on ensuring departments across the business are involved and empowered.
14. **Product Knowledge/Shift Brief** – This approach is for communicating and enhancing product knowledge and awareness across the business. The Flash Report is sent daily outlining the hotel's daily info as well as a shift brief article to assist departments in carrying out the briefings. Product knowledge quizzes are run by L&D each month to assess awareness and motivate colleagues to improve knowledge on our offerings and internal policies.
15. **Corporate Social Responsibility** – The objective for this approach is to create awareness and encourage practices to support CSR. CSR activities include annual blood donation drives, cardiology health camp, donations to the Philippine's Aid, Dubai Centre for Special needs, Dubai Foundation for Women and Children in Al Awir, The Angel Appeal.
16. **Communication Tools** – To keep all colleagues informed about relevant information on a timely basis through different communication channels so as to reach a wider audience. Communication needs are identified through colleague feedback. Some of our various means of communications to reach our colleagues are Shift Briefs, Tamieez, Town hall, Talk of the Towers, CCC, Ex-Comm Meetings, Big Engagement Workshops, Notice Boards, and Departmental Communication Meetings.

17. **Departmental Communication Meetings** – This approach is to keep all colleagues informed about relevant information pertaining to their departmental performance and updates. Each department conducts periodic communication meetings to cascade information, new developments, and strategy, and to celebrate success. These meetings are documented through minutes of the meeting, which are then uploaded into their respective team sites on Mercury.
18. **Multi-departmental Committees** – Discussing and contributing ideas and solutions to real business issues such as new policies, working practices, or any matters promoting the general interests of colleagues.

    There are several forums for which our colleagues can work in collaboration. Departmental representatives meet systematically to share best practices in an effort to enhance the effectiveness of the areas their committee represents.
19. **Big Engagement Workshop** – To keep colleagues informed about our top four priorities/goals for the year.

    At the beginning of each year, JET hosts the Big Engagement Workshop to communicate to colleagues (C2 and above) about the set goals and priorities for that particular year. We also have a Top 4 wall near the colleague cafeteria which outlines the set targets and is regularly updated so that all colleagues are aware.
20. **Jumeirah Pay and Benefits** – To define remuneration packages aligned with the development of the capabilities of the organisation. The headcount budget and salary band are accessible to all HODs. Our remuneration team conducts annual salary surveys and schedule reviews based on the performance of the business and the market rate. Jumeirah has a grading system with specific salary bands and benefit packages.
21. **Tamieez** – To recognise and motivate colleagues using recognition schemes

    Each quarter, an engagement activity known as Tamieez occurs and mainly focuses on rewarding and recognising colleagues who have excelled during the quarter. These awards occur systematically and periodically through the guidance of our recognition menu, which entails eligibility criteria as well as the prizes for all the awards available at JET.

22. **Engagement Activities** – To recognise and motivate colleagues using recognition schemes

    JET implemented several engagement activities aiming to raise health awareness and make JET a fun environment for colleagues: diabetes check, eye check-up, cardiology check, blood donation drives, movie night, management dance, anniversary celebration, annual party, and so on. All the engagement activities are directly linked to HR's KPI and BSCs.
23. **Diversity at JET** – To implement culturally connected engagement activities so as to embrace the diversity of our colleagues.

    Various activities are deployed as part of the HR BSC Actions on Colleague Engagement to promote diversity. HR organises celebrations of national days, museum and city tours, articles on chit chat, and so on.
24. **Thoughtful and Generous Events** – To understand the needs of colleagues and implement schemes to make the colleagues feel special and valued.

Partnership and Resources

1. **Strategic Supplier Selection and Evaluation** – To create a supply chain and logistics (SC&L) management structure to qualify and evaluate suppliers' performance, the company's SC&L segments JET suppliers into set categories according to the nature of the resources provided. Each segment is managed by a specific division within SC&L and there are established standards for acceptance and performance measurement of our suppliers.
2. **Yearly Budget Planning Process and Five-year Operation Plan** – To show sustainable economic growth year on year (YoY) in accordance with corporate objectives, our budget process is done yearly using a bottom-up draft, with budget guidelines. The plan is presented to relevant stakeholders and if targets are revised, a top-down approach is deployed to merge the gap.
3. **Health and Safety Executive (HSE) Department and Initiatives** – To promote a safe environment for our colleagues, customers, and business partners, our HSE Department oversees the quality of health

and safety standards in the property. This is done through periodic audits and a team of interdepartmental champions who train and inspect their areas periodically.

4. **BMS Management and Optimisation** – To ensure all assets are maintained and optimised for energy efficiency.
   JET utilises world-class Building Management System (BMSs), Johnson Controls, Messerschmitt RMS, and mechanical, electrical, and plumbing (MEP) system to control and monitor efficient use of water, electricity, and other utility supplies in order to optimise the use of resources.

Processes, Products, and Services

1. **Process Framework** – To establish a framework of core process, ownership, and measurements which supports the delivery of the organisation's strategy.
   Designed based on world-class models, it identifies the company's core processes, ownership, and expected outcomes. Provides a base for the departmental SOPs and JET products and service standards. Process ownership is identified at JET, which uses its IMPROVE tool to facilitate process improvement initiatives.
2. **Stay Different Brand Promise** – To create, communicate, and deliver a robust and attractive brand promise to support the realisation of the organisation's vision.
   Created based on a comprehensive study to align Jumeirah's value proposition with the brand image which involves input from the company's president and senior leadership. All colleagues receive a one-day training called Be the Difference and the dimensions are embedded in various other approaches.
3. **Lobster Ink** – Create training programmes for core customer processes to ensure all colleagues have the necessary resources to deliver the company's mission.
   The Lobster Ink training videos were tailor-made to suit the needs and brand promise of the Jumeirah group. The videos focus on core customer processes: manage arrivals, deliver personalised service, and

manage departures. All front-line colleagues have student IDs and have targets for training completion and exam scores.

4. **Medallia and Guest Feedback System** – Monitor customer feedback and ensure they are appropriately responded to.

   All guest feedback received is logged into the guest feedback system. Feedback is assigned for corrective action and response to relevant department heads and closure monitored on a daily basis. Top recurring comments are analysed at the end of each month and through sentiment analysis in the Medallia portal.
5. **Customer Results Meeting** – Review customer experiences through various performance indicators to understand trends and establish improvement actions.

Once a month, the hotel manager leads a review and discussion on the various customer perceptions and performance indicators to identify areas for improvement and lessons learned.

Overall, the excellence award-winning organisations demonstrated a number of practices relating to human capital. From another perspective, research on winning organisations of a human capital awards, for example, also demonstrated a number of strategies, which are illustrated in the following section.

Best Practice Examples from Dubai Human Development Award

Illustration 1 This illustration is about a bank based in the UAE. The bank holds a strong and loyal customer base of more than 250,000 with a strong profitable revenue. Their corporate value and organisational culture is the main area of differentiation from other banks and it ardently follows a belief that people, whether customers, stakeholders, or employees, are as important for the organisation as profit. Their values are possessed and promoted by the company associates, resulting in more employee engagement, feeling of passion, and togetherness. This belief is visible in their achievement of holding the best and lowest employee turnover rate as against the industry competitors and having an average employee service life of exceptionally 6.63 years. Their culture and best practices for empowering human resource are well evident as they hold a glorified title of Dubai Human Development Award for the year 2017.

Best Practices

The bank considers its value system as its differentiating factor. They guide their operations to achieve their organisational vision and mission under their '*Value-Driven Culture*'. In order to identify their core belief and make it the focal point of all business activities, in 2014, the bank's CEO and management announced a project and allotted it to the Business Excellence Team, which reflected the true culture of the organisation and would promote the behaviours necessary from all the stakeholders in order to excel. The project was determined to achieve a few key organisational objectives such as its significant impact on the achievement of the bank's vision and mission, enhancing employee engagement and overall satisfaction, improving the health of the workplace atmosphere to ensure employee satisfaction, increasing the average employee service span, and reducing employee grievances, which in turn would reduce employee turnover rate and enhance active employee participation in CSR initiatives making them more fruitful. The project plan aimed at ensuring interdisciplinary involvement focusing on articulating the organisational values with the behavioural indicators and assimilating the values of the human resource operations, such as recruitment, training, rewards, recognition, and CSR activities. The inputs captured during this session are assessed and reviewed to identify key themes of the bank and its culture. The bank designed an approach called *Integration with Recruitment*, which ensured that the bank drew attention and recruited the new joiners with the desired behavioural traits. This approach also ensured that the values were well integrated with the competency and skill-based interviewing process. The newly formulated values were also integrated with performance appraisal and rewards and recognition processes. The appraisal system was upgraded to include all the behavioural traits of the new core values. The bank associates were evaluated on the basis of their allegiance to the values. Rewards and recognitions were decided on the basis of the scores earned, and the extent of incorporation of the new values into this process. The bank was able to achieve all the outcomes that they anticipated and proposed at the start of the project. The rate of employee satisfaction with the organisation's career development activities increased from 41.12 in 2014 to 46.74 in 2016. The company observed the average service span to have increased to 6.63 years as against the target of 3 years. The employee satisfaction for their workspace environment saw an increment from 51 in 2014 to 54 in 2016, which was way above their benchmarked level, and the overall employee satisfaction improved from 54.18 in 2014 to 56.31 in 2016. The grievance rate observed the best outcome, reducing from 3 in 2014 to 0 in 2016. The overall impact of the initiative is evident from their employee turnover rate, which reduced from 11 in 2014 to 8.19 in 2016. In terms of CSR and the bank's commitment to CSR initiatives, the results observed saw improvement in the CSR initiative index by 2.8% in 2016 as against the rate in 2012, and employee participation in the organisation's CSR activities increased by 49% against the percentage in the baseline year 2014.

Illustration 2 This second example is about a conglomerate organisation established in 1998 in Dubai, UAE. This university operated by the group currently comprises students from over 75 nationalities and faculty from more than 22 countries. This well-dominated and acknowledged group of the region owes its success and strength to more than 3000 employees working in the group. The group guides all its operations with the values of excellence, trust, knowledge, innovation, and integrity, and considers service excellence as the factor for differentiation against all its industry competitors. They manage their services against internal and external challenges by their best practice of process mapping, also known as the Seismic Trigger Approach, adopted by the group in 2013, as a segment of its business improvement system that allows them to structure their project management and process improvement plans. This approach has been used by the organisation for many years and has led to exceptional improvements in most of the business operations. The organisation's aim in pursuing the process-mapping approach is to achieve many organisational objectives such as effective measurement and comparison of processes and organisational objects, alignment of the processes with organisational core values and capabilities, a better understanding of process interactions, and analysis of the process capacity to identify areas for improvement. This Trigger approach was a continuous process and was later extended to include the Clinical Review Process. Under this approach, quality management principles like Six Sigma and Lean Sigma were applied in refining the laboratory process, which resulted in many significant outcomes, one of which was a contraction of turn-around time (TAT). Within this approach, the group also utilised the value stream mapping tool to streamline and integrate the Incident Management System of the health-care organisations with the employee portals for offering easy access to the employees in all the health-care organisations. This online Incident Management System of the group focused on all the established Kaizen Bursts like ensuring on-time review of incidents with hardly any delays and capturing critical incidents in real time, communicating the Corrective Actions and Preventive Actions (CAPA) to all the departments simultaneously, effective data analysis to study the errors and their patterns, tracing the CAPA activities and intensification of unresolved actions. This system used by the group also proved to be a great cost-effective approach and provided feedback to the individual reporting the incident as an example to encourage others to consider it as a non-punitive reporting system. The group maintained a periodic assessment of process improvement activities and reviewed the hospital indicators data periodically in Hospital Administrative Committees. This allowed the organisation an opportunity to identify various areas for improvements. The group also conducted an annual review of selected hospital indicators where the continually low-performing indicators were identified as an area of concern and further improvements were directed to those indicators. The effectiveness of the indicators was ensured by regular monitoring by the group. Such evaluation and refinement processes led to an extension of their Lean Umbrella approach, which concentrated its effort in adding lean to all day-to-day health-care processes for which the staff was trained to attain required skills. Also, they developed a new tool for their staff called *My Lean Umbrella* to promote and sustain the culture of continuous improvement through lean principles.

Their approach to continuous process improvement through this easily accessible incident management system brought employees to contribute their efforts in this process. This non-punitive reporting system was deployed in February 2015 and encouraged the staff to report the errors without any fear of judgement. This resulted in an increase in incident reporting by the staff, which eventually led to a decrease in incident errors from 103 in 2015 to 89 in 2016. The total level of complaints registered with the organisation also reduced from 23 in 2015 to 6 in 2016. Clearly, their effort to map processes and improve them accordingly by the involvement of staff reporting led the group to optimise their performance.

Illustration 3 This case is about an organisation that operates several businesses and possesses 77 marine and inland terminals. They have been ceaselessly attaining unbeaten financial and non-financial outcomes in recent years, meeting and surpassing their industry benchmarks and different benchmarks of the generally comparative industry. Founded in 2005 and headquartered in Dubai, the organisation is a fundamental associate of worldwide supply chain activities exercising their activities crosswise over 31 nations and 6 mainland countries, providing access to more than two billion customers. The organisation's best factor is its Leadership *Development Program*, which was established to design processes to identify and develop a pool of talented employees in order to develop their leadership competencies for future placement into significant leadership roles. Through this initiative the organisation aimed to develop leaders and managers in a range of aspects such as developing better and in-depth knowledge about the business and its context, embellishing their people management and customer service skills, and broadening their business perspective and making it more holistic for them to perceive and allowing them to develop their extensive business networks. Aiming to develop participants for 'strategic roles', the advanced module developed by the organisation included the use of business simulation in the training, filed visits to Fortune 500 companies, mentoring from the members of Fortune 500 companies, an allocation of an executive coach for the participants, and a visit to Silicon Valley to learn about the culture of innovation in different organisations of Silicon Valley. The initiative also benefitted the organisation in terms of teamwork and networking amongst the departments that helped in participative problem-solving.

Illustration 4 This illustration is also about a bank, founded in 1969 in Dubai, UAE, offering a broad spectrum of products and services like retail and commercial banking. It offers three significant groups of services like corporate banking, consumer banking, and Islamic banking. The bank operates on its four significant values that include clients, consistent quality, teamwork, and enhancing capability through learning and innovation. Its best practices under these guiding core values are well recognised and have made them a winning organisation for the Dubai Human Development Award, for the 2013 cycle. The bank is also very strongly committed to various social initiatives and hosts various sports and athletic events for different schools and students, encouraging a spirit of healthy competition and togetherness amongst the youth of the region.

Best Practices

The bank's best practice emphasises continuous monitoring and measurement of performance to identify gaps. They pursued two best practices that focused on developing competencies of employees, specifically in terms of leadership skill. Their first best practice was planned with an aim to identify and rank the top employees in seven leadership skills. This assessment was composed of a series of interviews, case studies, and behavioural aspects in the performance during the assessment. An external assessment agency called AON Hewitt was involved in conducting the assessment and identifying, on the basis of predefined criteria, the right people, age, role, performance, and grade, and matching the leadership skill to their job roles. After the assessment, 65 managers attended the assessment and then developed an online profile testing called HOGAN, which highlighted particular reports that provided a baseline of leadership skills that are in line with the bank's strategic objective, following which an Individual Development Program is completed by the talent manager. The approach was developed to identify future leaders and potential talents through this continuous assessment activity. The assessment allowed the organisations to effectively perform career and succession planning that involved training and developing the skills of senior managers such that they could acquire the competencies to lead as well as to develop any aspiring talent. The managers were encouraged to participate in the initiative for their professional growth too. The assessment assisted the bank to identify the employees' personal need to develop their skills and to grow. The second-best practice was developed in aiming to create a culture of corporate coaching. The top managers were selected based on the previous assessment process on the basis of performance, skills, ability, and commitment. These two best practices were executed together and were incorporated into other training interventions. This corporate coaching culture was also linked to the organisation's five-year strategy, which focused on continuous growth and individual personal development needs. The Talent Manager along with the HR Director worked on these approaches to continuously develop the culture. These best practices of the organisation affirmed the continuous development of the employees and its potential future leaders.

Illustration 5 This fifth example is about a prominent UAE-based organisation founded in 1980 and headquartered in Abu Dhabi, primarily offering remittance services. It is a well-known brand offering worldwide remittance, foreign exchange, and a payment solution. The organisation has a significant reach to more than 28 nations with about 800 direct workplaces. They are a customer-oriented organisation driven by their empowered employees and practice great values to encourage their employees each day to take pride in their contribution to the organisation. Their constant HR-friendly best practices have made them a glorified winner of the Dubai Human Development Award for the year 2014.

Best Practice

Derived from the vision and mission of the organisation, this approach of Employee Volunteering Programme (EVP) was developed to inspire and encourage employees to act as volunteers under the endorsement and guidance of the organisation. This approach was undertaken by the organisation to become the best employer amongst its competitors. This programme was supported by various driving elements like the organisation's engagement culture, which encouraged all the employees to participate and be involved in community activities, evaluation of employees' efforts, implementation of fact-based improvements, and use of multiple communication channels like emails, announcements, events, social media, and internal fairs to create awareness of CSR activities and the importance of their contribution amongst the employees. Establishment of the Employee Volunteering Programme (EVP) required the organisation to clearly define the objective of EV, time commitment it needed, as well as an assurance that the organisation's as well as the employees' needs and inspiration for being a part of this programme are met. The organisation provided a clear written description of the programme as well as an opportunity to the volunteers to monitor how their efforts are benefiting the whole organisation. They also developed an EV charter that was composed of a statement of purpose defining the organisation's commitment to the EVP, volunteer expenses protocol, and the expectations from the whole programme. The organisation developed four types of EV, the first type being 'Employee Fund Raising', in which the employees could raise funds with the support of the organisation for various activities like disaster relief, supporting community groups before, during, or after natural calamities and emergencies. The second type was 'Mentoring', which focused on offering guidance and assistance to individuals, for example, providing training and knowledge about the financial sector for UAE nationals. The third type of EV developed by the organisation was 'Skills-Based Volunteering', which involved utilising employee skills to benefit the community by playing the role of an expert sharing knowledge for free. In line with this type, the organisation developed an awareness campaign for the public on Anti-Money Laundering (AML) compliance where employees got in touch with nearly 2500 customers to provide them training and information. The fourth type of EV planned was a Team Project, which involved team challenges and projects for the staff encouraging interactions and togetherness. The success and effectiveness of the EV was measured through various parameters such as Social Charter Framework, CBA, and employee and opinion surveys, and the outcomes of the programme were evaluated on the basis of perception scores, investment against the time spent, percentage increase in number of active volunteers, and number of new collaborations with government and non-government agencies.

In order to motivate people to actively participate, the organisation conducted internal recognition where employee achievements were also communicated through emails or Country Head's monthly messenger.

This initiative resulted in various kinds of benefits both for the organisation and for the employees. All through this programme, the employees learned various work-related skills such as project skills, budgeting, effective communications planning, presentation, and project management skills. They also developed their leadership competencies by learning skills such as the ability to influence, relationship-building, critical thinking, and teamwork. The result of the programme also led to many initiatives undertaken by the employees, one of which was the 'Blood Donation Drive' in which a total of 8550 employees participated, generating a blood donation of 1302 units. They also hosted an initiative called 'Helping Hand', which aimed at helping expats in different ways such as food and water distribution or booking flight tickets for ailing expats. One of their key initiatives which started as a result of this programme was 'Mission Zero Suicide', which was a six-month-long initiative to address the rising issue of expat suicides in the UAE, aiming to develop awareness about how people can deal with financial troubles in their tough times.

Another best practice by the organisation aimed at engaging customers in service delivery as well as creating a happy service delivery experience for all its customers. The organisation established their Customer Loyalty Month (CLM) for the month of June, which is an entire month focused on creating happy interactions with all its customers and celebrating their loyalty to the brand. Several special discounts, promotions, and big wins are created to give the customers an opportunity to engage and win amazing prizes that act as a stimulus to create loyalty. The strategic objective of the approach was to create customer experience and develop strong customer relationship. The approach required greater employee engagement as they were the main facilitators of this approach. The goal and the activity framework for the month were clearly communicated by the top management to each business unit. This framework developed by the top management categorised the activities into various segments: (a) customer service delivery standards, (b) people including both employees and customers, (c) premises, and (d) processes. The approach required innovations in customer engagement which were instilled through these activities. The business unit further captured various attributes for each category like name, people involved, time, duration, expected outcome, metrics to measure the effectiveness of the activities in terms of customer satisfaction, relationship management, and so on. Some of their activities conducted by the organisation in their Customer Loyalty month for the year 2014 included 'Serve with Sweet', 'Be a Customer Choice', and 'Serve with Fun'. The organisation used various marketing platforms like print media, digital and social media, and they also awarded their long-associated loyal customers to strengthen their relationship and to further act as a word-of-mouth marketing for the organisation. Later they also introduced the new channels to engage customers like Facebook and social media competition.

The approach produced some significant results with respect to customer engagement and involvement, such as the fact that the number of customers engaged in the CLM increased from 15,000 in 2013 to 200,000 in 2014. The organisation also recognised a greater number of customers as compared to previous years. The organisation also saw greater customer appreciation, as when this approach was implemented in 2014, the number of customer appreciation increased by 85%. The organisation's constant efforts also made them a winner for various glorified awards like People's Choice Award and Dubai Human Development Award amongst others.

Illustration 6 Founded as the Public Joint Stock Company in the year 1982, this illustration is about a pioneering domestic bank of the UAE. It offers a chain of products and banking and financial services to individual, corporate, and small and medium-sized enterprise (SME) customers with eight subsidiaries all across the Middle East and Asia. It offers a work space to diverse nationalities, cultures, and backgrounds and operates in such a way that they empower their staff members to show acceptable levels of professionalism and behavioural competencies in all their dealings in order to create satisfactory and happy customer interactions for the organisation. Based on their belief of empowering employees they expanded their human development strategy to need-based professional accreditation of the staff members at different functional levels. The bank ensures the implementation of their people strategy across the organisation, different business lines, as well as business partners. Their belief and best practices of taking care of their employees so that they take care of their current and potential customers were awarded in the year 2014 with the prestigious Dubai Human Development Award.

In order to create more positive and satisfactory customer experience, the organisation decided to accredit their different business customer interactive functions within Retail Banking, Corporate Banking, and Credit Management. This approach was planned to aim at closing the gap in credit skills of the staff members, structuring the high-quality profitable loans, and augmenting the selling skills of the employees while ensuring the delivery of customer value. The accreditation approach followed two separate roadmap and accreditation functions for the retail and corporate/credit management categories. The successful implementation of the accreditation approach required informed communication and decision amongst all the stakeholders and a complete agreement and commitment from the top management. Deliberate attempts were made to ensure that the targeted group had all the necessary backing, guidance, and encouragement from their line managers and business heads, as well as from the internal and external training faculty. To ensure that the staff considered this effort seriously, the cut-off percentage for qualifying for the certification was kept as 85% for the retail banking group (RBG) and 80% for the corporate banking group (CBG)/credit management group (CMG).

For the RBG the accreditation covered learnings that included history and achievement of the bank, banking sector in the UAE, commercial and civil legislation, retail services and offerings, new operations manual, competencies for successful selling, and people management skill (which was specifically meant for Branch Managers and Customer Service Managers). For the retail accreditation approximately 400 banking staff from all the branches were brought together for the in-house training, which included Branch Managers, Branch Operations Managers and Officers, Customer Service Managers, Customer Service Officers, Tellers, and Customer Service Representatives across all the seven Emirates. To design the training sessions the training department of the bank worked closely with the Heads of Retail Banking Group and the Branch Banking Division. The syllabus for the course and its content were selected on the basis of type of roles that are considered in the certification programme in the banking division and was recommended by the training department and examined by the Heads of Retail Banking and Branch Banking. The six area managers for retail banking were also training in this accreditation course. These area managers in turn provided knowledge and information about the product and service offerings and new operational manual to other targeted staff members by conducting focus groups and offering individual guidance. The in-house trainers ensured the efficient and consistent implementation of this approach across the retail branches. The training was conducted in the form of e-learning portals, self-study, focus group, and in-house activities, after which the trainees were put to the test through assessments constituting a series of multiple-choice questions that tested their understanding of various concepts covered in the training sessions. The objectivity and neutrality of the assessment were ensured by conducting the assessment on the same day for all the retail branches. By the end of the training, the organisation observed that overall 133 banking branch staff were being accredited on achieving the required cut-off marks.

Simultaneously, for the accreditation in the CBG/CMG, 20 managers were selected to form a pilot batch for the training. For conducting the training of the CBG/CMG, the bank collaborated with an external accreditation agency called M/s Omega, which was further certified as accreditation provider from the Chartered Institute of Bankers, Scotland. The external agency implemented the approach in two different phases, one of which was the Credit Skills Assessment (CSA) phase. In this phase they applied CSA, which acted as a diagnostic instrument to evaluate the current training needs of the employees and aimed at developing and validating the understanding of the employees about commercial lending, opportunity assessment, screening of applicants, loan management, and business and cash flow analysis. This articulation of the skill development module with the required objective ensured employees learn in-depth about their respective field of work. This phase allowed the participants to undergo this assessment in order to identify competency gaps. The second phase in the deployment of the training was the Credit Skill Development (CSD) phase, which was aimed at the employees who were involved in writing and evaluating credit proposals like relationship handlers and credit teams. The selected participants for this phase were equipped with the study material in the form of hard copies along with online access to the resources. The classroom training conducted was for a span of four days and covered the 15-course module proposed by Omega, following which an in-house facilitation was conducted, after which the employees were subjected to online final assessment under CSD. This programme conducted by the bank saw a successful outcome when 20 selected participants successfully completed their course and were awarded with the Advanced Diploma in Credit and Lending from the Chartered Institute of Bankers. Additionally, 43 Relationship Managers and Credit Managers were certified in successive batches. All the staff that successfully cleared the accreditation in both the RBG and the CBG/CMG were awarded by the organisation's CEO in the recognition ceremony. The effectiveness of this HR development training was reviewed after the completion of each phase, and many improvement plans were put in place to enhance employee participation in the programme. These improvement plans targeted concerns like work pressure and balance between training and job, as well as those employees who couldn't clear the assessment.

These best practices adopted by the bank with periodic evaluation and reviews assisted and benefitted the organisation to successfully achieve all their planned results across different functional levels. This approach enabled the employees to grow professionally and personally in their life and career and helped them to progress in their profession through various promotions and financial increments. This programme also resulted in enhancing employee product and service knowledge, their competencies and skills, and increased involvement in the branch operations, which in turn positively impacted the customer satisfaction level as observed through the Customer Satisfaction Survey, which furthermore resulted in enhanced business results.

Illustration 7 This last illustration is about the Middle East's largest chain of pre-school organisations and is the first to be an ISO-certified nursery chain. Launched in 2007, it functions all across the UAE with 15 accessible and convenient locales in Dubai, Sharjah, and Abu Dhabi. They follow a range of best practices in terms of recruitment, HR policy, transparency in performance evaluation of the staff, improvement through innovation, and creating a shared value culture. The organisation develops its annual business plan according to which the principal or manager formulates the annual manpower requirements encompassing all the details about the vacancies such as number and types of vacancies for each department in the organisation. The HR policies and procedures are well documented in the HR Manual, which helped in effective implementation of the people strategy across the organisation. The organisation and its leaders ardently believe that effective and constant communication with their staff and their stakeholders about the company policies and strategies is vital for them to achieve their vision and further develop organisational capability.

Therefore, to ensure that all the employees were aware of the policies and any changes, the Top Management Team communicated all the relevant details and procedures to all its staff members. To ensure the transparency of the performance evaluation and appraisal system the new hires underwent orientation where they were informed about the KPIs so that they were aware of all the expected targets and goals of their function, the procedure of performance assessment, as well as the organisation's expectation from their staff, before they begin with their contract with the organisation. The KPIs were also cascaded down to all functional levels and were deliberated through different communication channels ensuring clarity of HR and operational policies amongst all the staff members. The organisation's Senior Management Team was made responsible for identifying and defining key performance metrics on various business aspects such as Financial, People, Customer, Society, and Learning & Development. These KPIs also measured the company's and its relevant stakeholders' performance by utilising the BSC.

The organisation also translated their belief of creating shared value and vision amongst the staff members by aligning their company objectives with the individual employee by deploying the BSC within the organisation as well as through encouraging teamwork amongst the employees through various projects. This allowed the organisation to motivate employees to be proactive in their work and feel empowered to make their decisions. Annual reviews and refinement of budget, employee manuals, job role description, appraisal, and training were conducted by the organisation to ensure the employees are well supported and guided in delivering their responsibilities. These reviews and improvement conducted to ensure effectiveness of all the HR development and management approaches are supported by encouraging staff to provide their suggestions and improvement ideas on the ongoing activities. These suggestions were captured by the organisations through their upgraded staff survey forms, which included questions and suggestions to target service improvements. The organisation also implemented their suggestion box scheme and encouraged employees to participate by providing incentives for the most innovative and creative ideas. They also encouraged feedback from both the stakeholders and employees through their 360° mechanism to evaluate their activities. Owing to all these employee engagement activities in service improvement the organisation was able to improvise their HR policy and Customer and Employee Well-Being Policy. In order to ensure that the organisation's CSR policies are well communicated across the organisation, the organisation hosted communication sessions, training modules, displayed CSR polices on internal portal, and engaged their staff in all the CSR initiatives where they were empowered to put across their suggestions in formal as well as informal ways. To develop their organisational capability and quality improvement through innovation, the pre-school involved all their stakeholders in suggesting their innovative ideas to integrate in their system. They have developed a strong quality management system and a specialised Research and Development team that focused on prioritising and integrating innovation and improvement in their operations. This allowed them to improve their business process framework through comprehensive planning and assessment that resulted in increased outcomes for the students.

One of the significant outcomes from the organisation's best practices pertaining to innovation and improvement has resulted in 70%+ continual improvement in child development activities. Being an all-woman workforce organisation dealing with such sensitive activities, and adopting best practices such that they emerged as the winner of the Dubai Human Development Award in 2014, makes them an example for other organisations to look up to.

Conclusion

The five main cases illustrated in this chapter provide evidence of the important role of human capital. Engaged employees are not only an asset to their organisation but are also important stakeholders in creating a culture of high performance and excellence. Quality assurance is a responsibility of every employee within an organisation; hence it is important to develop its workforce to embrace quality. In doing so, the global excellence frameworks have a dedicated enabler or a criterion which the organisation must put into practice to achieve superior business results. Of the various strategies that will leverage this, most are actions aimed at successful employee management. Employee satisfaction rates are an important element in understanding an organisation's climate in terms of its employees, and these indicators must also be used to develop the strategies that will spur a spirit of continuous improvement. They should be used to seek feedback from its employees. Measuring the culture is another example discussed within the Abela case, which portrayed how it can help an organisation readjust itself to quality and excellence. Various quality tools and techniques are also essential for excellence initiatives to be successful. The road to excellence, however, can be drawn from the best practices to understand the current position of the organisation.

In summary, we conclude that essentially human capital is an essential ingredient in high-performing organisations. There is a strong association between human capital and excellence. Employee capability development should be a priority for high-performing organisations and it must be aligned with the organisation's key priorities. Motivated and happy employees are needed to create a culture of superior quality. Leaders play a key role is leveraging an organisation's human capital to its utmost potential. Leaders must therefore not only manage but also lead the people in the organisation for sustained performance. Organisations should ensure the embeddedness of performance indicators such as culture and satisfaction indexes.

8

Sustaining Business Excellence

In this chapter we reiterate the importance of sustainable business excellence (BE) for organisations globally. We do this through the lens of business models, customer happiness, total quality talent management, and innovative and creative initiatives. A business model is not only part of an organisation's strategic plan, but also its blueprint for creating and capturing value through a set of interlocking activities. We argue here that within these business models, organisations need to create a culture and space for BE. Our next lens in this chapter is the importance of customer happiness in businesses' attempts to excel and maintain a sustainable competitive advantage. We identify and envisage that when it comes to customer happiness, the focus has to be on four key areas, profitability, sustainability, reputation, and governance. Further, to be successful in implementing total quality management, organisations need talented human capital and hence organisations' focus on 'talent' becomes paramount. Our last lens is that of innovation and creativity, concepts which complement the other topics discussed earlier. Thus, creativity, the ability to conceive something original, alongside innovation, the implementation of novel initiatives, becomes crucial for organisations when it comes to them being sustainably competitive.

F. Lasrado, V. Pereira, *Achieving Sustainable Business Excellence*,
https://doi.org/10.1007/978-3-319-73314-2_8

Introduction

It is true that, even for excellent, high-performing organisations, the 'excellence' quest is an ongoing journey. Sustaining results in an extremely globalised market is not easy. As an organisation encounters growth, it faces a myriad of challenges in every sphere of its business activity. Thus, the looming challenges in an organisation today are of understanding its customer base and their ever-changing requirements so that products and services are customised, thus helping marketing efforts. Another challenge is ensuring the continuous flow of new ideas and fostering creativity so that new products and innovation are leveraged. At the same time, as a firm's employee base becomes increasingly diverse, it becomes more difficult to find ways to engage and retain staff, ensure superior productivity, and create a reputation or culture of excellence. Therefore, in order to sustain excellence, it is important to 'walk the walk' by considering emerging business environments and business models. Key enablers, such as leadership strategy, and customer and people focus are vital and centric to excellence, wherein organisations have to constantly find new ways to embrace them. An understanding of emerging new business models, knowledge of how to convert customer satisfaction into customer happiness that goes beyond loyalty, total quality talent management, and mechanisms to sustain the creative ideas to foster innovation is the way forward. In this chapter we explore these aspects that shape and portray a roadmap for sustained BE.

Towards New Business Models

The extant literature mainly defines a business model as *a firm's blueprint for creating and capturing value through a set of interlocking activities* (e.g. Malik et al. 2017). Business models provide firms with clear direction for managers to understand how a business generates and captures surplus through a range of activities. Thus, when firms embark on a BE strategy, prescribing a business model will be helpful and invaluable. Malik et al. (2017) argue that the role of human capital, through its human resources (HR), can support a firm in achieving greater BE through two dominant business models. First, through the 'Repetitive Efficiencies Model', wherein a model is developed that creates value for repetitive work often associated with efficient delivery and, second, through the 'Service Experience Model', which tends to focus on creating value for various services. In this book we investigate how human capital supports the processes of both value creation and value capture in the context of achieving BE. Thus, when it comes to a firm's business model incorporating BE, the role of human capital in *value creation* means providing sustainable processes, practices, and strategies that lead a firm to greater BE. Further, the role of human capital, by focusing on *value capture*, would mean undertaking actions that increase a firm's profit through achieving greater BE. But the role of human capital should go beyond creation and capture; it, in fact, should go on to *realise* value for a firm's business model. Thus, value *creating* and *capturing* human resource management (HRM) practices must be complemented by value *realising* HRM practices for delivering a sustainable business model. More specifically, human capital in a firm should, through BE in a business model, capture value and generate surplus/profit through four key HRM practices: efficient training, focused hiring, process-focused HRM, and project-based performance management.

Towards Customer Happiness

Aras and Crowther (2010) reiterated that the)way to manage a business for excellence and sustainable competitive advantage is to focus on the four key areas of profitability, sustainability, reputation, and governance. So, for organisations to succeed, they need to anticipate, define, implement, review, and improve the customer experience as a priority. If organisations are to achieve this, customer satisfaction has to be turned into customer happiness, going beyond loyalty. Customer happiness or experience is the key criterion in the search for excellence as organisations have entered the age of the customer, an era where customer experience is the only sustainable source of competitive advantage. Customers' perceptions have a strong impact on organisations' sustainability. Undoubtedly, the only way to beat the competition is through consistently 'delighting' the customer. To create delighted customers, organisations need to focus on adding value by meeting and exceeding their needs and expectations; customer focus is not just a total quality management (TQM) philosophy that envisages only understanding and fulfilling customer requirements. It is an increasingly critical business strategy that is being pushed to the forefront of forward-thinking companies, big and small, new and established, traditional and revolutionary. As defined by the European Foundation for Quality Management (EFQM), excellent organisations achieve and sustain outstanding levels of performance that meet or exceed the expectations of all their stakeholders and they sustain outstanding results that meet both the short- and long-term needs of all their stakeholders, within the context of their operating environment. In fact, the customer is a key stakeholder for any organisation, thus, excellent organisations need to meet or exceed their expectations and work towards delighting them by demonstrating a commitment to and seeking to optimise long-term relationships with them, by retaining customers and reducing their marketing efforts. Leaders play an essential role in driving the organisation towards achieving BE. They are responsible for establishing an effective customer relationship in which ethical behaviour is a crucial and compelling organisational norm. Hence, corporate governance is gathering more attention globally and in the Arab world in particular. Employee happiness entails the improvement of employee morale and workplace happiness is associated with increased productivity. Customer happiness or satisfaction measures how a service or a product that is supplied by an organisation meets or surpasses the expectations of customers.

Caterpillar Financial Services Corporation exemplifies customer focus. Caterpillar, Inc. received its Malcolm Baldrige National Quality Award (MBNQA) from President Bush after posting huge earnings within its parent organisation and achieving world-class customer satisfaction levels. Their secret to sustaining good results is that they implemented a customer account management programme, the Customer Relationship Review. It was deployed first to the Southern Region sales team and then to the rest of the United States. This experience helped to solidify the importance of consistent process to achieve consistent results, not just within one work group but across the company.

Another example is of a recent 2016 Baldrige Award recipient—Momentum Group. They use a proactive approach to obtaining input from customers, and in doing so their design team visits at least 60 customers per year to get face-to-face feedback on company products; these interactions go beyond customer visits by sales employees from the company.

Towards Innovation Management

Research on innovation and creativity has increased since these are considered to be the key pillars for building competitive advantage. In fact, it is also a challenge for organisations to sustain innovation internally. In particular, sustaining innovation within organisations involves several coordination challenges that centre on how ideas can be translated across space and time (Bartel and Garud 2009). Working with people and harnessing innovation, however, has proven to be effective in organisations. Innovation at work is essentially driven by employees' ideas, and successful implementation of new programmes, new products, or new services depends on a person or a team having a good idea—and developing that idea beyond its initial stage (Amabile 1996). The innovation process is a complex phenomenon, and many variables have roles to play in determining this process. Everyone has ideas all the time, but not all are creative; nor do they all lead to innovation (Vandenbosch et al. 2006). Organisational context can impede or support the generation of ideas (Amabile 1996): creativity needs to be nurtured to turn into innovation. Moreover, the organisational context of innovation—the work communities' culture, habits, and practices—is key to innovation success (Björklund 2010). In particular, an organisation structure that establishes the wrong authorities often hinders tacit knowledge-sharing (Seidler-de Alwis and Hartmann 2008). Companies aspiring towards innovative goals need to learn from the examples of highly successful companies such as 3M and The Body Shop whose leaders spend their energy and effort in building organisational cultures and climates which perpetually create innovation

(Ahmed 1998). Studies have shown that a traditional, autocratic management style results in low levels of employee engagement and motivation (Hayward 2010). Management must get actively involved by creating opportunities for employees to submit their ideas, have those ideas properly evaluated, give recognition when it is due, and implement them as soon as possible. Amabile et al. (2004) note that a leader who interacts daily with subordinates may, through certain behaviours directed at those subordinates, influence their daily perceptions, feelings, and performance, ultimately influencing the overall creativity of the work that they do. Transformational leaders emphasise enhancing the organisation's overall innovation and creativity and are willing to take risks to attain organisational success and eliminate ineffective processes and systems and manage their impact on the environment and society. Moreover, people need social, informational, and economic support to be able to create something new. It is also contended that creative ideas are more often the product of social interaction and influence than of periods of thinking in isolation (Yuan and Zhou 2008). Good ideas can come from anyone, at any level, from any place, and at any time (McConville 1990; Employees, therefore, need to be motivated and encouraged in their involvement and the involvement can be increased if employees develop a sense of belonging to the organisation (Martín Cruz et al. 2009). Happiness predicts creativity, and the composite hope measure also predicts creativity via the mediating role of happiness (Rego et al. 2009).

Finally, it is also important to organise the process of idea extraction to idea follow-up properly, otherwise employees will not be motivated to put their ideas forward and many ideas will be lost (Van Dijk and Van Den Ende 2002). Idea management systems more clearly underpin creativity, so to handle employee creativity effectively it is important to have a simple, formal, and effective system. The knowledge possessed by individual employees can only lead to a firm's competitive advantage if employees have the motivation and opportunity to share and utilise their individual knowledge in ways that benefit the organisation (Arthur and Kim 2005). Malaviya and Wadhwa (2005) note that creativity and innovation will only be sporadic occurrences and will not thrive without a supportive environment and culture.

To sustain excellence in business, innovation management must be at the forefront. The innovation context or culture must embrace new directions and take into consideration the organisational climate and culture, which are crucial to innovative success. Leaders are responsible and their jobs must also highlight a specific need to oversee this innovation and support efforts by ensuring they establish appropriate structures and opportunities for employees to share and learn. More clearly, the engagement of employees must not be just to ensure that they are happy but must be focused instead on creating happy employees.

- Leaders must have a clear vision of the ultimate goal of the company's innovation initiative and management responsibilities that work towards this.
- Leaders must set the goals and strategic objectives.
- Leaders must ensure sufficient and adequate resources are dedicated to the innovation process and its requirements.
- Leaders must hold their line organisation accountable for innovation and results.

Moving forward, project excellence models have brought in the aspects of employee happiness, customer happiness, innovation and creativity, sustainability, and risk management (Bolboli and Reiche 2013).

Creativity is the ability to conceive something original while innovation is the implementation of something new. Innovation and creativity are crucial for organisations which are looking to beat their competition in the market. Organisations also need to focus on sustainability since it inspires businesses and enables them to remain relevant in the market. An organisation that is sustainable has the potential to weather the challenges brought about by the ever-changing fast-paced twenty-first-century market environment. Risk management is a vital tool, identifying, analysing, and accepting or mitigating uncertainty in business prices (Garvare and Isaksson 2001). Risk management attempts to analyse and quantify the potential losses in a business investment as well as taking the appropriate actions dictated by the company's risk tolerance or investment objectives.

Finally, BE requires a transformational approach to deal with the continuous changes in an organisation's structure that companies are faced with today. It is also necessary for organisations to build an implementation roadmap of BE. Bolboli and Reiche (2013) proposed the process of change to manage BE: the process of implementation should begin with an orientation workshop which collects various opinions for informed decision-making. This should be followed by an economic analysis of this project. Once the decision has been taken, some preparatory works are necessary, such as establishing a team of specialists from different areas of the enterprise and creating a feeling of urgency for the change. The next step is to identify stakeholders and their interests, as well as environmental spheres. This will follow the optimisation step, which is to do with the assessment of the current situation and benchmarking of best practice. This phase will then lead to the stabilisation stage. This is a distinct categorisation of activities which provides a clear map to undertake the BE implementation. It is important to carry out an economic analysis that yields a decision process. Upon making such decisions, organisations then need to prepare a plan and act on it with a focus on optimising results and carrying out periodic reviews to ensure every quality loop has been closed.

Conclusion

BE frameworks are overarching frameworks within which other initiatives or approaches fit. The vice-chair of General Electric, Beth Comstocke, explained how the Baldrige Performance Excellence Criteria (BPEC) helps organisations to become emergent organisations, that is, to become adaptive organisations where solutions to problems and opportunities will spontaneously emerge before needs demand or exist. To sustain excellence, therefore, it is important that organisations become emergent and embrace customer happiness, employee happiness, and be ready to manage innovation within the organisation. Sustainable results, however, are rooted in core values of excellence, driven by leadership commitment, aligned with business objectives, and embedded throughout the organisation and its culture, which fosters customer and employee happiness and manages innovation.

Mehran Ferdowsian (2016) explains how, even six decades later (since excellence in organisations became known to be important), we find a number of fundamental commonalties in these frameworks based on the needs of the times, the interaction and dependencies of requirements, and the significance and impact of ethics and social responsibility on how results are delivered. For example, it has become evident that the achievement of excellence is highly unlikely if leadership overlooks any of the following: the overall welfare, satisfaction, engagement, and alignment of the workforce with the overall goals and objectives of the organisation; the needs, requirements, and expectations of their market and customer base and the responsible way in which leadership plans, executes, and delivers products/services that add meaningful value to society.

Finally, to be successful in implementing TQM, organisations need talented human capital and hence organisations' emphasis on 'talent' becomes paramount. Our last lens is that of innovation and creativity, and these concepts complement the other topics discussed earlier. Thus, creativity, the ability to conceive something original, alongside innovation, the implementation of novel initiatives, becomes crucial for organisations when it comes to them being sustainably competitive.

References

Ahmed, P. K. (1998). Culture and climate for innovation. *European Journal of Innovation Management, 1*(1), 30–43.

Amabile, T. M. (1996). *Creativity in context: Update to the social psychology of creativity*. Boulder: Westview Press.

Amabile, T. M., Schatzel, E. A., Moneta, G. B., & Kramer, S. J. (2004). Leader behaviors and the work environment for creativity: Perceived leader support. *The Leadership Quarterly, 15*(1), 5–32.

Aras, G., & Crowther, D. (2010). Sustaining business excellence. *Total Quality Management, 21*(5), 565–576.

Arthur, J. B., & Kim, D. O. (2005). Gainsharing and knowledge sharing: The effects of labour–management co-operation. *The International Journal of Human Resource Management, 16*(9), 1564–1582.

Bartel, C. A., & Garud, R. (2009). The role of narratives in sustaining organizational innovation. *Organization Science, 20*(1), 107–117.

Björklund, T. A. (2010). Enhancing creative knowledge-work: Challenges and points of leverage. *International Journal of Managing Projects in Business, 3*(3), 517–525.

Bolboli, S. A., & Reiche, M. (2013). A model for sustainable business excellence: Implementation and the roadmap. *The TQM Journal, 25*(4), 331–346.

Ferdowsian, M. C. (2016). Total business excellence – A new management model for operationalizing excellence. *International Journal of Quality & Reliability Management, 33*(7), 942–984. https://doi.org/10.1108/IJQRM-08-2014-0109

Garvare, R., & Isaksson, R. (2001). Sustainable development: Extending the scope of business excellence models. *Measuring Business Excellence, 5*(3), 11–15.

Hayward, S. (2010). Engaging employees through whole leadership. *Strategic HR Review, 9*(3), 11–17.

Malaviya, P., & Wadhwa, S. (2005). Innovation management in organizational context: An empirical study. *Global Journal of Flexible Systems Management, 6*(2), 1–14.

Malik, A., Pereira, V., & Budhwar, P. (2017, forthcoming). Value creation and capture through human resource management practices: Gazing through the business model lens. *Organizational Dynamics.*

Martín Cruz, N., Martín Pérez, V., & Trevilla Cantero, C. (2009). The influence of employee motivation on knowledge transfer. *Journal of Knowledge Management, 13*(6), 478–490.

McConville, J. (1990). Innovation through involvement. *The TQM Magazine, 2*(5), 295–297.

Rego, A., Machado, F., Leal, S., & Cunha, M. P. E. (2009). Are hopeful employees more creative? An empirical study. *Creativity Research Journal, 21*(2–3), 223–231.

Seidler-de Alwis, R., & Hartmann, E. (2008). The use of tacit knowledge within innovative companies: Knowledge management in innovative enterprises. *Journal of Knowledge Management, 12*(1), 133–147.

Van Dijk, C., & Van Den Ende, J. (2002). Suggestion systems: Transferring employee creativity into practicable ideas. *R&D Management, 32*(5), 387–395.

Vandenbosch, B., Saatcioglu, A., & Fay, S. (2006). Idea management: A systemic view. *Journal of Management Studies, 43*(2), 259–288.
Yuan, F., & Zhou, J. (2008). Differential effects of expected external evaluation on different parts of the creative idea production process and on final product creativity. *Creativity Research Journal, 20*(4), 391–403.

Index

F. Lasrado, V. Pereira, *Achieving Sustainable Business Excellence*,
https://doi.org/10.1007/978-3-319-73314-2

The manufacturer's authorised representative in the EU is Springer Nature Customer Service Centre GmbH, Europaplatz 3, 69115 Heidelberg, Germany. If you have any concerns regarding our products, please contact ProductSafety@springernature.com

Printed and bound by CPI Group (UK) Ltd, Croydon, CR0 4YY
30/09/2026
02225195-0002